Welfare Theory

Also by Tony Fitzpatrick

Freedom and Security*
Welfare Theory (*first edition*)*
Environmental Issues and Social Welfare (*co-editor*)
Environment and Welfare (*co-editor*)*
After the New Social Democracy
New Theories of Welfare*
International Encyclopaedia of Social Policy (*editor*)
Applied Ethics and Social Problems
Voyage to Utopias
Understanding the Environment and Social Policy (*editor*)

* Also published by Palgrave

Welfare Theory

An Introduction to the Theoretical Debates in Social Policy

Second Edition

Tony Fitzpatrick

First edition 2001
Reprinted eight times
Second edition 2011

Published by
PALGRAVE MACMILLAN

Palgrave Macmillan in the UK is an imprint of Macmillan Publishers Limited, registered in England, company number 785998, of Houndmills, Basingstoke, Hampshire RG21 6XS.

Palgrave Macmillan in the US is a division of St Martin's Press LLC, 175 Fifth Avenue, New York, NY 10010.

Palgrave Macmillan is the global academic imprint of the above companies and has companies and representatives throughout the world.

Palgrave® and Macmillan® are registered trademarks in the United States, the United Kingdom, Europe and other countries.

ISBN: 978–0–230–27202–6

This book is printed on paper suitable for recycling and made from fully managed and sustained forest sources. Logging, pulping and manufacturing processes are expected to conform to the environmental regulations of the country of origin.

A catalogue record for this book is available from the British Library.

Library of Congress Cataloging-in-Publication Data

Fitzpatrick, Tony, 1966–
    Welfare theory : an introduction to the theoretical debates in social policy / Tony Fitzpatrick. — 2nd ed.
        p. cm.
    Includes index.
    Summary: "This fully updated new edition of a trusted text retains the accessibility and engaging style of its predecessor. With analysis of the key concepts and theories of welfare, this book examines the potential impact of globalization and the financial crisis, making it core reading for all those studying welfare and the welfare state" — Provided by publisher.
        ISBN 978–0–230–27202–6 (pbk.)
    1. Social policy – Philosophy. 2. Public welfare – Philosophy. I. Title.
HN28.F57 2011
361.6'501—dc22   2011016908

10 9 8 7 6 5 4 3 2 1
20 19 18 17 16 15 14 13 12 11

Printed and bound in Great Britain by the MPG Books Group, Bodmin and King's Lynn

Quomodo sedet sola civitas

Contents

List of Figures and Tables

Figures

Tables

Acknowledgements

I continue to be grateful to all who contributed to the first edition, especially Jo Campling who sadly passed away several years ago. Not much has changed, otherwise. Having failed to learn from experience Catherine Gray commissioned this edition too. Many thanks to the reviewers for their enthusiasm about the subsequent proposal. And, having put me in the spotlight in the first place, 12 years ago, Chris Pierson was kind enough to read and comment upon an earlier draft of the second edition. I should also express my gratitude to the many students over the years who have taught me how to be a better teacher.

Introduction to the Second Edition

The ideas of economists and political philosophers, both when they are right and when they are wrong, are more powerful than is commonly understood. Indeed the world is ruled by little else. Practical men, who believe themselves to be quite exempt from any intellectual influences, are usually the slaves of some defunct economist. Madmen in authority, who hear voices in the air, are distilling their frenzy from some academic scribbler of a few years back.

Keynes, 1954: 373

What does John Maynard Keynes mean by this and why is it important?

On 27 February 2002, in the British House of Commons, a backbencher asked the then prime minister an apparently innocuous question:

Will he provide the House with a brief characterization of the political philosophy that he espouses and which underlies his policies?

Tony Blair struggled for several seconds, obviously at a loss for words, and then replied:

The best example that I can give is the rebuilding of the National Health Service today under this government – extra investment. For example, there is the appointment today of Sir Magdi Yacoub to head up the fellowship scheme that will allow internationally acclaimed surgeons and consultants from around the world to work in this country. I can assure the House and the country that that extra investment in our NHS will continue under this government. Of course, it would be taken out by the Conservative party.

This reply, let us be clear, does *not* espouse a political philosophy and does *not* help to illuminate the fundamental ideas underpinning government policies[1].

My intent here is not to chuckle at the ineptness of Blair's response. I suspect most of us – even battle-weary philosophers – would fail to pinpoint our

---

[1] A full transcript can be found in Hansard: http://www.publications.parliament. uk/pa/cm200102/cmhansrd/vo020227/debtext/20227–03.htm#20227–03_ spnew10

social and political philosophies effectively, succinctly and comprehensively. Yet this is a task that we must perform, especially (as tends to be the case) when governments cannot or will not perform it themselves. Government is too important to be left to politicians. And although there are many ways of analysing what a government stands for, we would deprive ourselves of important tools were we to ignore the significance of social and political theories and concepts.

This is partly because most of us already have a basic philosophical map in our heads. Conservatives? They stand for lower taxes, a smaller state and a disciplined economy. Lefties? The state, equality and lots of compassion. However sketchy, many people may in fact have a firmer grasp of the broad principles that motivate political parties than they have of those parties actual policy commitments! Our job in this book is to take such rough sketches and sharpen them so that we have a much clearer image of how the land lies, who populates that landscape and why they stand where they stand. It will also help you to work out where you locate yourself and why.

In asking 'how', 'who', 'why' and 'where', we begin to explore the theoretical ground upon which all of us – whether we appreciate it or not – rely. This is what Keynes was getting at in the quote which heads this introduction. The idea is that we are rooted in a soil that we often fail to comprehend, appreciate or even notice. The challenge we face is therefore even greater than the backbencher realized. Nor is it simply a matter of what 'underlies' a policy, but of what justifies, drives and accounts for it. Theoretical inquiry and debate is active rather than passive. There are at least three ways in which social and political theories relate to the work of 'practical men'.

Explanation

Theories help to provide explanations, reasons and justifications for why individuals, governments and other organizations behave and believe as they do. Keynes proposed that ideas influence us without our really knowing it. Sometimes, perhaps. Yet we often think explicitly about our place in the world and how we do and should act upon it. Theories, concepts and principles help us to orientate ourselves. A rigorous theoretical analysis takes what can often be an inchoate series of ideas and instincts, examines how well – or how badly – they fit together and clarifies the extent to which they are rooted in solid ground.

Assessment

Theories therefore also provide a basis for assessing and judging whether our beliefs, values, interpretations and actions are or are not reasonable. We might evaluate a government according to its level of health expenditure. But is *more* spending necessarily better than less? What are the principles that higher expenditure is meant to serve? In other words, a policy can be assessed in terms of the extent to which it enables its objectives to be achieved. But what substantiates those objectives in the first place?

Reform

Having made our explanations and assessments, what should we do next? Do we conclude that existing principles and aims are okay? Should they be modified, radically revised or even abandoned? Where would that take us? Ultimately, social and political theorists ask questions like 'what is the best form of society?' and 'how do we get there?' These are substantial normative questions about the nature of what is right and good. How ought we to live and how should we strive to live together?

We have already made reference to policy and it is doubly instructive that a particular *social* policy was the lifeline for which Tony Blair snatched. This is because a large part of what government does *is* social policy. In 2010, the UK allocated approximately £697bn to its welfare state (income protection, healthcare, housing, education, social care); this was about two-thirds of total public spending and about 29% of total national wealth (measured as GDP). Across developed nations, some countries spend less and some spend more. In other words, two-thirds of what British people are asked to vote about during national elections is social policy! In truth, this is to underestimate the importance of the subject because the scope of social policy, as a field of research and scholarship, ranges much wider than the welfare state and beyond a simple number-crunching exercise. (I say more about this in Chapter 1.) *Welfare Theory* offers an account of that scope.

In short, (1) the map with which political philosophers and social theorists in general are concerned overlaps to a considerable extent with (2) the particular territory occupied by social policy. This book starts from the premise that you cannot properly understand the one unless you understand the other.

Before outlining its aims I should say something about this, the second edition.

Since writing the first edition of this book, in 1998–2000, I've taught it as a key text every year. Only I hadn't re-read it. It was always open in front of me, but I relied mainly upon memory and my own changing impressions of how to explain things. So, after being asked by Palgrave Mcmillan to produce a second edition, I settled down with it for an evening's entertainment, expecting to experience a few tears of laughter and enlightenment. And several hours later? Well, there were lots of tears anyway. What arrogance to have written the damn thing in the first place! Three years after my PhD and convinced I knew everything worth knowing. When the offer came to write a textbook I couldn't resist. Actually, I thought that parts of it held up fairly well. My understanding is different now to what it was, but I'd hesitate to call it superior. Turns out it makes as much sense to write an introductory text at the start of your career as it does later on.

In terms of how I've revised the book, the basic aims remain the same as before:

- To make a case for 'welfare theory' as distinct from social and political theories; the former is heavily dependent on the latter, yet since social policy asks specific questions about specific subjects, without reference to the former I believe the latter are incomplete. Welfare theory (the philosophy of social policy) is not quite the same as social theory (the philosophy of sociology and social science) and political theory (the philosophy of politics and government).
- To map and help you to understand the historical origins, key concepts, most influential debates and recent developments of welfare theory.
- To encourage social policy students and researchers to take a greater interest in the theoretical foundations of their chosen field.

This said, some debates have been dropped and new ones added. I have tried to reflect recent major developments without chasing each and every fashion. I have tightened the narrative and I have also restructured. For instance, Chapter 10 has been redistributed into the rest of the text and replaced with a new chapter on global justice and environmentalism, both of which are beginning to reframe the fundamental assumptions and procedures of social policy.

Overall, at least 30% of the second edition is new and the rest has been extensively revised and updated.

In each chapter we review long-established questions, some more recent debates and contemporary developments.

Chapter 1 deals with wellbeing and examines several concepts that help us to understand what the term means and implies: happiness, virtue, preferences, needs, desert. Particular attention is given to the recent interest in happiness. Running throughout the chapter are a series of contrasts: individual and social, subjective and objective, reason and emotion. We review such debates in order to enrich the meaning of wellbeing.

Chapters 2–4 offer three perspectives on justice. In Chapter 2, we are concerned with equality, the possible relationship between equality and liberty (with particular reference to John Rawls), several versions of egalitarianism and with objections to egalitarianism. Chapter 3 directs our attention to questions of liberty and freedom by looking at libertarianism, justifications for free markets and the arguments of Robert Nozick and Friedrich Hayek. Chapter 4 investigates issues of citizenship and community, eventually taking us beyond liberalism to ideas associated with communitarianism, republicanism and deliberative democracy.

Chapters 5 and 6 then apply many of these earlier debates to specific political and sociological topics. Chapter 5 establishes a narrative which links the state, various perspectives on the meaning of power and the themes of poverty and social exclusion. Chapter 6 explores the contrast between structures and agents in order to understand the nature of society, before examining class, class society and post-class debates.

Chapters 7 and 8 cover some old and new debates that relate to what we know and how we know. Chapter 7 reviews some key ideological positions: the Radical Right, Conservatism, Social Democracy, Marxism and Feminism. Chapter 8 considers questions of identity, identity politics, the politics of recognition (including the work of Nancy Fraser) and some 'new social divisions'.

Finally, Chapters 9 and 10 explore two questions: 'what are the constraints and opportunities of globalization?' and 'in what kind of global society do we wish to live?' Chapter 9 deals with the multifaceted nature of globalization, the recent financial crisis and the possible implications of both for social policy. Chapter 10 presents two debates which are becoming ever more important – global justice and environmentalism – which in many respects return us to the concerns of the earlier chapters.

Let me reiterate that theory is something you *do*. You stick your head inside and see what happens. Yet all too often it is seen as a chore or, alternatively, as a bit of decoration to be draped somewhere out of the way before real research (generating data, managing budgets, and supervising personnel, don't you know) can begin. Oh, everyone *says* that the theoretical and the empirical need one another, but fewer people do it than *think* they do it.

I should add, finally, that teaching the subject has been invaluable. There's nothing like having to convince a room full of nervous and sceptical students that, yes, it will improve their lives to know about interpersonal comparisons of utility, to make you realize when philosophy works and when it doesn't. Not all have been converted but many have and the first edition helped the light to switch on inside their heads.

I hope you too will enjoy the challenges and rewards of the subject.

1
Wellbeing

- Two Utopias of Social Policy
- Welfare Theory
- What is Wellbeing?
- Subjective Wellbeing
- Policy Implications

- Reasons and Emotions
- Social Wellbeing
- Public Goods
- The Prisoners' Dilemma
- Collective Action

Discussions about wellbeing have become prominent in recent years. Dean (2006) argues that, while the study of social problems remains important, social policy should also be based on understanding and promoting those values and attributes which enable a life to go well rather than badly. To some extent, this interest in wellbeing is due to a shift in economics away from mathematical models and towards psychological analyses of how and why people behave as they do. Within this literature, 'welfare' and 'wellbeing' are sometimes used synonymously; sometimes they have different, though complementary, meanings; and sometimes they point in opposite directions—e.g. in the U.S. 'welfare' continues to signify failure and dependency. In this book, the terms are typically used interchangeably ('faring well' and 'being well' are similar), though 'the welfare state' also denotes a particular socioeconomic regime of institutions and services.

What is wellbeing, then? The principal perspectives are reviewed on pp. 5–16, preceded by a discussion of the relevance of social and political theories to social policy. We then go on to address some key issues. Is there such a thing as *social* wellbeing (pp. 16–18)? What are public goods (pp. 18–19)? Can individual wellbeing be aggregated into collective forms of wellbeing (pp. 19–22)?

Two Utopias of Social Policy

As an academic subject social policy is still relatively young. It was established in the 1950s and 1960s under the title of 'social administration', largely as a response to the increased role and responsibilities of the post-war state. Yet its concepts, principles and ideals have roots that stretch back many centuries.

For instance, during the years 1515–16 Thomas More (1478–1535) said the following about poverty and inequality:

> If you don't try to cure these evils, it is futile to boast of your severity in punishing theft. Your policy may look superficially like justice, but in reality it is neither just not practical. If you allow young folk to be abominably brought up and their characters corrupted, little by little, from childhood; and if you then punish them as grownups for committing the crimes to which their training has inclined them, what else is this, I ask, but first making them thieves and then punishing them for it? (More, 1989: 21)

In short, if crime is a product of unjust social conditions then the only moral and effective way of tackling it is to eliminate those conditions. More gives a hypothetical description of such a perfect society in his book *Utopia*, a term he invented which literally means 'no-place'. More's observation captures an idea about social injustice which has endured throughout the intervening centuries. Think of Bauman's (1998: 97) metaphorical distinction between 'tourists' (the affluent and economically secure) and 'vagabonds' (the poor and socially excluded):

> *A world without vagabonds is the utopia of the society of tourists.* Much of the politics in the society of tourists – like the obsession with 'law and order', the criminalisation of poverty, recurrent spongers-bashing, etc. – can be explained as an ongoing, stubborn effort to lift social reality, against all odds, to the level of that utopia.

Like More, Bauman is accusing politics of seeking the elimination of the *poor* rather than the elimination of the *conditions that create poverty*. What both men have arguably done is to articulate the normative parameters of social policy.

What parameters do I mean? It could be claimed that modern society exists somewhere between two extremes, two absolutes, two dreams of perfection. On the one hand, there is a 'social' utopia where social problems are explained in terms of social conditions; on the other, there is a 'pathological' utopia where social problems are attributed to the supposed failings and immorality of individuals. Social policies are a means by which society moves itself in one direction or the other: some address the social (in)justice of underlying conditions; some are concerned with improving the behaviour and habits of individuals. Of course, it might be claimed that we must always fall short of either extreme (utopias are, by their very definition, unattainable). To ignore this point is to risk creating one of two *dystopias*: either a collectivist society that stifles individuality (More's utopia is a fairly unpleasant place) or an individualistic society that fractures the interdependent ties that hold us together. This may imply that social policies are somewhat paradoxical. We use them to aim at utopia but, if we are not to create utopia's opposite, they must always fall short of their target.

In any event, this focus upon deliberate social change is the essential theme of social policy. In this book, a 'welfare system' is defined as set of socioeconomic and cultural relations that effects social change by trying both to address social problems and to promote wellbeing. A 'welfare state' is defined as a welfare system within which the state plays a central role (cf. Goodin, 1988: 11). All welfare states are welfare *systems* but not all welfare systems are welfare *states*; although the state habitually plays an important role, some nations give prominence to other sectors (markets, families and civic society). In this book, 'social policy' sometimes refers to the particular services contained within welfare states (income maintenance, health care, etc.), sometimes to the more general processes of deliberate social change and sometimes to academic research and teaching. Sometimes to all of them! The meaning should be clear from the context.

In the twentieth century there were two attempts to drive society in the direction of the social utopia. The first of these was communistic, the belief that since social injustice derives from the private ownership of property, abolishing the latter will help abolish the former. The failure of that project does not necessarily invalidate the basic idea, or suggest that the social approach is redundant. A question mark hangs over the second attempt and we will see why throughout this book. The endeavour to create and maintain state welfare systems in liberal democratic societies continues into the twenty-first century, in the face of conditions and challenges barely envisaged by the architects of what we now call the 'classic welfare state'. Thus, many contemporary debates (political, economic, sociological, philosophical, etc.) deal with the question of whether this experiment is worth continuing and, if so, in what form. The last few decades have been dominated by the 'pathological' utopians' attempt to recreate people as independent, self-sufficient and responsible agents, as consumers utilizing economic rationalities within free market capitalism. This book will address many of those key debates.

Welfare Theory

There are basically two types of theoretical inquiry.

Firstly, theory can be interpreted as a form of 'transcendence'. Throughout our lives we inhabit certain locations, know certain people, trust and believe in certain things and accumulate a certain familiarity with the world and our societies. In one sense, theorizing is the attempt to transcend our immediate contexts, to look beyond the particular, the apparent, the visible: we understand the social world by trying to look at it from the outside. The very first philosophical inquiry was supposed to have been made by Thales (625–545 BC) when he asked the question 'What is the world made of?' Since it is not obvious, just by looking around us, what the world is made of, we need philosophical theories that will enable us to explore beyond the immediate.

In our time one of the most brilliant exponents of such theorizing is the German philosopher and sociologist Jürgen Habermas. Secondly, theory can also be interpreted as a form of 'immanence'. This means that rather than transcending our contexts, theorizing enables us to delve into those contexts still further: we understand the social world by looking at it from the inside.

Let me illustrate this distinction. What does the study of history involve? According to 'transcendence theorists' we should be identifying the underlying causes of historical progression. A Marxist, for instance, says that the fundamental dynamic of history is class struggle. But according to 'immanence theorists' that kind of approach risks being too abstract and ignoring the way in which the messiness and disorderliness of past events cannot be forced into neat categorical boxes without distorting the very processes we are trying to understand. The French intellectual Michel Foucault (1926–84) believed that knowing something requires us to immerse ourselves in the contingencies of the intended object of knowledge (Foucault, 1984). But for Habermas (1984) knowledge requires us to achieve a critical distance from the object of knowledge and from the immediate contexts within which knowing takes place.

My own view is that we need recourse to both theoretical methods. Thus, when we seek explanations and ask normative questions, we sometimes transcend our particular positions within the social world and sometimes we immerse ourselves more fully within them.

This throws some light on the subject of social policy. Scholars and researchers search for explanations. How did what *is* the case come *to be* the case? When we trace or apply those explanations to fundamental concepts we are engaging with welfare theory, with the deepest philosophies of social policy. We also need such 'depth analysis' to ask normative questions. What *ought* to be the case? Where do we go from here? In short, welfare theory is integral to one tradition of social policy. A second tradition is that of social administration, which is basically concerned with the descriptive, the 'how' and the 'what' of social policy; e.g. how do welfare services operate and what effects do they have on individuals and society? It is difficult and probably meaningless to ask one type of question without also asking the other; the traditions are not always easy to disentangle. That said, we can arguably denote the philosophical investigation of social policies as trying to gain

> [t]ranscendent and immanent knowledges of the concepts and principles that underpin the design and delivery of social policies in order to understand the ways in which those policies either improve or adversely affect the wellbeing of individuals and society.

My shorthand for such theorization – 'welfare theory' – distinguishes the topic from political, economic and sociological theories. Welfare theory draws substantially upon them, yet social policy has its own identity, history, literatures, premises, agendas and critical frameworks.

If you can see that this raises yet more questions you have learned an important lesson: the point of theory is not to ask questions that will receive correct answers (though that has been known to happen!) but to ask questions more intelligent than those we would ask otherwise and to detect which answers are likely to be *incorrect*. Theoretical debate resembles an endless, ear-splitting conversation that goes on amongst countless numbers of people, across vast reaches of time and space. This book invites you to join that conversation. We start by returning to our initial question.

What is Wellbeing?

Theorists have been struggling with this question for centuries. This section introduces five of the main perspectives.

Happiness

Happiness has two definitions. In a 'shallow', hedonistic sense, happiness is a direct mental and physical experience, e.g. the pleasure experienced when winning a prize or receiving a promotion. Although happiness obviously can involve such immediate feelings, there is also a second, 'deeper' definition. This is to regard happiness more as a general state of living, one not necessarily reducible to a particular feeling of euphoria or joy but which is most often referred to as long-term satisfaction, contentment or equanimity. The ancient Greeks called this *eudaimonia* ('good spirit'), which can be understood in modern terms as 'being and doing well'. It means that I may be happy in general, perhaps because my ambitions are being realized, even when I suffer day-to-day sadness and frustrations (Kraut, 2007).

Shallow happiness is an inadequate candidate for wellbeing. Although we would hesitate to describe as being well someone who *never* experienced joyful feelings, shallow happiness is a transient condition. Hedonism's very intensity makes it short-lived. Someone who expected a romance to deliver such pleasure indefinitely is likely to be very disappointed. And so the pursuit of shallow happiness might make it harder to achieve deeper forms of happiness. Addicts are typically people who try to recapture with every 'hit' the feelings they experienced with the first one. This may prevent them from pursuing valuable things in life. And hedonists may become vulnerable to all sorts of social and psychological conditioning by those who promise them instantaneous exhilaration.

Should we therefore define wellbeing in terms of deeper happiness?

Virtue

Deeper happiness avoids the above problems. It is enduring, not limited to physiological and emotional sensations, and is much more definitive of our identity and life plans. But what does this really imply? *Eudaimonia* is a state of flourishing and fulfilment that comes from satisfactorily realizing my goals in life. Yet does this mean that *any* goals will do? What if my sole purpose is to watch television? What if everything else in my life is sacrificed to that one goal? Would achieving it leave me in a *eudaimonic* state, or would you be tempted to suggest that goal realization is, by itself, insufficient, i.e. that the quality of my goals matters as much as their fulfilment?

For Aristotle (384–322 BC), what is most important is the exercise and contemplation of wisdom (Aristotle, 1955; see Fitzpatrick, 2008a: ch. 4). To be *eudaimonic*, a life must be a virtuous life of judging and acting wisely. This implies avoiding extremes. Aristotle defines a virtue as a middle way between two vices; e.g. courage is the mean between cowardice and reckless bravado. It also implies realizing the chief human 'function': to live excellently. Virtue is therefore a property of character, a disposition or propensity to act in ways that embody 'the good'. Some dispositions and goals are therefore better than others. The person who is a successful coward cannot be described as experiencing *eudaimonia* because cowardice is not a virtue.

We seem to have two options. Either we can leave the meaning of deeper happiness to individuals or we can try and define it objectively. If we leave it to individuals then we risk their valuing trivial goals, such as dedicating their lives to watching television. But if we define deeper happiness objectively then we risk dictating *to* individuals the kind of life they should lead. Aristotelianism could be condemned as elitist since the exercise of Aristotelian virtue requires prior instruction into such practices by those said to possess the requisite wisdom and experience. This potentially offends against liberal principles which state that individuals have a right to define for themselves what it means for their lives to go well.

Preferences

It seems reasonable to describe someone whose preferences have been satisfied as enjoying more wellbeing than someone whose desires have been left unfulfilled. If I want to buy a new car and can afford to do so then my 'want-satisfaction', and therefore my level of wellbeing, is higher than the person who also wants that vehicle but cannot afford it. The attraction of defining wellbeing in this way is that it potentially renders the concept quantifiable. According to some welfare economists the value of something depends upon how much an individual would be willing to pay for it in the market. If you and I are equally wealthy and I am willing to spend 10 per cent of my wealth on a Picasso whereas you would only spend 5 per cent then the ownership of that painting enhances my wellbeing by twice the level it would enhance yours.

There are, though, several difficulties here. It might be that my preferences are (a) distorted, (b) superficial or (c) manipulated, in which case want-satisfaction does not increase my level of wellbeing after all. If I am (a) addicted to smoking then I may experience more moments of sheer want-satisfaction than a non-smoker, yet my wellbeing may still be considerably lower due to the long-term health risks. Or (b) if my preference is to spend my life watching TV or (c) purchase whatever gadget advertisers tell me is now fashionable, then want-satisfaction may not bring substantial, long-term fulfilment. In each case, such preferences may correspond to the kind of shallow happiness examined above. We also have to remember that the satisfaction of my desires may reduce the ability of others to satisfy theirs; e.g. I want a cigarette whereas you want clean air to breathe. Preferences may, then, be too narrow and individualistic a concept to fully capture what is meant by wellbeing.

Needs

Within social policy a popular candidate for wellbeing is needs (Lister, 2010: ch. 6; cf. Goodin, 1988: 27–50, 278–305). This is because a need seems to describe something about human nature that is more essential, universal and egalitarian than preferences. We explore needs further on pp. 24–5 and Chapter 5; for a discussion of needs in relation to security see pp. 25 & 110.

Needs are distributed along several, intersecting dimensions. There are arguably universal needs, i.e. for food, water, shelter, which all people possess at all times. But there are also relative needs which are in some way dependent upon social contexts; the need for Internet access is less urgent in countries which lack clean water. There are also basic needs and non-basic needs. My need for food will usually be more important than your need for a cigarette. And needs can be objective or subjective. Subjective needs are defined primarily by the person who possesses them, while objective needs are needs irrespective of whether people experience and recognize them as such. These are not the only relevant dimensions (see Doyal & Gough, 1991; Dean, 2010) but they already highlight the difficulty of defining wellbeing in terms of needs.

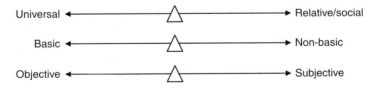

Figure 1.1 Needs and wellbeing

If in Figure 1.1 the triangular dials are aligned then the picture is fairly simple:

Universal needs = basic needs = objective needs.

Relative needs = non-basic needs = subjective needs.

But philosophers disagree on where the dials should be placed. A philosopher who turns the top dial to the right and the middle dial to the left is someone who defines needs as universal and sees them as incorporating a lot of non-basic needs. By dialling the scales in various directions we could generate dozens of different configurations, in other words. That would leave us with a much more complex task of defining needs and therefore wellbeing.

Desert

Given difficulties such as these, perhaps desert would make a better candidate. Desert implies an equivalence between contribution and reward. If I contribute twice as much as you to the design of an invention, my share of the profits should be twice as high as yours. If I receive more than this amount then you have suffered an injustice; if I receive less then I have suffered an injustice.

Yet desert is also a moral principle. Conservatives often appeal to desert as a concept that allows us to sanction those who take more from society than they contribute. Others on the Right point out that desert is a remarkably difficult value to quantify. If consumers prefer to buy my substandard sketches to your expert oil paintings then the fact that you might deserve more than I do in an artistic sense means absolutely nothing in a market context. Markets are about entitlements rather than desert (Nozick, 1974: 159). This might suggest that if the principle is to be preserved then we need to look beyond the market. Indeed, some on the Left think that desert implies social justice. Marx appealed to desert as well as need: under socialism people would be rewarded according to their labour, whilst in a subsequent communist society resources would be distributed according to need.

It might well be that wellbeing is closely related to desert. Someone who receives less than they deserve fares less well than someone whose rewards are proportionate to their contributions. The problem lies in deciding who is deserving. For some, the poor are undeserving because they are held to take from society more than they give; yet we could use much the same argument against the wealthiest! So, although desert is a principle to which we constantly appeal, the value of such appeals is heavily dependent upon the ideological context within which they are made.

Subjective Wellbeing

However it is defined, why have debates about wellbeing recently exerted such an influence (see A. Offer, 2006)? Firstly, there has been increasing dissatisfaction with the economic model of free market capitalism where people are defined as calculative maximizers of their self-interest. The view that wellbeing derives mainly from the competition for, and acquisition and consumption of income, wealth, possessions and property seems less attractive than it once did. Secondly, a general view has arisen that long-established means of measuring prosperity, e.g. gross domestic product (GDP), are inadequate. Many now believe that economic growth does not, by itself, guarantee wellbeing. Some governments are becoming interested in developing national *wellbeing* accounts. Finally, the challenges of the twenty-first century may require new socioeconomic priorities, including a greater sense of responsibility for the natural world (see Chapter 10). It was often environmentalists who pioneered criticism of the economic orthodoxy that 'more' is always 'better' (Jackson, 2002).

Happiness revisited

This led to a renewed interest in happiness. Layard (2005) has sought to revive happiness as a useful tool for economists, social scientists and policy-makers and promote a *Utilitarian* understanding of it (see Chapter 2). Layard addresses a paradoxical feature of modern times: we are wealthier than we have ever been and yet we don't necessarily *feel* much happier as a result. Growth and affluence have soared since World War Two and yet levels of depression, substance abuse and general social anxiety have not fallen correspondingly. This divergence between living *standards* and the *quality* of life was first examined in the 1970s and is known as the Easterlin Paradox. Easterlin (2005) found that

- those in higher socioeconomic groups were generally happier than those in the lower ones, but,
- beyond a certain level of development, wealthier countries are no happier than poorer ones, and
- overall levels of happiness within a country remain fairly stable over time.

The conclusion? Once absolute levels of deprivation have been surpassed, economic growth seems to matter less than we usually imagine.

What explains this paradox? Several explanations have been formulated (cf. Diener et al. 2009: chs. 6 and 7).

Set-points

One possibility is that individuals are 'programmed' by nature – genetically determined, perhaps – to experience a given level of happiness which remains stable, regardless of circumstances. How often have you considered that some people seem naturally happy and others naturally unhappy? Thus, after the thrill of winning a prize has faded a habitually gloomy person will revert to their default (or 'set-point') level of (un)happiness.

Hedonic treadmill

It may be that as circumstances improve so our expectations rise, cancelling out the improvement. If I receive a pay rise then for a while I am pleased with my higher income. But as I become accustomed to my higher income – as I adapt to my changed circumstances – its novelty fades until I am no happier than before. Perhaps I spend more until higher spending becomes the norm, or perhaps I yearn for another pay rise and consequently feel impoverished. It is not unusual to hear quite wealthy people claim that they would be truly happy if only they possessed a 'little more'. And yet if this happened, their expectations, habits and aspirations might also evolve upwards to counterbalance that objective improvement in their circumstances.

Intersubjective comparisons

The level of wellbeing that I experience is dependent upon the relative levels of wellbeing experienced by my 'comparison group'. If I own two goats and compare myself with those who own three then I may feel badly off; if I compare myself with one-goat households then I may feel affluent. My sense of wellbeing changes, though the number of goats I own remains the same in both cases. Thus, what matters are not just objective conditions but my *perception* of others' wellbeing. This is the 'spotlight' phenomenon. At a party you worry because you don't believe yourself to be as witty or well-dressed as the other guests. In truth, the other guests are not really noticing *you*; they are themselves obsessed with how *they* look in your eyes! There is a gender issue to these relative, 'psychosocial' comparisons. Due to widespread ideals of feminine beauty and desirability, women are more vulnerable than men to the emotional-physical problems that attend a 'failure' to measure up to those ideals. Women are much more likely to experience eating disorders or seek cosmetic surgery.

Counter-reactions

Perhaps socioeconomic development resembles walking up a rapidly moving *downward* escalator. For every advance there is a corresponding downside which makes it difficult to raise happiness overall. As society becomes wealthier there is more to steal. The more we possess, the more fearful of losing those possessions we may become. We can take measures to protect our property – insurance, burglar alarms, CCTV. But such measures may become another source of anxiety as it has been demonstrated that people are more concerned to avoid losses than to make gains (Kahneman et al. 1999). And as economic activities and mobilities increase so we become aware of having lost important things like job security, familiarity with neighbours and a slower pace of life.

Recently, the Easterlin Paradox has been criticized, with some insisting that the relationship between affluence and wellbeing is more complex and others concluding there is no paradox (Graham, 2009: 12–14). This research is ongoing. Few, though, now imagine that individuals and societies resemble 'happiness vessels' where pouring more wealth into the vessel automatically creates more happiness.

There are several problems, though, with any emphasis upon happiness. Firstly, as we saw above, it possibly legitimates shallow definitions. Layard (2005: 113, 118, 200, 234), for instance, argues that no type of happiness is intrinsically better than another; to imagine otherwise is paternalistic. Yet because the 'sources' of happiness *are* identifiable we ought, he insists, to promote them through education about moral truths and values. As a Benthamite Utilitarian, Layard believes that paternalism is only justified if it corresponds to what people feel. Yet, putting aside the suspicion that promoting some forms of happiness may be *less* paternalistic than promoting 'moral truths and values', feelings can mislead.

Consider this, secondly. You are given the option of plugging yourself into a happiness machine which will guarantee you immense, endless pleasure. Want to live a life of wealth and fame? Sign the contract! Unfortunately, these experiences will only occur inside your mind and you can never unplug yourself! When asked whether they would contract to this most of my students decline. Why? Because such pleasures would be unreal and inauthentic. They value happiness, for sure, but they value freedom and authenticity even more. This suggests that while wellbeing and happiness are related we have to go beyond indiscriminate, hedonic feelings.

Thirdly, and similarly, could a concern with happiness make us less interested in justice? Searle (2008: ch. 3, 102–3) observes that manual workers are more likely to report high levels of wellbeing than non-manual workers, despite the generally increased wealth, status and consumption of the latter. In the hands of some – but not Searle herself – this might imply we ought to be more concerned with soothing middle-class anxieties than with class inequalities. Or, perhaps if people are in deprived circumstances then rather than addressing those circumstances we ought, instead, to lower their expectations so that they are experienced as desirable. Perhaps through policies of 'adaptive preferences', of psychological conditioning, we can train the poor to be happy with their poverty. Yet slavery cannot be justified just because a few slaves are happy. In short, ensuring that our conception of wellbeing is sensitive to justice seems to require a focus beyond happiness *per se.*

Life satisfaction

Such considerations lead some researchers to redefine happiness as life satisfaction, a *eudaimonaic* notion of flourishing and contentment. What matters here are long-term assessments of what makes a life go well or badly which draw upon wider, more pluralist notions of wellbeing. Dependent upon longitudinal panel surveys, this kind of research is still in its early stages, though existing findings are pretty much in line with common sense. It is generally better

- to have a higher income than a lower one;
- to have a job, or some form of meaningful work, than to be unemployed;
- to be in a secure relationship than to be lonely;
- to be healthy than to be unhealthy;
- to have close friends and access to social networks than to be socially isolated.

And so on.

For philosophers the controversies arise when we consider the following. Firstly, is wellbeing, in this sense of life satisfaction, subjective or objective (Sumner, 1996)?

The problem with formulating an objective list of wellbeing is that it is potentially elitist, deriving from the views of 'experts'. Even if that list derived from panel surveys it might overlook the fact that wellbeing is an 'inner-state' experience whose meaning is dependent upon the relevant agent. And experiences differ. Social conditions that allow me to thrive may be debilitating for you.

But if, alternatively, we define wellbeing subjectively (Diener et al. 2009: 20) – as purely dependent upon agents' feelings, perceptions, ideals and experiences – then we may run into similar problems as above. People can be mistaken about their own wellbeing. A husband oblivious to the fact that his wife has been cheating on him for the last 20 years might report high levels of wellbeing – ignorance is bliss. Those who know about the infidelity might hesitate to assess his life as going as well as he imagines. Furthermore, wellbeing is inevitably politicized. A fear of crime adversely affects wellbeing (cf. Graham, 2009: 202–12), but such fears can be manipulated by those newspapers and politicians wishing to promote a draconian, law-and-order agenda. And perhaps considerations of freedom and justice should make us prefer *lower* levels of wellbeing. The abolition of slavery after the American Civil War will have lowered the wellbeing of many white Southerners for decades, but we surely regard this as a desirable change.

By and large, then, most commentators believe that we should refer to both subjective *and* objective notions of wellbeing.

Yet, secondly, this solution does not resolve the question of scope. Is wellbeing the same for all people, regardless of their location in space and time, or is it context-dependent, i.e. relative to the era and places in which we live? If we defined wellbeing in universal terms, we might miss the extent to which our perceptions, feelings and experiences are conditioned by the particular environments in which we live. However, if wellbeing is purely context-dependent then we may lose the ability to speak meaningfully about it, e.g. if everything is relative then 'basic needs' may not exist if by *basic* we mean 'that which is common to everyone'. By and large, we are likely to regard wellbeing as universal *and* relative.

What all of this implies is difficult to decide.

Policy Implications

There are two broad options.

We can allow empirical data and philosophical debates to 'inform' the policy-making process, on the grounds that there is a distinction between facts and values. The fact of *x* does not dictate what we ought to do about *x*. The fact that 'cream cakes contain lots of calories' does not permit the judgement that 'cream cakes should be taxed more than lower-calorie desserts'. We may reach that conclusion, of course, but it does not follow from the fact alone. Therefore, the fact that *q* usually creates happiness or wellbeing does not automatically mean that *q*-promoting policies should be introduced. The normative gap between facts and values implies that while wellbeing research can improve our knowledge of what makes lives go well, the practical implications of this will rely upon lots of other issues, deliberations and priorities.

The alternative is to propose that where the evidence is strong enough we *should* allow wellbeing research to determine policy decisions. Note that we can place the problem of causation to one side. Are people happy *because* they are healthy or are happy people more likely to be healthy? Does health cause happiness or is it the other way around? For policy-makers the difficulty of distinguishing the dependent from the independent variable may not always matter. If we postulate a two-way reciprocity – health creates happy people who are then motivated to live healthily – policy-makers can simply design and implement policies accordingly.

Yet even if we leapfrog over the specifics of causation we are still left with the difficulty of deciding where to go politically. One of the earliest critics of the 'growth is always good' orthodoxy was Hirsch (1977) who insisted that there are 'social limits' to growth. Although the material economy grows, the 'positional economy' remains stable. By the time you have bought an HD television, which five years ago was *the* symbol of success, those consumers you were trying to emulate have purchased 3D Internet TVs. Your *relative* position has remained the same (you may even reduce your quality of life by continually playing catch-up with others). For political radicals the implication is that we ought to re-evaluate our values and create a society based less upon 'having' and more upon 'being' and 'caring'. For some, this means a different socioeconomy entirely, where the emphasis is taken away from employment and growth (Jordan, 2008); but for others we ought to prod people into jobs in the interests of improving their social attachments and mental health (Layard, 2005). The gap between fact and (political) value reappears.

My view is that we ought to address the most obvious sources of unhappiness as a means of enabling people to lead the best kind of lives they can. This means drawing from wellbeing research without allowing it to dictate our conceptions of justice. Not only should we allow individuals to decide largely for themselves the direction of their lives – even when this means lives go less well than they might otherwise have done – we should be sensitive to the pluralistic, ambivalent, even self-conflicting nature of wellbeing. Wellbeing cannot be reduced to a quantity. If we criticize hedonism on the grounds that it is possible to be simultaneously happy *and* sad, perhaps we ought to recognize that a life can simultaneously fare well *and* fare badly. Life does not distribute into neat boxes.

Reasons and Emotions

The fact/value distinction derives from Hume (1711–76) who believed that humans are motivated by passions rather than rationality (Hume, 1969: 507–21). This is a long-standing debate. Wellbeing has become a popular subject partly as a reaction to the 'economic rationalism' of free market liberals, who are criticized for ignoring the role played in life by the non-rational (moods, love, prejudices, compassion, etc.).

That economic rationalism manifested itself in a number of ways. Take rational choice theory (RCT) (Coleman & Fararo, 1993; Elster, 2007: ch. 12; Taylor-Gooby, 2009: chs. 6–8). This asserts that

1. people are primarily self-interested agents,
2. who respond rationally and predictably to incentives and disincentives,
3. in order to maximize the benefits and minimize the costs of their behaviour to themselves,
4. by satisfying whatever preferences they hold.

RCT therefore regards all forms of social, group and organizational behaviour, including co-operative and collective forms of action, as reducible to the individual actions of *homo economicus*. RCT sits well within individualistic societies that regard market choice to be the highest expression of personal freedom because markets are assumed to be far more efficient and sensitive to liberty than state bureaucracies and public sectors.

RCT is now less influential than it was in the 1980s and 1990s (Sen, 2009: 185–90; cf. Zey, 1998: 87–113). Firstly, by treating individuals as 'economic agents' RCT merely reproduces the Robinson Crusoe figure beloved of classical economics and ignores the extent to which we are interdependent and socially determined beings. RCT treats preferences and values as given, uninterested in the social process through which they are constructed and potentially manipulated. Therefore, secondly, the theory is not very good at accounting for power. By treating inequalities of power as the product of rational, self-interested decisions, it overlooks the role that coercion, violence, exploitation and oppression play in human affairs; e.g. people may remain in situations where the costs outweigh the benefits because of a real or perceived lack of choice. Thirdly, the theory is not very good at explaining the inherent value of altruism and collective behaviour, or why people can be motivated by those values. Finally, RCT underestimates the extent to which market exchange and activity is dependent upon non-quantifiable qualities such as trust, friendship and co-operation.

The reaction against RCT is arguably part of a broader swing away from any doctrine which ignores or downplays the role of emotions and feelings in social life (Elster, 2007: ch. 8; Haybron, 2008). This is not a shift in favour the *irrational*. Instead, some have argued for a rebalancing of the rational and the emotive in social theory, research and reform. Goleman (2007) argues that emotional and social intelligence derives from an interactive harmonizing of the affective and the cognitive. Others have proposed that our choices are often non-rational, especially when we are confronted with too much choice and so feel confused and inadequate (Schwartz, 2004: 99–116). Thaler and Sunstein (2008: 1–52) agree that choice is often about intuition, impulse and inertia; e.g. people are more likely to select short-term benefits and ignore long-term costs. Therefore, institutions should subtly guide people towards the best options.

The legacy of economic rationalism remains, though it has been subject to various revisions. From a Centre-Left perspective, Le Grand (2003) presents a taxonomy of public motivations. To assume that people are fundamentally self-interested is to assume that they are *knaves*; if they are assumed to be basically altruistic and public spirited then they are *knights*; if people are thought of as passive, with little capacity for independent action, then they are *pawns*; whereas if they are active agents then they can be defined as *queens*. Le Grand thus makes room for altruistic motivations, without abandoning the rational choice perspective; e.g. his claim that competition between public sector providers is desirable corresponds to aspects of the above RCT list (Le Grand, 2007).

Alternatively, a rebalancing of reason and emotion may imply a greater role for care (see Chapters 2 and 7). Thus, Nussbaum (2001: 401–54; Darwell, 2002) has argued for greater compassion in our welfare systems, social institutions and public life. Compassion has to be a matter of both psychology and institutional design. Welfare services may have been designed by compassionate policy-makers but unless the producers and users of those services are also motivated by compassion then they are less likely to be effective. Yet having compassionate *people* is not enough either. Institutions are required to ensure an environment of social and distributive justice. A society which is more compassionate towards the unhappy millionaire than towards his underpaid housekeeper is not a just one. Compassion is an intangible, elusive, cultural construct that we cannot simply legislate into being, though Nussbaum (2001: 425–33; Fitzpatrick, 2009) proposes that a liberal, humanistic and multicultural education system, based around the imaginative empathy of the creative arts, is more likely to create such compassion than one based upon fact-gathering, rote learning and exam-passing.

Social Wellbeing

We are still left with an old problem. What is the relationship between individual and social wellbeing? Is there even such a thing as 'social wellbeing'? Is society largely the sum of individuals' actions and beliefs? Or does society have its own identity which in some way 'precedes' that of individuals? We will revisit these questions throughout the book.[1] For now, we can concentrate upon welfare and wellbeing. There are four key theorists who have argued that the concept of social wellbeing is meaningful.

Jeremy Bentham (1748–1832) viewed society as the sum of its parts but thought it possible to speak meaningfully of social wellbeing (Bentham, 1984). For Bentham, wellbeing was equivalent to utility, by which he meant 'measurable happiness': he formulated an 'hedonic calculus' where my pleasure at eating chocolate is measured against your pleasure at dieting. It is the measurability of utility which allows us to add individual wellbeings together and so quantify the aggregate level of social wellbeing, i.e. the 'greatest happiness of the greatest number'. For Bentham, this approach has three advantages.

Firstly, it enables us to evaluate different social states-of-affairs and supplement market outcomes with a system of statutory social and public policies. Secondly, it permits us to make rational and deliberate decisions as to which are the most efficacious policies. Finally, we can compare different societies in order to decide which corresponds most closely to the principle of the greatest happiness of the greatest number.

The basic problem with his philosophy is that it reduces 'wellbeing' to utility and reduces utility to a shallow notion of happiness. To measure your love for ice cream against mine for yogurt, Bentham has to appeal to basic, neurophysiological sensations. But if this is too facile a notion of wellbeing, as argued earlier, then there is a question mark as to whether social wellbeing can be regarded as the simple and mechanical aggregation of individual wellbeings.

Similarly, one of the most contentious aspects of this 'Utilitarian' account of wellbeing concerns the claim that we can make inter-personal comparisons of wellbeing, e.g. between the pleasure of watching TV and reading *Ulysses*. If wellbeing has a strong subjectivist element then how is this possible? How can my experiences be reliably compared with yours? The welfare economist Pigou (1877–1959) argued that inter-personal comparisons *are* possible because wellbeing is a matter of desire and *desire can be measured in monetary terms*: the more I am willing to pay for something then the more I desire it and the higher will be my level of wellbeing should I achieve/acquire it (Pigou, 1965). Therefore, individual wellbeing is closely related to market choice and social wellbeing can be said to rise and fall when national wealth rises and falls. Yet, as we saw above, numerous criticisms have recently been made of this viewpoint.

The economist Vilfredo Pareto (1848–1923) was one of those who argued that inter-personal comparisons are *not* possible, but that we can nevertheless talk meaningfully about social and collective states of wellbeing. According to Pareto, a society that is making at least one person better-off can be described as improving its level of wellbeing so long as nobody is becoming worse-off as a result (Aron, 1970). However, there will come a time when it can only make some better-off by making others worse-off.[2] At this time the society in question has reached the point of 'optimum efficiency', making any further change unwarranted. Therefore, we can have a meaningful discussion of 'social wellbeing' without having to make Benthamite comparisons between my utility and yours. But the problem with defining social wellbeing in terms of Pareto efficiency is that it is biased in favour of the status quo: if a change makes just one person worse-off then the change is unjustified *no matter how unequal the society in question and how rich the 'worse-off' person remains*.

A more recent attempt to define social wellbeing without reducing it to Pareto efficiency has been made by the political philosopher John Rawls (1921–2002). We shall examine Rawls in Chapter 2 but it is worth observing that he directs the discussion away from the criterion of efficiency and back towards non-Utilitarian accounts of justice and morality. For Rawls, a society with a just distribution of resources is better than one with an unjust distribution, a just distribution being that which is to the benefit of the least advantaged. Social welfare therefore requires the elimination of *unjust* inequalities, rather than inequality *per se*, and Rawls's arguments offer an important justification for redistributive social policies.

Figure 1.2 illustrates how these theories of social wellbeing relate to one another: one axis defines social wellbeing in terms of either ethics/justice or efficiency/economics; the other axis relates to whether it is or is not possible to make inter-personal comparisons of wellbeing.

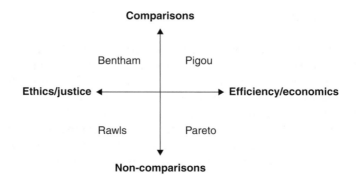

Figure 1.2 Four perspectives on social wellbeing

Public Goods

Another relevant debate concerns public goods.

Public goods are distinguishable from private goods. A private good is excludable: my consumption of the good prevents you from consuming it. Public goods are non-excludable: my consumption of the good does not and cannot prevent you from consuming it also. Food is an obvious private good (once I swallow this doughnut it's gone for ever). Food *safety* is a public good because ensuring hygiene is too costly and complicated a business for each individual alone; and my consumption of safe food does not prevent – nor is it devalued by – you consuming safe food too. *Social policies are concerned with the production and distribution of public goods.*

The question is this: what counts as a public good? There are obvious candidates such as clean air, street lighting, national defence, law and order, but should we also include health care, education and minimum income maintenance? By and large the free market Right believes that these latter items are not public goods because they are privately consumable. Consequently, the market should play a large and perhaps exclusive role in their provision (Shapiro, 2007). Most on the Left believe that the private consumability of education, etc. does not contradict their status as semi-public (or *lumpy*) goods, i.e. goods typically too expensive for individual purchase and from which public benefits can be derived (known as *merit* goods). Consequently, collective action is necessary because in a market economy such goods are underproduced: a political authority (like the state) is needed to compel payment for such goods. *The welfare state is a system of collective action that facilitates the production and distribution of public, lumpy and merit goods designed to increase the sum of social wellbeing.*

Part of the problem with public goods is that they are invitations to free-riders. Imagine that all the inhabitants of a port agree to build a lighthouse for reasons of public safety but that 10 per cent of the town then refuse to take part in financing its construction (White, 2003: 61). Unless we resort to coercive measures inconsistent with a free society, those 10 per cent cannot be excluded from enjoying the benefits of the lighthouse: they are free-riders. *Free-riders enjoy the benefits of social co-operation without shouldering the burdens of co-operative activity.* Although free-riders probably cannot be abolished altogether, one of the arguments of the Right is that a welfare state is an invitation to free-riders, e.g. benefit fraudsters, and leads to a society where people are more prepared to take rather than give and where the hard working are exploited by the lazy (de Jasay, 1989). Some on the Left accept this logic. Others reply either that some free-riding is a necessary price to pay or that the Right have too narrow a definition of free-riding; e.g. Fraser (1997: 62) argues that an extensive welfare system is needed to correct the free-riding of men on the undervalued work of women.

The Prisoners' Dilemma

These issues lead us towards a discussion of the nature of social co-operation. The prisoners' dilemma is a branch of 'game theory', a mathematical understanding of social interaction. Any game includes a number of components – players, rules, strategies and outcomes – that are heavily inter-linked. My strategy will develop and alter depending upon my perceptions of your strategy, and vice versa. So, a game is a constant feedback process of mutual re-adjustments, and game theorists believe that social interaction can be understood as a complex game in which each participant tries to secure the best outcome for herself based upon her interpretations of, and responses to, the 'moves' of others.

There are basically two types of game: conflictual and co-operative. Conflictual games are those in which there is a fixed stock of resources to be won (a zero-sum game or 'negative game'), meaning that players are more likely to fight it out than to collaborate. Co-operative games are those in which the stock of resources is not fixed (a non-zero-sum game or 'positive game') so that there may be a benefit for all if all agree to work together (resources may increase as a result of co-operation). This co-operation may be associative and spontaneous (bottom-up) or it may be enforced and centralized (top-down). *A welfare state may be defined as a liberal democratic form of enforced 'top-down' co-operation.* The prisoners' dilemma is a theoretical means of debating social conflict and co-operation.

Two criminals have been arrested and separated from each other. The police are already in a position to convict both of robbery but they need a confession if either is to be convicted of the murder that was committed during the robbery. Both prisoners are informed that they have two alternatives: each can either stay silent or confess that they both committed the murder. Prisoner 1 is then offered a deal and told that prisoner 2 is being offered the same deal.

If both he and his partner confess to murder then they will each receive 15 years in jail; if he stays silent but his partner confesses then he will serve 20 years whereas his partner will go free; if both men stay silent then they will only be convicted for robbery and serve two years. Prisoner 1 reasons that the best alternative is to stay silent and hope that his partner does the same. But can his partner be trusted to do so? If not, it would be best to confess and at least serve five years less than he would serve if he stayed silent while his partner betrayed him. Prisoner 2 follows the same reasoning. So although it is in the best interests of both men to stay silent, self-interest and a lack of communicative trust leads each prisoner to confess, condemning them both to 15 years in jail. The prisoners' dilemma illustrates how individual self-interest can lead to a worse situation for everyone but also why it can be a more rational strategy than selfless altruism (Axelrod, 1984).

In this version of the prisoners' dilemma the conflictual model of social interaction predominates; e.g. RCT suggests that markets are the best way of co-ordinating the self-interested actions of rational individuals. However, it is possible to revise the above thought experiment so that co-operation is the more rational strategy; perhaps the prisoners are allowed to communicate, or the rules of the game are altered, or the players are naturally more altruistic, or the game is played several times (allowing the players to learn from past mistakes). In short, game theory is a means of theoretical modelling and does not tell us which social model is superior. Society is neither inherently conflictual nor co-operative: it is not inherently anything. Therefore,

Social policies are not responses to social facts; they are means by which social 'facts' are constructed in the first place according to normative deliberations concerning the kind of society we want to create.

Collective Action

If the prisoners' dilemma permits some social co-operation what might this imply?

An influential account of the 'collective action problem' was offered by Hardin (1977; also Elster, 2007: ch. 24). Imagine an open pasture, a commons, on which farmers graze their cows. One day, Farmer Joe reasons that he should buy more cows and graze them on the commons because he will fully reap the benefits of doing so while the burden (overgrazing) will be distributed to everyone. But what if every farmer then copies Joe's example? The commons would be ruined. Now imagine that the commons represents the earth's ecosystem. Each of us gains personally through our economic activity while the diswelfares (or 'externalities') of pollution, resource depletion, etc. are distributed to everyone (see Chapter 10). So, a collective action problem arises when what it is reasonable for an individual to do *as an individual* may not be reasonable *for the group* to which that individual belongs.

According to Hardin, there are two solutions to this 'tragedy of the commons' and he advocates the second. (1) We could make people act responsibly through a system of 'mutual coercion, mutually agreed upon' (Ophuls, 1977), i.e. laws, taxes, regulation and 'command-and-control' governance of the commons. (2) We could raise the costs and lower the benefits of acting irresponsibly by abandoning any notion of collective action and privatizing the commons, i.e. parcelling out bits of land to everyone on the basis that people care most about what they personally own. Such arguments resemble those of Olson (1965) who observed that people are unlikely to act for the common welfare because if each individual knows that they cannot be excluded from enjoyment of a public good then nobody has much of an incentive to contribute to their creation and maintenance.

Is this the conclusion to which we are inevitably drawn? Perhaps not. Firstly, we have recourse to the objections already mentioned. The advocates of rational self-interest are too simplistic in their view of social agents, too naive in their interpretation of power, too reductionist when it comes to altruism and selflessness and too facile in their interpretation of markets (it might be possible to privatize land, but how can we privatize the sea and air?). Secondly, we might treat the proposed alternatives as too polarized. What if people can engage in egalitarian, democratic debate with their neighbours about the best way of using the commons and minimizing the risk of free-riding? If, in short, we alter the terms of the hypothesis then Hardin's pessimistic conclusions about the efficacy of collective action *can* be avoided (see Ostrom, 1990).

Recent debates about state welfare and social policy have thus been dominated by two views. Some insist that wellbeing is individualistic concept because collective aggregation is not possible, because most goods are private in nature, because of the danger of free-riders and because individual self-interest is the most rational strategy for people to adopt (N. Barry, 1999). Social policies should therefore be based upon free market principles. But others argue that wellbeing is individualistic *and* collectivist because there *is* such a thing as social wellbeing, because there are numerous public, lumpy and merit goods, because we are all free-riders to some extent and because co-operation is the most rational strategy if and when the circumstances are right. Social policies must therefore be geared towards the collective interest of all, implying the involvement of the state. By and large, the advocates of the first view are on the political Right and those of the second are on the Left.

In this chapter we have wound our way through some of the more intricate and complex aspects of social policy. We saw that welfare theory is a crucially important aspect of the discipline, resembling an open-ended discussion that does not provide a set of easily digestible solutions. We suggested that wellbeing has no single, simple meaning or defining quality. Those debates have challenged familiar models of economic rationalism. We then identified a contrast between those who interpret wellbeing in terms of private goods, individual self-interest and market provision, and those who interpret it in terms of public goods, altruism, co-operation and collective provision.

Throughout this chapter we have alluded to a number of further concepts and debates, principal among which has been that of justice. The next three chapters weave in and around the most influential perspectives on the meaning and implications of justice. We begin by introducing debates about equality.

Questions for Further Discussion

- If individuals plugged themselves into a 'happiness machine' to what extent might it increase their wellbeing?
- Does the 'hedonic treadmill' suggest that improving levels of happiness should not be an objective of social policies?
- Does 'social welfare' refer primarily to the wellbeing of a society's *individuals*?
- Are my needs more important or less important than your preferences?

2

Equality

Throughout Chapter 1, we saw that some debates are politically charged. Chapters 2–4 elucidate a series of perspectives on justice: equality, liberty, citizenship and community. These debates, too, are characterized by highly contested and politicized ideas. Understand also that these chapters are interdependent. What you think about equality will influence, and be influenced by, your views about liberty and both will intersect with discussions of citizenship and community.

In this chapter we look at why equality is such an attractive yet controversial concept (pp. 23–4), examining what it is that should be equalized (pp.24–31), outlining some key theories of egalitarian justice (pp.31–8) and the relevance of equality to social policy (pp.38–41), and concluding with a look at some recent theoretical developments (pp.42–4).

Introducing Equality

Equality is a philosophical concept and a political principle (Callinicos, 2000; Kymlicka, 2002: ch. 3; White, 2006; Holtung & Lippert-Rasmussen, 2007).

The concept of equality is central to philosophical discussion. Aristotle (384–322 BC) distinguished between numerical equality (sameness in number or size) and proportionate equality (an equivalence in terms of ratio) (Aristotle, 1988: 111). Imagine Aristotle has a pie to divide between four hungry people. If everyone is equally hungry then it seems fair to divide the pie into numerically equal parts, i.e. quarters. However, if two people are twice as hungry as the others, then the division of the pie should not be strictly numerical but should be proportionate to this ratio between the hungry and the not-so-hungry. In short, the pie should be divided into *unequal* slices in order to ensure that all appetites are *equally* satisfied. Aristotle's distinction seems to suggest that equality be defined as *the appropriate distribution of shares in respect of x* (hunger, in the above example). The nature of equality therefore depends upon the nature of *x*.

However, such philosophical distinctions do not require us to actually *support* equality. We might prefer to let hungry individuals fight for the pie, irrespective of any considerations of equality. To treat equality as a principle is to regard it as possessing ethical and political values which ought to motivate action. One of the first people to recognize that equality had been adopted as an organizing principle of modern society was Alexis de Tocqueville (1805–59) who, in his travels around America in the 1820s, recognized that the French and American revolutions had made equality an irreversible, institutional feature. In this sense, most of us are egalitarians because most of us are democrats. However, de Tocqueville (1990) also recognized the tensions to which the principle can give rise and he correctly anticipated that modern societies would spend much of their time, energy and resources attempting to resolve them.

Before we go any further, several points should be understood. Firstly, we will be mainly concerned with *social* equality, i.e. the distribution of socially produced goods. Secondly, we should remember that social equality is not an absolute. It is common to hear people object to equality on the grounds that it would be unrealistic for everyone to have the *same* income or the *same* wealth. Yet by social equality we might mean not a crude, numerical equality but a degree of equalization to eliminate unjust *in*equalities. Finally, some claim that we cannot all be equal because we are all different. Yet this objection confuses equality with uniformity. An egalitarian can acknowledge that there are many qualities in respect of which humans are different from one other (see p. 42).

Why Support Social Equality?

What is it that justifies social equality (Goodin, 1988: 51–69)? Why should social goods be distributed accordingly? Perhaps the most common answer has centred around the relationship between the natural and the social: if there is such a thing as natural equality then we have a substantial reason to support a corresponding social equality.

In the above examples, what justified a fair distribution of the pie between the four people was, firstly, that they each belonged to the same group (they were all hungry) and, secondly, they each had a legitimate claim on what was to be to be distributed. Is it possible to justify social equality on a similar basis? More specifically it could be explained as follows:

- If, in the above example, *x* denoted hunger then is it possible to identify a property or characteristic that can be said to belong to all humans?
- Would this common property give rise to a legitimate claim on the part of all humans for a socially equal distribution?

In one prominent attempt to address such questions Doyal and Gough (1991) argue that all humans possess basic needs – health and autonomy – those being the preconditions for a meaningful human life. These basic needs can therefore be said to constitute a universal 'core' which defines what it means to be human. Is this a possible candidate for the *x* that we were looking for: the common denominator that we all share and which marks us out as members of the same (human) group? If so, then we have addressed the first of the above questions: *x* denotes basic needs that are universally common to all humans. As Chapter 1 noted, many social policy commentators make this kind of assumption.

However, even if the existence of basic needs justifies equality in some form it does not necessarily justify a *social* equality. We could potentially provide for everyone's basic needs without such social equalization (see the discussion of prioritarianism in Chapter 3).

One possible bridge between basic needs and social equality concerns what Doyal and Gough call 'needs-satisfiers'. If humans have needs, they require the means to satisfy those needs, e.g. nutritional food, clean water, housing, non-hazardous environments, health care and education, physical and economic security.[1] Now recall the argument of pp. 13–14. 'Positional goods' are those whose value to an individual, depends greatly upon their location within the overall distribution of such goods. The value of a degree is higher when few people attend university than when many do; if a spectator stands to improve his view of the game, requiring everyone else to follow suit, then eventually no-one's view will be any better than it was when everyone was sitting. Status competition for positional goods is frequently futile – like always having to run faster just to remain where you are; the implication being that the fair distribution of – rather than competition for – such goods would reduce the privations of a positional economy. Therefore, if at least some needs-satisfiers are positional goods then this suggests that a politics of basic needs *can* justify social equality.

Even if we can justify social equality, however, considerable disagreement amongst egalitarians exists about what type and level of social equality is preferable.

Equality versus Liberty?

Many disputes concern the relationship between social equality and individual liberty. Some view equality and liberty as a negative or 'zero-sum' game. Imagine two piles of stones, one pile labelled 'equality' and the other pile labelled 'liberty'. Assuming that no other stones are available, the only way we can enlarge the equality pile is by taking some stones from the liberty pile and *vice versa*. On this interpretation, the two are mutually exclusive and our task is to decide which of the following options we prefer:

1.   A strong commitment to social equality over individual liberty.
2.   A strong commitment to individual liberty over social equality.
3.   A more balanced trade-off between equality and liberty.

The social policy implications of this are wide-ranging. The first option might demand a closely regulated economy and society with extensive redistributive welfare services and extremely high rates of taxation. The second option might suggest a laissez-faire economy and libertarian society with few welfare services and very low rates of taxation. The third option might imply any number of welfare systems depending upon the nature of the balance preferred.

Alternatively, we might think of social equality and individual liberty as being engaged in a positive or 'non-zero-sum' game where we can *increase* the size of both piles over time. This has long been an argument advanced by many Left egalitarians. R. H. Tawney (1880–1962) famously argued that it is unequal societies which reduce the scope of liberty. Within capitalism, people have to spend so much of their lives making money, avoiding poverty and aspiring to consumerist lifestyles that they have little time left for anything else. Therefore, it would be a society of socialist equals that would embody the diversity which anti-egalitarians wrongly attribute to capitalist societies with their vast inequalities of wealth and power. 'Freedom for the pike is death for the minnows', Tawney (1964: 164) once famously said. Tawney is here giving voice to a longer tradition in which equality and liberty have been regarded as mutually supportive.

Take the work of Jean-Jacques Rousseau (1712–1778). Rousseau (1973: 28) was concerned to reconcile 'the equality which nature has ordained between men, and the inequality which they have introduced'. A return to a state of nature is out of the question, he believed. Therefore, the task should be to remodel society so that its institutions no longer hold us in chains. Rousseau thought of society not as a collection of individuals but as an expression of the 'general will': something that transcends the sum of individual wills. So, whereas representative democracies establish their authority on the basis of majority voting, Rousseau (1973: 175) calls for a *direct* democracy where citizens place themselves 'in common under the supreme direction of the general will'. The authority of the common good therefore derives ultimately from the individual consenting to surrender his or her freedom to it, but this 'surrender' is not so much the negation of individuality as it is its highest realization.

Equality of What?

But we can only really decide the extent to which equality and liberty are in conflict by examining what it is we are trying to equalize. 'Equality of what?'

is the simple yet profound question which egalitarians set out to address. What is the 'metric' or 'currency' that we should use to categorize and measure equality? Should we be liberals who are attracted to egalitarianism or egalitarians who are attracted to liberalism? Let's make sense of these questions, beginning with the latter.

Opportunities and outcomes

A distinction is commonly made between opportunity and outcome. Think of the following analogy. For any race to be fair, two conditions must prevail:

- The same rules should apply to all runners without bias.
- Each runner should be required to compete over the same distance as everyone else.

Now, there can be little doubt that existing societies frequently fail to embody these conditions. The existence of both direct and indirect discrimination suggests that different rules are applied to different groups. Furthermore, the existence of poverty and systemic inequalities implies that, in effect, some runners have further distances to complete than others. The principle of equal opportunities is therefore a means of trying to correct these deficiencies (Jacobs, 2004): applying the same rules to all might involve introducing anti-discriminatory legislation; giving everybody an equal start in life (starting-line equality) might imply introducing a system of publicly funded education so that success derives from 'efforts of will' and hard work rather than luck and accidents of birth.

However, there is reason to believe that equality of opportunity is insufficient (Baker, 1987). Subjecting everyone to the same rules *now* might not be enough to compensate for many of the injustices inherited *from the past*. Poverties, unjust inequalities and disadvantages may be so deep, so endemic and systemic, that an emphasis upon the starting-line is inadequate. Also, the principle implies an equal opportunity for people to become *unequal*, potentially contradicting the very point of egalitarianism. Even if you eliminate luck and accidents of birth, new inequalities may lead to their reappearance further down the race-track.

Critics therefore propose that equality of opportunity has to be supplemented by an equality of *outcomes*. This is where we intervene throughout and at the end of the race (finishing-line equality) to ensure that any injustices left uncorrected at, or which materialize after, the starting-line are repaired. We might require employers, government departments and other public organizations to favour the interests of the least well-off. We might redistribute income and wealth to narrow the gap between the social top and bottom. And we might tax inheritances to ensure that people have to rely on their own merits and not those of their parents or grandparents.

However, equality of outcome is criticized by those who insist that to determine the results of the race artificially is to interfere with something that should, strictly speaking, be left to the determination of individual effort and choice (N. Barry, 1987). If I work hard, then what right has the state to tax the wealth that I freely choose to leave to my children? Furthermore, perhaps outcome equality would require us to interfere with the race so often and so powerfully that important liberties would be undermined.

By and large, advocates of egalitarian social justice appeal to both opportunities and outcomes on the grounds that each will counterbalance the other. As such, the line between liberalism and egalitarianism is sometimes blurred. At the risk of over-simplification, we might say that those who emphasize outcomes are liberal *egalitarians* (for whom social equality is the priority), while those who emphasize equal opportunities are egalitarian *liberals* (for whom liberty is the priority). However, such categories are not set in stone.

Within recent egalitarian theory an equally significant distinction involves that between welfare, resources and capabilities (see Figure 2.1).

Equality of welfare

If equality of welfare is our objective, then we achieve this once all members of the relevant group experience the same state of wellbeing (see Chapter 1 for definitions). For instance, if our division of Aristotle's pie successfully satisfies all appetites equally, then we may be said to have achieved an equality of welfare. Or, if welfare implies happiness then equality of welfare implies an 'equality of happiness'.

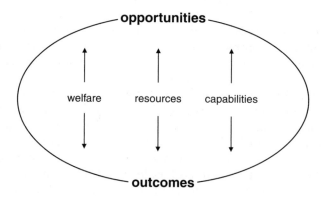

Figure 2.1   Welfare, resources, capabilities

It is not difficult to criticize equality of welfare. There is the sheer impracticality of creating it, for one thing. Recall the difficulties in trying to measure the wellbeing experienced by different people (see pp. 9–13, 16–18); now ask yourself whether an equality of happiness, say, is a realistic aim. Furthermore, equality of welfare presumably requires the subsidy of expensive tastes (Dworkin, 2000: 49–59). If I wish to learn the piano and would be dissatisfied by not being able to learn, then any government committed to an equality of welfare has a duty to fund my piano lessons. Yet, because piano-playing is an expensive taste, this doesn't exactly square with the egalitarian impulse. There is a debate over the extent to which those possessing expensive tastes can be held responsible for them. If they cannot – if my desire to play the piano was determined by my upbringing – then perhaps an injustice *would* be committed if the state refused to fund my lessons (Roemer, 1993). However, many egalitarians are not persuaded by the idea that tastes are devoid of choice (see below).

One way of salvaging equality of welfare is to redefine it as 'equal *minimum* welfare'. If welfare refers to needs, then an equal minimum level of welfare might imply ensuring that everyone's basic needs are met. Another alternative is to concentrate less upon outcomes. An 'equality of *opportunity* for welfare' acknowledges the importance of welfare and facilitates its pursuit without imagining that its actual achievement can or should be guaranteed (Arneson, 1989).[2] The state does not have a duty to fund my piano lessons but to provide me with decent opportunities, e.g. for a job, out of which I can fund my own piano lessons if I choose.

Equality of resources

Critics of welfare egalitarianism sometimes prefer to treat 'resources' as the currency of equality. Rawls (1993: 181), for instance, defines 'primary goods' as including basic rights and liberties, freedom of movement, freedom of occupation, income and wealth, and the social bases of self-respect. Resources can be external to the person (income, wealth, property) and internal (talents, abilities, aptitudes); some resources we acquire through choice and some through luck and circumstance.

Dworkin (2000: ch. 2) is a 'resource egalitarian'. Imagine some people become stranded on a deserted island. Having to invent their own society from scratch the islanders decide to use clamshells as their means of exchange. Everyone is given an equal initial amount and they then start trading with one another. Some people will spend their clamshells recklessly; some will hoard their stock; others will work hard and accumulate more clamshells. The point is that, given the initial distribution, nobody later on can reasonably envy anybody else's holdings. If you waste your clamshells you cannot reasonably complain at being poorer than those who were more prudent.

Therefore, Dworkin's equality of resources implies two things. Firstly, we should be sensitive to people's desires, tastes and choices (ambition-sensitivity). A resource-egalitarian distribution is that which accurately reflects the choices that people make – as when the reckless end up with fewer clamshells than the prudent.[3] Secondly, we can only reward good choices, or penalize bad ones, by not allowing the distribution of resources to be affected by those factors over which people have *no* control (endowment-insensitivity). If I am disabled by a falling tree then it seem unreasonable to leave me as poor as the imprudent. Perhaps, when agreeing on an equal initial distribution, each islander decides to contribute a percentage of their clamshells to an insurance pool in order to compensate those who later become disadvantaged through no fault of their own. This contribution would be equivalent to social insurance premium or a rate of taxation.

Of course, it may be that these twin requirements are too unrealistic. Perhaps we can never entirely eliminate the effects of undeserved advantage or disadvantage. If so, then an equality of opportunity for resources may be the second-best option. If, for example, we can never fully compensate for falling trees, then our insurance system might at least approximate to that ideal – perhaps by allowing individuals to determine their own insurance premiums over and above what is socially mandatory.

Capabilities

Another approach is satisfied with neither welfare nor resources – though it may incorporate them – and instead treats 'capabilities' as the preferable metric.

Sen (2009: 231–90) believes it possible to identify basic human 'functionings', but argues that the capabilities needed to realize those functionings will be highly diverse and context-specific. Thus, functionings are sets of 'beings' or 'doings' which are essential to human life, including being adequately nourished, being healthy, possessing self-respect and participating in social networks. A capability implies the power and freedom to achieve such functionings. Yet, because what it means to achieve health, say, varies across space and time – health in 2011 means something different to what it meant in 1911 since, as longevity lengthens, degenerative diseases become more frequent – so health-related capabilities also change.

Therefore, while it is important to recognize the importance of wellbeing we should not imagine that there is just one form of wellbeing appropriate for everyone. And although resources are important we should not confuse justice with the distribution of material *things*. An equality of income would imply an inequality in capabilities because, for instance, a disabled person typically requires a higher income to achieve the same functionings as an able-bodied person. Egalitarians should therefore be concerned with the 'space of capabilities' rather than with a single indicator of justice.

This, though, arguably gives the capabilities approach an unhelpful imprecision. How can we ensure a *space* of capabilities? Nussbaum (2006: 392–401; Burchardt, 2008) offers a list of capabilities which she holds to be universally applicable. These include being able to control one's environment, being safe, being able to reason, and so forth. Yet, while this gives us some idea of what is meant by a space of capabilities it is still highly generalized. For instance, we might agree that play, recreation and enjoyment are important, yet welfare egalitarians can argue that their importance derives from an overarching conception of *wellbeing*, e.g. needs (Dean, 2010: 85–9; recall Doyal and Gough's argument). Resource egalitarians might argue that income and wealth are not 'things' but social relations central to the opportunities which structure individuals' life-experiences (Fitzpatrick, 2008b).

Welfare, resources and capabilities all capture some aspect of egalitarianism but none seems entirely satisfactory on its own. There is, at present, no meta-theory which incorporates the insights of all three. We now go on to see how these metrics have influenced the main schools of thought in recent theorizing about justice and equality.

Distribution versus Solidarity?

The landscape chartered by John Rawls is one that all subsequent philosophers have been – sometimes reluctantly – forced to explore (Miller, 1999). If we wish to appreciate the significance of Rawls we first have to understand what it was he was challenging.

Utilitarianism

Utilitarianism is a normative moral and political philosophy (see pp.16–17). Characterized by Jeremy Bentham and John Stuart Mill (1806–73), Utilitarianism is concerned with how to maximize utility. Utility is a notoriously difficult concept to define. As we saw in the last chapter, Bentham (1984) took it to mean happiness, or an excess of pleasure over pain. Because Bentham believed that pleasure and pain could be measured, he concluded that utility was quantifiable: something had utility if it could be shown to contribute to the sum of human happiness. The problem, as Mill observed, is that this is only a shallow version of happiness which neglects the more complex pleasures and satisfactions of human life.

Subsequent Utilitarians have often adopted a non-hedonistic account of utility, e.g. as denoting some form of preference-satisfaction. If I am dining in a restaurant, then any of the meals on the menu may have utility: if I am ostentatious, then I am likely to value the most expensive meal; if I am a food connoisseur, then the most exotic meal might hold the greatest utility; if I am on a diet, then the meal with the fewest calories will be most valuable. Whatever my preference, the meal I select will possess utility for me.

Utilitarianism qualifies as an egalitarian doctrine because it states that equal consideration should be given to everyone's happiness and/ or preferences. This is partly because equality is held to have an intrinsic value – relating to Bentham's insistence that each person should count as one and nobody as more than one – but also partly because equality has an instrumental value: treating people equally is the best way of maximizing overall utility.

Imagine a society of 100 people, 50 of whom possess £1 million each whilst the other 50 possess nothing. According to Utilitarians, if by redistributing £10,000 from the richest to the poorest, the pleasure/ satisfaction experienced by the latter is greater than the displeasure/ dissatisfaction experienced by the former, then we are entitled to perform such redistributions until such time as the increasing utility of the poorest fails to outweigh the decreasing utility of the richest. Therefore, Utilitarianism is concerned to maximize utility and so has the potential to be strongly egalitarian.

But critics allege that Utilitarianism does not respect the rights, integrity and 'separateness' of persons (Fitzpatrick, 2008a: 30–9). What if our society contained 50 people with two arms each and 50 people with no arms? A strictly Utilitarian calculation seems to demand the compulsory redistribution of one arm per person from the fortunate to the unfortunate. But this hardly seems consistent with the requirements of liberty. Liberty would demand a lower level of utility. That 50 people have been dealt a bad hand (terrible pun, sorry) by life's lottery is certainly regrettable but this does not necessarily justify a compensatory redistribution that trumps the freedoms of others. Or, what if the satisfaction 90 people derived from torturing the other 10 was greater than the pain experienced by the tortured? A strictly Utilitarian calculation would demand that we allow torture. We could solve this by defining utility in a way that respects individuals' freedoms but this takes us away from the straightforward ideas defended by Bentham and Mill.

Is there a better way of ensuring social justice while also protecting individual liberties? Rawls believed there was.

Rawls

Rawls asks us to imagine ourselves as a group of people who have to decide what kind of society they would prefer to inhabit. In making this decision it is necessary to prevent bias, otherwise each of us is likely to prefer only that society which rewards the attributes that we individually possess. Therefore, we have to imagine ourselves behind a 'veil of ignorance' which means that nobody can have any knowledge of things such as their intelligence, skills and abilities, class position and social status, gender, race and ethnicity, and so forth (Rawls, 1972: 12). In this way, fairness and impartiality can be ensured because bias-motivating attributes have been factored out. So, in this 'original position', what kind of society should we choose to inhabit?

Rawls insists that we should choose to live in a society that protects our freedoms but which also maximizes the position of the least well-off – the maximin principle. Because, behind the veil of ignorance people do not know whether they are rich or poor, a rational person should decide to play it safe and support the maximin principle just in case they themselves turn out to be one of the poor when the veil is removed. A Rawlsian society would therefore embody the following two principles of justice:

- First Principle – Each person is to have an equal right to the most extensive total system of equal basic liberties compatible with a similar system of liberty for all.
- Second Principle – Social and economic inequalities are to be arranged so that they are both:
  (a) to the greatest benefit of the least advantaged, and
  (b) attached to offices and positions open to all under conditions of fair equality of opportunity. (Rawls, 1972: 302)

The first principle is the most important: liberty. A society cannot restrict liberty in the name of either equality or utility and be considered just. This is why Rawls opposed Utilitarianism. The second principle concerns equality and Rawls insists that fair equality of opportunity must take precedence. However, some equalization of outcomes is justified in terms of what he calls the 'difference principle': the notion that inequalities should be arranged so that they are to the benefit of the least advantaged.

Consider the alternatives in Table 2.1.

Which of these should we prefer? An anti-egalitarian prefers Blue because this is the *least* equal distribution, whereas an egalitarian prefers Red because

Table 2.1 Three distributive alternatives

	AMANDA	BILL	CAROL
BLUE	12	6	1
PURPLE	10	5	3
RED	4	3	2

this is the *most* equal. But according to the difference principle, we should prefer Purple because it is the one within which Carol, the least-well off in each society, possesses the most units, even though it is less egalitarian than Red. According to Rawlsian justice, if the wealth and income of the richest do not benefit the poorest, then we are justified in redistributing that wealth and income up until the point when such redistribution would no longer work in favour of the poorest. We might decide to introduce higher levels of taxation and spend the revenue raised on the least well-off; but if we reached a point where raising still more taxation only harmed the poor's interests, e.g. by damaging economic growth, then we should stop redistributing.

In sum, Rawls's theory of justice incorporates a strong element of social justice (the difference principle) that seems to require redistribution and the equalization of income, wealth and power (and other 'primary goods') but not equality for equality's sake.[4]

What kind of economic and social policies does this theory of social justice prescribe (Daniels & Sabin, 2002)? Rawls (1972: 274) states that his ideas are biased neither towards capitalism nor towards socialism. More often than not, though, he has been interpreted as giving support to the tradition of Centre-Left social democracy. If the object is to improve the material circumstances of the poorest, then private ownership and free markets might be required to generate wealth and ensure the *efficient* allocation of goods; but redistributive taxation, egalitarian welfare services, (some) socialized ownership of property and market regulation are required to ensure the *just* allocation of those goods. In social policy terms, Rawls might be thought of as a supporter of welfare state capitalism.

Rawls has been subjected to considerable criticism (Freeman, 2007: 72–9, 115–25). The Right charge Rawls with ignoring the role that individual entitlement should play in society (see pp.49–50). The Left charge Rawls with ignoring the value that social equality can have in and of itself (see p. 37). In addition, some have alleged that Rawls's ideas derive from assumptions which are inherently biased in favour of white ethnicity and masculinity (Pateman & Mills, 2007: 118–32). Communitarians (see Chapter 4) criticize Rawls's interpretation of the 'self' by insisting that we cannot be regarded as disembodied beings, even for the purposes of an imaginary exercise, because who and what we are depends upon the particular social and historical contexts within which we are rooted (Sandel, 1982; cf. Rawls, 1993; also Schaefer, 2007). Theorists favouring the capabilities approach believe that justice must imply more than material resources and primary goods (Nussbaum, 2006). Other critics suggest that it is naïve to assume that people in the original position should play it safe and adopt the maximin principle, e.g. they may prefer an extremely unequal society, taking the risk that they themselves will turn out to be poor.

Luck egalitarianism

Important criticisms have also been made by resource egalitarians. According to Rawls, we do not deserve our natural talents (like intelligence) any more than we deserve our social resources (like inheritances). They are both arbitrary 'from a moral point of view' because they are both due to accidents of birth. However, Dworkin (2000) argues that this neglects the importance of choice. Even if you do not deserve your intelligence, you still choose to use it in one way rather than another and so surely deserve something of whatever flows from such decisions.

Dworkin distinguishes between 'brute luck' and 'option luck'. Brute luck categorizes those events over which individuals have no control and so for which they cannot legitimately be held responsible; option luck categorizes those events for which an individual *can* reasonably be held responsible. There can be 'bad brute luck' and 'good brute luck'. If 50% of the houses on a street are damaged by a tornado, Peter and Petra experience bad brute luck if their houses are hit and Greg experiences good brute luck if his is not. There can also be 'good option luck' and 'bad option luck'. Peter experiences the former if he previously chose to take out appropriate insurance and Petra experiences the latter if she did not.

What has come to be called 'luck egalitarianism' makes two basic claims (Segall, 2010: 10–24). Firstly, social distributions should not derive from brute luck. Individuals should not be advantaged or disadvantaged because of circumstances they did not choose; chance, natural talents and socioeconomic backgrounds (such as parentage) should not determine social distributions. Egalitarian measures are justified in so far as they eliminate, or at least compensate for, the dis/advantages deriving from brute luck. Secondly, if and when brute luck has been neutralized people should bear the consequences of the choices they make. Peter and Petra may both be due some assistance. However, all things being equal, because Paul chose to pay insurance premiums he would deserve higher compensation than Petra.

In other words, justice demands a combination of endowment-insensitivity and ambition-sensitivity. Luck egalitarianism therefore captures the long-standing intuitions of the Left while rescuing notions of choice and responsibility from the Right (Matravers, 2007). Three key objections have been made to it, however (Scheffler, 2003; Fleurbaey, 2008).

Firstly, luck egalitarianism is arguably too severe in that, once brute luck is no longer a factor, it would presumably require someone who chooses unwisely to bear the full costs of that decision. Anderson (1999: 295–6) claims that luck egalitarians must leave someone injured on the side of the road if she was responsible for the accident. This therefore conflicts with recent attempts to incorporate an ethic of care into principles of justice (see below). Luck egalitarianism thus offends against feelings and duties of compassion, dignity, respect, empathy and benevolence.

Secondly, it is also charged with being too demeaning, intrusive and paternalistic (Anderson, 1999: 300–2). In counteracting the effects of brute luck, luck egalitarianism must compensate those whose initial endowments are poor. But this involves prying into the personal circumstances of those who have experienced brute luck disadvantage. In effect, luck egalitarianism says 'your talents are below an acceptable threshold, have some money as compensation'.

Finally, there is arguably an obstructive indeterminacy about the brute/ option distinction (Hurley, 2003). How much brute luck really operates in people's lives? How can we know when a choice is not a product of brute luck? Could we ever really neutralize brute luck inequalities? Luck egalitarianism requires us to take a stance on complex questions of free will and determinism which only problematize equality and egalitarian politics.

The debate does not end there and luck egalitarians make spirited responses to their critics (Arneson, 2004; Segall, 2010: 37–44, 59–73). Knight (2009) argues that luck egalitarians *are* motivated by values like respect and benevolence but simply wish to think through the consequences of no longer basing social distributions upon accidents of birth.

Relational egalitarianism

Others insist that Rawlsians and luck egalitarians possess too limiting an approach to questions of justice. Perhaps, as we saw on pp.27–31, there is no single metric of justice that will suffice for all people in all places at all times. Some egalitarians therefore believe that we should not associate social justice so closely with just *distributions*. *Social* justice has to imply more than *distributive* justice alone since the appeal of egalitarianism resides in its values; its humanitarian emphasis upon compassion, interdependency, care, togetherness and fraternity (Schmidtz, 2006: 114–19). The *quality* of social relationships is what matters and not a mechanical reorganization of economic goods. There is no consensus, however, over what this might imply.

Anderson (1999) proposes a 'democratic equality' that resists social oppression and natural injustice by defending an ethos of equal recognition and a capabilities-based version of social relationships. However, it can be argued that this fails to embody the very compassion which Anderson charges luck egalitarians with ignoring.

Wolff and de-Shalit (2007) have tried to combine distributional and relational approaches. They are influenced by Michael Walzer's (1983; Miller & Walzer, 1995) notion of complex equality. Instead of fitting a diverse range of social goods into a single 'sphere' of distributive justice, Walzer envisages each good operating within its own distributive sphere according to norms that are not necessarily shared by other spheres. This implies that dominance in one sphere would not engender dominance in others. I may be dominant in terms of wealth, for instance, but this should not mean that I am similarly dominant in terms of access to health care or educational opportunities. Wolff and de-Shalit also draw from the capabilities approach.

They argue that a just society is one which gives priority to the least advantaged, i.e. those who experience and become trapped within a 'cluster' of disadvantages. To be disadvantaged is to lack 'genuine opportunities for secure functionings'. Such disadvantages are likely to be corrosive in that one will often create or intensify others. For instance, a lack of access to social networks may affect access to job opportunities, reducing that person's income and so having knock-on effects on health. The job of government should be to 'de-cluster' those disadvantages so that it gradually becomes harder for us to identify who the least advantaged are. The corrosive interaction of disadvantages needs to be challenged, though social policies need to be pluralist since it is unlikely that just one redistributive method will suffice.

Wolff and de-Shalit provide a welcome contribution. However, it can be argued that they fudge the luck egalitarian's concern with choice and responsibility. Nor do they have much to say about property, capital and capitalism.

Another attempt to reconcile the distributive and the relational is provided by G. A. Cohen (1941–2009). While happy to describe himself as a luck egalitarian, Cohen (2008) attacks Rawls' approach. Rawls says that talents and inheritances are morally arbitrary because they are undeserved, but would permit inequalities so long as they are to the benefit of the least well-off. Rawls' assumption is that, unless we allow them to retain a large slice of their earnings, the richest will become demotivated and work less hard, so that fewer resources will be available to distribute to the least advantaged. We have to appeal to their incentives if we want to benefit the poorest. But, for Cohen, this is tantamount to allowing the powerful (and lucky) to hold everyone else to ransom. The rich in effect say, 'I'll allow you to tax me only once you pay me lots of money.' But such economic blackmail is not what egalitarian justice should imply. You don't regard a thief as acting morally just because he donates some of the money he stole to charity. Cohen therefore detects a contradiction in Rawls's philosophy. It asks us to be concerned with the least advantaged while appealing to an ethos of self-interest. We ought, instead, to be concerned with the cultural values and social morality of justice, while reviving the socialist aim of long-term social transformation.

This is a powerful argument, but it has to be questioned whether and to what extent this culture of justice can be created. Rawls (2001: 10) was concerned with what he called the 'basic structure of society', i.e. the main political and social institutions. The basic structure is concerned with social cooperation but does not assume that everyone can or should be motivated by a similar political ethos of altruism and mutualism.

There are many different kinds of egalitarianism, then. Indeed, some are fond of quoting Bernard Williams when he suggested that equality implies a plurality of ultimately incommensurable ideas (White, 2006: 97). It is, however, possible to anticipate some of these disagreements being resolved in the future. Those concerned with distributions need to appeal to social relationships; those concerned with the latter need to specify an appropriate distribution of social goods.

Social Policy and Equality

It is sometimes tempting to throw in the philosophical towel, though. With few exceptions (e.g. Van Parijs, 1995), the vast majority of the brilliant minds who have theorized about equality and justice in recent decades have *not* dealt with real-world problems or policy prescriptions. There are one or two signs that fashions are shifting (Barry, 2005; Craig et al., 2008) but social policy commentators are entitled to feel rather frustrated with their philosophy colleagues (cf. McLaughlin & Baker, 2007). Perhaps we should bypass such debates altogether.

Wilkinson and Pickett (2009) present a considerable amount of evidence which suggests that equality is almost always better for you. This is because – morally, emotionally, materially and socially – inequality creates insecurity, vulnerability, selfishness, anxiety, shame and fear. Unequal societies are ones in which everyday bonds of trust begin to fray as people see others as strangers, obstacles and competitors. As social ties erode so we try to fill the vacuum created with materialistic substitutes. To maintain its wellbeing, the self becomes dependent upon consumption in a life which feels more and more like an unwinnable race (an hedonic treadmill?). The costs of inequality surround us: impoverished communities, rising rates of depression, ill-health, crime and low-level hostility. Thus, whatever equality is we need more of it. Even the wealthiest benefit from living in equal societies.

However, this does not mean that we should set philosophical complexities to one side. Recall the society where 50 have two arms and 50 have none. We could create equality by compulsory redistributing one arm from the fortunate to the unfortunate, or by cutting off all arms. In other words, not all forms of equality are desirable as there are many other principles that we need to promote and protect.

Furthermore, post-2WW reforms were often driven by what Tawney (1964) called a 'strategy of equality'. This strategy required the establishment of institutions that would guarantee equal access to those goods without which life is impoverished and incomplete. Tawney favoured classlessness as the ultimate goal of social and economic reform and so was a supporter of comprehensive education. By contrast, T. H. Marshall (1893–1981) defended the welfare state as something which equalized status and eliminated undeserved advantages, but which could safely leave *just* inequalities alone because these are necessary to a healthy economy and reflective of individual differences and abilities. In short, despite their shared concern with social justice, Tawney believed that equality implied classlessness while for Marshall a citizens' society could still include considerable inequalities. Social policy cannot be indifferent to such alternative social philosophies, therefore.

We must also remember that support for social equality was not universally shared, even amongst those who founded the welfare state. Bismarck set up pensions and unemployment insurance in the Germany of the 1870s to forestall the possibility of socialists gaining power. It seems, then, that although a desire for greater social equality motivated many welfare architects, it would be simplistic to interpret the welfare state as a straightforward strategy of equality.

Consequently, and as we shall see in Chapter 6, the welfare state's record on equalizing wealth, income and power is often modest. Le Grand (1982) makes this argument by identifying five types of equality:

Equality of Public Expenditure
Public expenditure on the provision of a particular social service should be allocated equally between all relevant individuals, e.g. two state schools of equal size should receive equivalent amounts of public money.

Equality of Final Income
This implies a vertical redistribution from the rich to the poor. (In contrast to horizontal redistribution (a) within the life-course, i.e. from the wealthier parts of your life to the poorer, or (b) between occupations.)

Equality of Use
The amount of a public service used by all relevant individuals should be the same, e.g. two people who are equally ill with the same condition should receive equivalent medical treatment.

Equality of Cost
All service users should face the same private (or opportunity) costs, e.g. an inequality of costs arises if Jack is able to take time off work to visit his doctor, whereas Jill's employer docks her half a day's wages.

Equality of Outcome
This refers to an equivalency in the consequences that a welfare service has for its users.[5]

Le Grand believes that the welfare state has failed to deliver on any of the above. For instance, he insists that the wealthiest receive up to 40 per cent more in terms of UK healthcare expenditure than the poorest. Essentially, this is because the welfare state is caught in a contradiction: it was intended by many to embody an ethos of equality without fundamentally challenging the profound inequalities of capitalist society.

Similarly, Hills (1997) finds that most of the benefits that people derive from the welfare state originate out of the taxes and contributions that they themselves have paid; only one-quarter of what the welfare state delivers could be defined as 'Robin Hood' redistribution from rich to poor. For Le Grand, this is not necessarily a bad thing (Goodin & Le Grand, 1987) because if the welfare state were to equalize resources too much then it could easily lose the support of those from whom such resources would be taken. By pursuing only modest redistribution, the welfare state has been able to retain the broad support of the middle classes and it is this which enabled it to survive the radical Right onslaught of the 1980s and 1990s.

By and large, then, we should think of the welfare state as being mostly concerned with equality of opportunity. It is, at best, an egalitarian liberal set of institutions. The debate does not end there, however, for even within the context of equal opportunities there are many different ways of organizing welfare services. To illustrate this point look at two important debates.

Universalism and selectivism

According to Richard Titmuss (1907–1973), the principle of universality refers to

> ...the aim of making services available and accessible to the whole population in such ways as would not involve users in any humiliating loss of status, dignity or self-respect. There should be no sense of inferiority, pauperism, shame or stigma in the use of a publicly provided service; no attribution that one was being or becoming a 'public burden'. (Titmuss, 1968: 129)

Access to universal services is therefore 'triggered' by the demonstration of some kind of need, irrespective of one's income level, e.g. a medical exam might reveal the need for hospitalization. By contrast, selectivism is usually taken to imply a means-test (such as Food Stamps in the USA) and/or a charge for the service at the point of use (having to pay a fee to consult a doctor).

Now, from an egalitarian point of view, both universality and selectivity have their attractions. Universal services embody an ethic of citizenship: the notion that we are all part of the same society and should all have access to welfare provision (Rothstein, 1998). The trouble is that, apart from being expensive, universal services may also contradict egalitarian aims. If the Duke of Westminster is entitled to receive the same provision as his chauffeur then this might perpetuate, rather than eradicate, the inequalities between them. Therefore, selective services are more vertically redistributive. Means-tested benefits are funded out of taxation and are provided only to those who fall below a stipulated income level. Selectivism therefore implies that people should be *treated* unequally by virtue of the fact that they have unequal incomes. The trouble is that selectivism, too, can contradict egalitarian aims for such services divide people into haves and have-nots with a considerable stigma being attached to those who depend upon selectivist provision.

Positive discrimination

Policies of positive discrimination are associated largely with the USA (Sandel, 2009: 167–83). The idea is that where certain groups have been disadvantaged in the past, we have a duty to ensure that existing institutions and practices give a preferential form of treatment to those groups so that the injustices to which they have been subjected will be eliminated. We might decide, for instance, that companies and colleges have to admit a certain percentage of women, black people and disabled people.[6] This is consistent with an equal opportunities attempt to assemble everyone equally at the starting-line.

Critics of positive discrimination allege that such policies ignore merit and so are unfair to talented individuals. Let us say that Jeff, who is white, male, able-bodied, and has five qualifications, applies for a job which is subsequently given to a black, disabled women with three qualifications for reasons of positive discrimination. Is this fair? Nobody could seriously deny that black disabled women are not discriminated against in society, but this is not Jeff's fault, so why should he lose out because of some quota system? Furthermore, positive discrimination could mean that well-off individuals from disadvantaged groups may gain at the expense of poorer individuals from *both* advantaged and disadvantaged groups. It may also mean that talented individuals from under-privileged groups are incorrectly assumed to owe their success to quotas rather than merit. Finally, by creating a backlash against social equality *per se*, positive discrimination may distract from a more radical egalitarian agenda.

However, defenders of positive discrimination argue that the short-term injustice to a privileged individual like Jeff is out-weighed by the long-term interests of the disadvantaged group. Dworkin (1977: 223–39) goes further and contends that because institutions such as colleges can be thought of as *social* institutions, with duties to the wider society, it is no more unfair to admit someone on, say, racial grounds than it is to do so on the grounds of IQ. If black communities need more black doctors, then a few less white medical students is a small price to pay.

One possible compromise between these two positions is to give preferential treatment to *low-income* individuals. Somebody with three qualifications might well possess more merit and suitability for the job than someone with five qualifications if the latter grew up in a mansion and the former grew up in a slum. However, placing an emphasis on low-incomes might neglect the specific *cultural* injustices to which many are subjected (see below and Chapter 8).

Recent Developments

Equality of differences

Differential equality is an idea we have already encountered. The capabilities approach identifies basic human functionings but claims that the capabilities needed to realize them will vary across different socioeconomic, political and cultural-historical territories. But the basic concept preceded this approach and to some extent reflects the changing priorities of the 1970s and 1980s when identity politics came to prominence. We explore identity in Chapter 8. For now we can say the following:

Although many egalitarians have acknowledged the importance of plurality and diversity, many egalitarian politics and policies have imposed a conceptual 'blanket' upon society, smoothing over certain valuable differences. Oppression, it is argued, can often result from benign intentions. For instance, gender equality has long been a goal of progressive movements, but unless such equality is sensitive to the differences between white/black women, straight/ lesbian women, Western/non-Western women, able-bodied/disabled women, and so forth, then gender equality may inadvertently institutionalize subtler, more cultural forms of discrimination and prejudice.

Differential equality, then, is about breaking down the conceptual difference between 'difference' and 'equality' and about trying to develop appropriate social, public, economic and political practices. The theoretical work has been performed largely by postmodernists, often influenced by feminist theory (e.g. Young, 1990, 2009; Fraser & Honneth, 2003). The social implications of differential equality can be wide-ranging, but usually imply a retention of what the welfare state can do best (provision for basic needs) combined with a call for the democratization of welfare services so that these differential identities can gain a new and powerful voice. Some insist that it is a differential or postmodern social policy, based around the new social movements, that should inspire future welfare reform.

Caring for equality

Care is both a good to be distributed fairly and an expression of the respect and dignity which are owed to people. In short, care is a matter of distributive, relational and differential justice.

There is a long-standing debate over whether care should be included within the idiom of justice at all (Fitzpatrick, 2005: 44–6). Gilligan (1982) famously argued that justice is an inherently masculine concept. Just as masculinity implies separations between mind and body, culture and nature, so justice implies that people should treat each other as strangers who relate to one another through impersonal rules and codified systems of behaviour. The very language of justice speaks with a masculine voice. By contrast, an ethic of care is more suited to a feminine emphasis upon connection, communication, empathy and mutual identification. Care implies emotional intimacy and is not something that can be abstracted into commandments, regulations or formal rights and responsibilities. Care implies a particular relationship between the carer are the cared-for but, even more than this, a moral society is one in which people all care for one another.

Few commentators have accepted Gilligan's framework uncritically. Her categories (justice = masculine, care = feminine) appear to imitate the very masculinist hierarchies that she wishes to overturn. Furthermore, care is that to which conservatives have long appealed in the form of a sentimental attachment to history, authority, locality, home, family and country. Yet most feminists are aware of the oppressive gender relations which frequently lurk within each of these terms. Many philosophers have therefore sought a rapprochement between care and justice.

As such, care has been promoted as an egalitarian concept. If people care for one another, they are less likely to see others as competitors in a free market environment. And egalitarianism has made room for care. As we saw above, luck egalitarians value such notions too. There are now few theories of egalitarian justice which make no allowance for a political economy of care.

Equality of assets

A great deal of emphasis has recently been placed on 'assets' among those philosophers concerned with the practicalities of policy reform (White, 2003). Egalitarians have always been interested in redistributing wealth and, for a long time, this was taken to refer to 'capital'. For Marxists, justice was associated with a socialization of the ownership of productive resources. To redistribute wealth, you needed a collective control of the commanding heights of the economy. Whatever the merits of this position, by the 1970s it held less purchase in the popular mind than the radical Right's appeal to more personalized forms of wealth: consumerism, home ownership, shares. Some egalitarian theorists have therefore sought to shift social justice onto a similar political agenda, albeit one which is less individualistic.

'Assets' typically refer to a stock of resources and endowments such as inheritances, investment capital, education entitlements, property, shares/ stocks and savings/trusts. To redistribute wealth according to the precepts of social justice implies ensuring that such assets are available to all and so not possessed disproportionately by the economically advantaged (Schram, 2006: ch. 5). Imagine that everyone is entitled as a right to an annual dividend generated out of the profits of their nation's most successful companies. Citizens are here defined as stakeholders with equal rights to basic assets.

Proposals for a guaranteed minimum income have appealed to such notions of asset-based welfare (Wright, 2006). Thus, a monthly income paid to all unconditionally could be considered as a basic right of citizenship, an inalienable entitlement to a proportion of economic growth. Others have proposed that such entitlements should generate a lump-sum capital grant, paid to all high-school graduates (Ackerman & Alstott, 1999). Such grants could be used to finance a university degree, create a small business or simply fund a wild night at the local casino. If asset egalitarianism was a means of eliminating the influence of brute luck, then an array of such activities would be permissible, so long as the individual accepts the consequences of either choosing well or badly!

Readers should now possess a clearer idea as to why the principle of equality has enduring appeal. Yet the concept is undoubtedly a complex and controversial one. This chapter traced some of the main controversies and explained how these translate into competing theories of social justice. As such, we risk misinterpreting social policies unless we appreciate the extent to which welfare services struggle to reconcile social equality and liberty, a struggle that is likely to continue as new theories and perspectives of social equality become influential.

Lurking throughout the above discussion, though, was another concept crucial to any understanding of justice and it is this which we now move on to explore in more depth.

Questions for Further Discussion

- Offer a critique of what John Rawls meant by 'fair equality of opportunity'.
- On Monday everyone in the country owns one house. On Tuesday everyone in the country, except yourself, is given another house. Are you now worse off than you were on Monday?
- In a society where 50% of people are millionaires and the other 50% are billionaires, should we redistribute wealth from the latter to the former?
- To what extent is it credible to debate 'equality of opportunity' without reference to 'equality of outcome'?

3
Liberty

- Libertarianism
- The Invisible Hand
- Nozick and Hayek
- Equality versus Liberty?
- Negative and Positive Liberty
- Further Thoughts
- Recent Developments

Equality and liberty are reference points for disagreements about the nature and social implications of justice. As such, we will be revisiting many themes from Chapter 2 and anticipating some of the ideas and debates we encounter later in the book.

The central questions are the following:

- What is liberty?
- How does liberty relate to social equality?
- How can a society be free while avoiding chaos and anarchy?

There are many answers that have been given to these questions (cf. Goodin, 1988: 306–31; Schmidtz & Brennan, 2010: 1–18).[1]

Plato (427–347 BC) insisted that freedom could not imply people doing whatever they wanted, for this would lead to the blind dominance of the appetites (Plato, 1955). Instead, justice demands that the characteristics of individuals and of society chime with one another harmoniously. Aristotle (1988) also distinguished between ordered liberty and anarchic liberty. He equated freedom with citizenship and, in the Ancient world, free citizens were predominantly male, Athenian property-owners, in contrast to non-citizens (slaves, foreigners and women). For Plato and Aristotle, therefore, freedom seemed to demand restrictions on the number of people definable *as* free.

Such restrictions have become less and less acceptable in the modern world. Indeed, by 'the modern' we mean a process of liberalization and emancipation where the former bonds of exclusion are broken and freedom becomes a universal principle. Over the last two hundred years, fewer and fewer reasons have been found for limiting the principle to a lucky elite and, one by one, regimes based upon slavery, apartheid, limited suffrage, despotism, female subjugation and religious oppression have toppled. But with each extension of freedom the above questions have become more prominent.

We first review libertarian and economic liberal theories of liberty; pp. 46–54 explore how and why liberty has been used as a weapon with which to attack social equality and state welfare; pp.54–5 contrasts negative with positive liberty; pp.55–8 then complicates matters by reviewing how those definitions can be rearranged and refined; pp.59–64 then explores some recent theoretical developments.

Libertarianism

Libertarians regard liberty as freedom from interference by others (Narveson, 2001; Kukathas, 2003; see Kymlicka, 2002: ch. 4). It involves equality only in so far as liberty is distributed equally to all. However, 'equal liberty' does not imply 'equality of outcomes'. People are free in so far as they are not restrained by others, where interfering with the distribution of goods, income, wealth, etc. constitutes such a restraint. Free individuals are also more likely to respect the freedoms *of* others. Yes, we need an enforceable rule of law to ensure, for instance, that private property is respected. But a free society is one that protects the voluntary exchanges and relationships of individuals.

Libertarianism has attracted several important theorists and we explore its most persuasive proponent, Robert Nozick (1938–2002), shortly. Traditionally, it can be thought of as having free market, right-wing implications. Indeed, libertarianism might be thought of as a reinvention of 'classical liberalism', i.e. the liberalism of early capitalism which defended free markets, the minimal 'nightwatchman' state, private property and self-help individualism (Mack & Gaus, 2004).

In this respect, it has a dog-eat-dog quality to it. Herbert Spencer (1820–1903) proclaimed the advantages of egoism (J. Offer, 2006: ch. 2). As a 'social Darwinian' he insisted that what we call society is a constant process of struggle, a never-ending fight for survival. For if only the strongest survived would humanity become stronger. This suggested that people should be left alone to prosper (or not) as best they could, as any interference into these natural processes would only leave humanity weaker. Spencer (1969) regarded a market free-for-all as the ideal medium for this evolutionary struggle, with the state having little role to play.

However, note that not all Right libertarians necessarily say that we are motivated primarily by self-interest. Like Nozick, Mack (2009) states that individuals have a right of self-ownership and thus to private property. This generates an economic and political liberalism in which self-interest will play a central role, but not necessarily a dog-eat-dog free for all!

But the Right have not monopolized the libertarian agenda. Spencer himself subverted a Left–Right framework, arguing in the mid-nineteenth century that women should be regarded as free beings. In addition to the Left-libertarianism outlined below, a counter-cultural libertarianism emerged in the 1960s. Some of the radical politics of that decade was driven by the desire to tear down repressive conventions and celebrate drug-taking, non-marital sex and so forth.

Elements of that spirit continue to exist in a kind of 'cyber-libertarianism' where the freedom to exchange information, e.g. via the Internet, is defended against those who would prefer to control information flows.

In any event, it is not difficult to object to libertarianism. Firstly, why define freedom as doing whatever you wish to do? Perhaps the exercise of freedom demands that we respect and observe the needs of others. Freedom may be a moral category which implies reference to obligations and care, rather than just self-interest and property rights. Secondly, if we ignore the importance of equalizing the distribution of income, wealth and all other goods which affect human wellbeing, then any doctrine of equal liberties may be 'formal' rather than 'substantive'. Someone is formally free if they are not being restrained yet, nevertheless, lack the resources needed to translate that freedom into a meaningful and purposeful life. Indeed, it may well be that libertarians are blind to the *de facto* restraints that a lack of real opportunities involves. If a pauper is free to dine at the Ritz *if only he had the money*, then what kind of freedom is that? Defining freedom in such terms might only benefit the powerful and advantaged. Thirdly, the risk of freedom having immoral and/or deleterious consequences cannot be wished away. To be consistent, libertarians surely have to recommend the legalization of *all* drugs, *all* pornography, etc. Some do, but it is much more common to find libertarians hedging their principles. Block (1994) argues that whereas such activities should not be proscribed they *should* be discouraged.

In short, it is rare to find someone advocating a pure, unqualified libertarianism. Even within the confines of libertarianism, therefore, we can see that there is no simple, answer to the question 'what is liberty?'

The Invisible Hand

To this end, Right libertarians often support free market economics.[2] Unregulated capitalism may not represent the perfect expression of libertarian freedoms, but it might be the best that we can reasonably expect. Thus, it is difficult to specify where right-wing libertarianism ends and economic liberalism begins (Friedman, 1989).

The problem of how to ensure that a market-based society remains ordered became particularly acute by the eighteenth century. As the power of the aristocracy was undermined, as democratic movements gathered momentum and as the economy became industrialized, so people were faced with the problem of how to reconcile private interest with the public good. Some identified self-interest as the overwhelming source of human motivation. Mandeville (1670–1733) insisted that what everyone desired, first and foremost, was wealth and luxury for themselves (Mandeville, 1988). Public benefits could not be the result of *deliberately* trying to create such benefits; instead, if everyone pursued their own private interest, then the sum of such interests would inevitably generate the public good. By benefiting themselves the selfish would benefit others too.

Hume (1969) took issue with this view. He also believed in a system of private property and market exchange but observed that such a system could only endure if there were certain moral, social and legal rules binding on all. Hume identifies an empathetic impulse where I project myself into the role of a neutral spectator in order to provide an impartial assessment of my own actions. In a society of purely egoistic selves there would be nothing to stop me from harming others if it were to my advantage to do so; but the system of private property and market exchange would then quickly destroy itself, since the same would be true for everyone else! The capacity to empathize and to imagine myself as an impartial spectator motivates me to curb such tendencies. The system of rules, which only government can guarantee, is simply a way of formalizing this capacity.

Adam Smith (1723–1790) extended Hume's political philosophy and virtually invented 'classical' economics with its insistence that the free market was the means by which: (1) private interest was translated into the public good and (2) my freedom is made compatible with yours (Smith, 1970). In a competitive market, hat manufacturers, let us say, will have to lower their prices if they are to attract customers and, by doing so, everyone gains: producers will make a profit and consumers will be able to buy hats at affordable prices. There are two scenarios where this will not be true, however. Firstly, where the supply of hats is too high (or the demand for them too low, which is the same thing). Here, the market will be flooded to such an extent that the low price of hats will not enable everyone to make a profit. Secondly, where the supply is too low (or demand too high) customers will have to pay exorbitant prices. However, these scenarios should cancel each other out over the course of time. If, for instance, the supply of shoes was too low, then those who failed in the hat market would be able to step in and try their luck in the shoe market, supplying that demand and bringing the prices of shoes down. In short, a free and competitive market should always balance itself out over time and achieve an equilibrium of supply and demand. By producers trying to make a profit and consumers trying to save money, everybody should gain in the long run. Therefore, market competitors are led by an 'invisible hand' to promote the general welfare even though this was no part of their original intention. Like Hume, though, Smith attaches this invisible hand to a visible arm: namely, certain moral and social codes of behaviour ('moral sentiments') that are underwritten by the rule of law and guaranteed by the state.

This moral philosophy has often been neglected by those eager to claim Smith as a straightforward economic liberal and some claim that Smith's moral justification for market economics actually serves Left-wing as much as Right-wing agendas (Stedman Jones, 2004: 231–5; Satz, 2007). Therefore, while economic liberalism *may* approximate to libertarianism, it is more common for economic liberals to prefer an active role for the law and the state.

We therefore have two perspectives on liberty. Freedom can be regarded as the pursuit of self-interest that translates into the public good without much need for collective intervention (definition 1). Freedom can also be regarded as the pursuit of self-interest that translates into the public good via a free market based upon moral, social and legal rules that are actively protected by the state (definition 2). Definition 1 appeals to those, whether on the left or right, who view freedom in black-and-white terms; recall the zero-sum game mentioned on p. 19. Definition 2 adds a degree of complexity into the picture, such that freedom becomes 'multipolar', i.e. stretching along multiple axes and dimensions. The next section outlines the ideas of two of the most important theorists of recent decades: Robert Nozick, who defends 1, and Friedrich Hayek, who defends 2.

Nozick and Hayek

Nozick (1974) criticizes the stance of pure anarchists and libertarians for their complete rejection of the state. There has to be some agency upon which all can rely, for their physical and legal security, otherwise we would experience the endless proliferation of private police forces, private armies and private legal systems with irresolvable conflicts emerging between them. Nozick then defends definition 1 from the political Right.

He starts with the inviolability of individual rights: put simply, he holds something to be just if it derives from the exercise of such rights and unjust if it involves their infringement. This gives rise to an 'entitlement' or 'procedural' theory of justice which Nozick contrasts favourably with what are called 'patterned' or 'end-state' theories.

Imagine that six people are playing poker. Each player starts the game with equivalent amounts of money and poker skills. Let us say that when the game ends Alan and Betty have done very well, Carl and Daisy have broken even and Edgar and Fran are almost bankrupt. Do we have any grounds for regarding this state of affairs as unjust? According to Nozick, we do not. Since each player chose to play and play in a certain way, the result of the game can be interpreted as perfectly fair. In short, *if in a series of exchanges each individual transfer and transaction is just, i.e. does not violate anyone's rights, then the outcome of that series is also just, even if massive inequalities have been created.* This entitlement account can be contrasted with patterned justice, where the focus is upon the end-state of a series of transactions (the result of the game) rather than the process out of which the end-state was produced. According to Nozick, if we forcibly redistributed some of Alan and Betty's winnings, this would violate their rights and constitute an injustice. (Note that this has nothing to do with desert as Alan and Betty may simply have been incredibly lucky: *but even though they may not deserve their winnings they are entitled to them and should be able to dispose of them as they wish.*)

Formulated in response to Rawls, Nozick's arguments challenge all forms of redistributive and egalitarian politics. End-state theories, he believed, disrespect a fundamental right to own private property. Imagine that I walk through the woods one day, pick up a fallen branch and whittle it into an attractive sculpture.[3] This combination of nature and labour is the source of what is now my private property. You wish to purchase the sculpture and we agree a price of £5. I didn't steal the branch, no-one forced me to take the time and effort to create the sculpture and no-one forced you to purchase it. What right, then, does the state have to come along and tax my £5? None, according to Nozick. If someone stole the sculpture then that would be theft. Well, so the state's taxation is also a form of theft, or what Nozick calls 'forced labour'. Just as I own my capacity to labour ('the principle of self-ownership'), so I surely own whatever my labour creates. Yet, through taxation, the state has forced me to work for it. So although it seems humane to take my money and redistribute it to the have-nots, this is actually a violation of what it means to be a person.

After all, imagine that it would benefit the least advantaged to redistribute talents or body parts. If I am a talented piano-player should the state force me to give piano lessons to poor people who wanted to learn? And recall the society in Chapter 2 where 50 people have two arms and the other 50 have none. Should we force redistributive surgery on the fortunate 50? Most of us would resist such coercions. Yet why should we then permit the redistribution of the products of my labour through taxation?

As such, the dismantling of state welfare systems, and their replacement with market-based forms of security and insurance, would be entirely legitimate. Rather than a pool of social insurance, each individual could use their earnings to purchase, from competing insurance companies, whatever levels and types of insurance protection they prefer.

Whereas Nozick's commitment to neo-anarchic liberalism demands the almost complete withdrawal of the state, Friedrich Hayek (1899–1991) defends a constitutional reorganization that would, in some respects, leave it more centralized and powerful than before. The principle of social justice is also anathema to Hayek (1976). The redistribution of income and wealth is certainly ruled out by his political philosophy, but so too is an equality of opportunity. This is because, like Nozick, he regards justice as something that refers to actions and exchanges, and not to end-states or collective circumstances.

If I am walking along and, completely by accident, a brick falls off a wall and hits me on the head, then that is unfortunate for me, *but it is not an injustice*. If no injury was intended then I can moan about fate, but I can't claim to have been treated unjustly. Hayek insists that the market (though his preferred term is the 'spontaneous order') is just the same. There can be *actions* which are either just or unjust, but justice cannot refer to society and social environments. Society is simply an aggregate of the unintended consequences of individuals' acts and exchanges, and it is this lack of intention that renders the concept of social justice meaningless. The market does not drop a brick on my head because a market is not an 'agent'; it is a process of countless millions of decisions and exchanges which produce unintended consequences. If inequalities are the result, then such inequalities cannot be morally condemned; in the spontaneous market order there is no central, sovereign agent determining who wins and who loses.

Instead, it is only the egalitarian, managerialist state which imposes such patterns upon society. Ironically, it is the proponents of social justice who have contrived to propagate injustice: every attempt to equalize material resources and opportunities gives too much power to the state, the state being a perennial source of injustice (and inefficiency and incompetence). By handicapping the free market, the welfare state has created far more destitution than would otherwise have been the case. Imposing some kind of ideal, utopian pattern of distribution upon society can only lead to the infringement of individual liberties by a state exceeding what should be its proper role: namely, guaranteeing national security, the rule of law and the rules of just conduct.

Initially, Hayek (1944) imagined that the state should simply be restricted and the economy privatized and deregulated. Later, he came to believe that economic reform alone was not enough, that a wide-ranging constitutional, political and legal reorganization was needed to minimize the possibility of the free market being damaged by those who advocated redistribution and state ownership, e.g. Hayek (1979) recommends the exclusion of trade unions from the political process. He is therefore opposed to a strong state that *threatens* the market but not to a strong state which bolsters and protects it.

Equality versus Liberty?

Are these criticisms of state welfare convincing? The last chapter spelt out several arguments which suggest that liberty and equality are mutually reinforcing and interdependent, perhaps suggesting a third definition. We shall critique Nozick and Hayek, then, once we have seen how liberty has been viewed by other influential theorists within the liberal tradition.

Immanuel Kant (1724–1804) was a liberal in that he did not believe that notions of what is the 'good life for man' should be imposed on individuals. The modern period was one of freedom from the subjugation of monarchs and despots. Freedom implies obedience to the moral law which is revealed to us through reason, plus a recognition that all agents (autonomous beings) can similarly obey such laws. A free society, according to Kant (1996), is a 'kingdom of ends' where people do not relate to one another simply as 'means', i.e. as instruments or vehicles that I use to advance my own interests. Instead of the selfish individualism all too often defended by apologists for early capitalism, the Kantian individual is concerned to live morally with, and offer public justifications of their behaviour to, others. This requires a state which respects the dignity of its citizens.

Influenced by Kant, but also critical of him, Georg Hegel (1770–1831) initiated a tradition of thinking, which to some extent represents an alternative to liberalism. Prior to Hegel, freedom had usually been defined ahistorically, i.e. as the same for all people in all places and at all times. Hegel (1967) regarded freedom as something which evolved with the unfolding of history and the self-realization of *geist*. *Geist* is a difficult concept to define, referring to absolute spirit or mind. It is that which 'authors' and infuses the material world and historical development can be explained as *geist* coming to consciousness of itself through three stages.

The first stage is the stage of collective, historical unconsciousness: the primitive state of humanity. The second stage consists of succeeding periods of alienation and conflict as humanity comes to recognize itself as an object of study and the source of its own evolution. The final stage is that of infinite and endless self-consciousness, the overcoming of alienated being, the reconciliation of dialectical opponents, the transparent union of self and essence. The meaning of freedom therefore changes with every unfolding 'moment' of history. During stage two, it is articulated within the spheres of the family (the emotive bonds of kinship) and civil society (the contractual bonds of rights and duties). But as we move into stage three, so the opposition between family and civil society is reconciled within the state. The state therefore represents the transcendence of 'individual' versus 'collective', and freedom comes to mean the realization of the self within and through the realization of others.

Hegel's thinking echoes the liberal attraction to freedom. But he also wants to transcend the cruder, 'atomistic' interpretations of individualism. The formation of the malleable, private self was a necessary stage in the emergence of humanity from centuries of religion and superstition. But to view individuals as primarily insular, independent, self-interested, Robinson Crusoe figures, is to misunderstand the relational, solidaristic nature of the self. Hegel therefore reiterates Kant's point, about the mutual recognition of interdependent selves, but would also inspire those socialists and conservatives who are highly critical of liberalism.

As Hegel's influence spread, others were developing the liberal tradition. Mill believed that the burden of proof was upon those who would inhibit rational adults from exercising their freedoms. It is very tempting to try and make others do what you want them to do, especially when you are convinced that you are acting in their best interests. If someone was about to walk onto an unstable bridge, wouldn't you try and stop them? But according to Mill's 'harm principle' (1962: 135–8), we are not entitled to interfere unless the wellbeing of others is at stake. If Bob is harming Seth, then we may take steps to prevent this. But if Bob is harming no-one but himself, then we are not entitled to force him to behave differently (Mill, 1962: 138).

There is a lengthy debate over when we might be entitled to act paternalistically towards someone like Bob (Fitzpatrick, 2011a). We wouldn't simply allow him to walk onto the dangerous bridge, would we – even if he knew it to be unsafe? If we prevent children from harming themselves, are there not instances where we are allowed to similarly intervene in the case of adults? And is it not too simplistic to distinguish between harming oneself (which Mill permits) and harming others (which he does not)? Whatever the rights and wrongs, Mill's influence upon liberalism has been considerable and he, himself, tried to steer it towards socialist and feminist priorities.

Therefore, it is not ridiculous to interpret T. H. Green (1836–1882) as reconciling Hegelian and Millian ideas. Green (1986) was a seminal figure in the development of social, or welfare, liberalism, arguing that a conception of the 'common good' had to occupy a central place in liberal thought. Individuals, he argued, are *social* beings and the principle of liberty was implicated within communal, convivial forms of association. My wellbeing is therefore dependent upon your wellbeing and the good of the one is inseparable from the good of all. Therefore, rather than regard the state as a danger to individuality, it could be interpreted as a promoter of the common good and therefore of freedom also. By establishing individuals' legal commitments to the law and their moral commitments to each other the state enables us to overcome the dichotomy between liberty and social equality that those such as Nozick and Hayek regard as irreconcilable. As such, a welfare state is that which establishes strong links between the demands of individual liberty and the imperatives of the common good.

Despite their differences, Kant, Hegel, Mill and Green lead us towards a third definition of freedom. Here, liberty implies a degree of interdependency and solidarity among social beings (Anderson & Honneth, 2005). The asocial individual is a fantasy invented by free market economists. An agent is both the effect of social processes and someone who, in turn, shapes their social environments. The relationship between individuals and society is organic: you can no more separate a person from 'the social' than you can chop off a leg and expect it to walk. Therefore, freedom has to imply reference to the wellbeing of others and maintaining just social conditions is mutually beneficial.

Nozick and Hayek revisited

This third perspective allows us to critique Nozick and Hayek. In addition to objecting to his justification of private property (see below), we might accuse Nozick of ignoring the extent to which individuals are products of their social environments. If individuals are not atoms who pop into the world with fully-formed rights, then procedural theories of justice cannot entirely capture what we want justice to mean. Nozick *stated* that individuals have rights, but never justified why (cf. Lacey, 2001: 21–7; also Schmidtz, 2002). The players in the card game are not equal participants: their internal and external resources will have been largely determined by accidents of birth. If so, then the exchanges within the game cannot be regarded as fair since some players will have undeserved advantages over others. But if this is the case then even on Nozick's own reckoning the outcome of the game must be unfair also, i.e. if the exchanges are unjust then the outcome must also be unjust. Therefore, principles of social justice and redistributive egalitarianism might well be justifiable after all![4]

The intriguing thing is that Nozick himself allows for the possibility that existing patterns of distribution may well be unfair due to the illegitimate acquisitions and transactions that have occurred in the past. He therefore indicates that a massive, one-off redistribution of resources may well be warranted: a redistribution, in fact, that goes way beyond anything envisaged by the welfare state that he spends so much time attacking (Schaefer, 2007: 168–9). In conclusion, by ignoring the interdependency of the self, the mutuality of freedom and social equality, and the extent to which liberty is a social construction, Nozick leaves himself with a procedural theory of justice that gets tangled in its on philosophical and ideological knots. His critics point out that the means cannot, of themselves, justify the end.

Similar considerations apply to Hayek's thought. Powerful companies, cartels, networks and individuals *do* manipulate markets and so do intentionally drop bricks on our heads. Because the injustices of capitalism distort market outcomes in favour of the already-powerful *then it is as if* a deliberative mechanism is at work. In short, there are class-specific market *structures* that subtly guide the invisible hand in particular directions, i.e. in favour of the wealthy. But whereas Nozick is at least sensitive to the possibility of past injustices, Hayek is not. A Hayekian society would reduce welfare services to a few residual safety-nets whilst introducing an autocratic state to ensure than market losers have a minimal influence within market society. Many, however, struggle to understand why this would be preferable to a democratic welfare state, or even to the communist state that Hayek abhorred.

So, just as Nozick can only dismiss welfarist politics by allowing for the possibility of a redistribution that exceeds anything ever accomplished by the welfare state, so Hayek can only abandon social justice by replacing one kind of centralized state with another. The arguments that are raised against the welfare state on the basis of definitions 1 and 2 can be challenged by invoking definition 3.

Negative and Positive Liberty

Many of you will detect that definitions 1 and 2 correspond to what has been called 'negative liberty' and definition 3 to 'positive liberty'. The distinction is most famously associated with Isaiah Berlin (1909–1997). Negative liberty is the freedom which we experience when we face an absence of constraints. If I imprison you in a cell, then I am depriving you of liberty in this sense, whether I do so legitimately (as a prison warden) or illegitimately (as a kidnapper). Positive liberty is the freedom we experience when we possess the capacity to pursue some end or course of action. Those who lack access to goods which are vital to social participation may lack positive freedoms because they are less able to control and determine their lives.

Berlin drew this simple but influential distinction in order to warn against the dangers of defining liberty in the positive sense, because when we start to associate freedom with something that people *must* possess in order to be free, then we may start to sanction measures which interfere with the private space of personal liberty. If positive freedom implies the internal, psychological disposition to control one's destiny, are we permitted to intervene with those who lack such dispositions? If so, we are close to Rousseau's recommendation that we 'force people to be free', which carries worrying authoritarian overtones. Yet Berlin (1984: 25) was not advocating the abandonment of positive conceptions of freedom (in fact, he believed that coercing individuals in order to enhance their liberty was sometimes justified); he was advising us to proceed carefully whenever the state is called upon to perform redistributive and interventionist roles.

But the negative/positive distinction has sometimes hindered rather than helped understanding. As indicated above, right-wing liberals have been adamant that positive liberty is chimerical and that the institutions, policies and practices that it inspires are a considerable threat to (negative) liberty. Redistribution does not enhance anybody's freedom because *freedom and its lack have got nothing to do with the distribution of income and wealth*. A lack of money may lead to a reduction of opportunities but does not imply a lack of freedom: you are still *free* to fly to Australia even if you cannot *afford* to do so.

By contrast, the Left have denounced this equation of 'liberty' with 'negative liberty'. Being prevented from doing something implies more than physical constraints, it also implies financial constraints (so a beggar *is* less free than a banker). But this does not mean that we should abandon the concept of negative liberty either. Unfortunately, some on the Left have dismissed negative liberty as a bourgeois construct, as an inferior, deceptive type of freedom that can and should be superseded by allegiance to, in Marxist terms, the inevitable development of history.

Further Thoughts

So, where does this leave us? Should we favour definition 3? Are we led back to the kind of liberty-respecting egalitarianisms we explored in Chapter 2? Not necessarily.

Libertarianism revisited

For instance, there are other, more left-wing versions of libertarianism and anarchism available (Vallentyne, 2009). Remember the wooden sculpture that you bought from me? This implied a defence of private property that Nozick adapted from John Locke (1632–1704).

Locke (1960) imagines that in the pre-social 'state of nature' the world was originally unowned. The branch that I pick up does not belong to anyone. And although I am excluding others from acquiring this particular branch, the forest (the state of nature) is abundant with branches and natural resources for others to acquire. Therefore, when I start whittling and sculpting with my knife I am 'mixing my labour with the fruits of the earth' to create an item of private property out of what was previously unowned. No-one else's rights have been violated; unlike the thief who steals my sculpture or the government who steals part of my earnings. Thus, if the original acquisition of the earth's resources was just then, according to Nozick, every freely agreed upon transaction that follows is also just.

But what if we assume, instead, that the world was originally owned in *common* (recall the similar argument on pp.20–1 when discussing Hardin)? This would call my acquisition of the branch into question. In effect, Nozick assumes that private property and the right to create it are both 'pre-political' and 'pre-social', that property rights *precede* the formation of government. But if, instead, we assume that a system of property is a social good subject to political determination, then the social community has a say in how property should be distributed (Murphy & Nagel, 2002: 31–7).[5]

For instance, those who regard anything above minimal taxation as akin to socialism, will typically complain about government taking away 'my earnings'. But my earnings are only partially due to my efforts and decisions. If workers in developed nations earn, on average, 100 times more than those in developing nations living in extreme poverty, does this mean they work 100 times harder? Should the global poor simply start pulling their socks up and stop lazing around? Or, do wages derive from factors which go beyond the efforts of the worker, e.g. the fact I was lucky enough to be born in an already-affluent nation? If so, if property does not derive from individual effort alone, then a system of property requires other, non-Lockean justifications (H. Steiner, 2002: 348–53).

Thus, if the forest is commonly owned, then even my acquisition of the branch *may* violate the interests of the community. It might well be that no form of private property is permissible.[6] Or, perhaps private property is justified only in so far as it serves an end-state conception of justice.

Alternatively, we might assume that the world *was* originally unowned but insist that only an egalitarian acquisition of its resources is permissible. I am allowed to pick up the branch and make money from it, but only if in doing so, I recompense the rest of the community since I have now reduced the stock of natural resources available to others. Taxation of my £5 is, therefore, simply the state collecting such compensation on behalf of the community. Left-libertarians, for example, propose that although priority be given to individual liberty this must be set within the context of a fair and equal distribution of the earth's resources (H. Steiner, 1994). This, then, is a libertarian philosophy of equal shares which can have many different implications for welfare reform.

Some Left-libertarians support the proposal for lump-sum grants – mentioned on p. 44 – where people receive a one-off pot of money to squander or invest. The catch is that if you squander the grant you would have no safety-net to fall back on. A more paternalistic version of the lump-sum grant idea is a Basic Income – an unconditional income paid periodically to every man, women and child. This is the option favoured by Philippe Van Parijs (1995; Fitzpatrick, 1999) who describes himself as a 'real libertarian'. So Left-libertarianism favours egalitarian distribution but not necessarily a welfare state as it has traditionally been defined.

However, Left-libertarianism could be accused of neglecting the less materialistic aspects of social justice. As proposed on pp. 36–7, we ought to be concerned with the quality of social relations and not with mechanical distributions of income and wealth. Distributive justice may not exhaust everything which is relevant to *social* justice.

Priority and sufficiency

Nor have we yet considered prioritarianism. Egalitarians often object to liberalism on the grounds that it neglects the interests of the poorest. But perhaps we can imagine a liberalism which weighs the interests of the least advantaged, more highly than those of the well-off, without being egalitarian. In fact, we have already encountered such a liberalism. Rather than viewing him as an egalitarian, some argue that Rawls is a 'prioritarian' (Parfit, 2001; see Fitzpatrick, 2005: ch. 2).

For 'prioritarians' justice consists of improving the position of the least well-off. Doing so will often be compatible with egalitarianism in practice, if not always in theory. For instance, in a country with just two inhabitants we could only give priority to Paul Poorman by redistributing from Richard Richman. We help Peter *and* narrow the gap between him and Richard. Since prioritarian distributions will often resemble egalitarian ones, perhaps we should not worry too much about the theoretical differences between them. Rawls is a kind of egalitarian after all.

That said, perhaps prioritarianism is less vulnerable to the charge anti-egalitarians direct at egalitarian theories, i.e. the levelling-down argument. Imagine two countries where everyone in Country A owns two houses while in Country B 50 percent of the population own two houses and the other 50 percent own three. On strict egalitarian grounds Country A is preferable and yet this appears to be counterintuitive. After all, those in Country B who own two houses are no worse off than anyone in Country A; their possessions are still the same even though there are others who possess three houses. The egalitarian support for Country A therefore represents a levelling down in comparison to Country B. Indeed, if the choice were between Country B and Country C (where everyone owns one house) then egalitarians will prefer Country C even though the absolute position of the least well-off has now been worsened.

Perhaps, therefore, prioritarianism resembles egalitarianism without being vulnerable to the levelling-down objection (Holtung, 2007; Segall, 2010: 118–20; cf. Christiano, 2007).

However, the following question arises: should we *always* give priority to the least advantaged (see Arneson, 2002)? In country B, would it really be worth our while to try and improve the position of those who 'only' possess two houses? Doesn't there come a point where the least advantaged are nevertheless so well-off that we don't need any more redistributions? For theorists of 'sufficiency' what matters is not the distance between the badly-off and the well-off but the fact – if it is a fact – that the badly-off do not have enough to live a decent life. Once a point of sufficiency has been attained, then social justice falls off the agenda. We can argue about where the line of sufficiency should be drawn, but the idea that the interests of the least well-off should always be prioritized is misguided, as is the egalitarian argument that equality is always better.

Egalitarians have offered rebuttals to both viewpoints (Temkin, 2009: 168–75). Take sufficiency, first of all. Is it unreasonable to prefer the interests of those in Country B who own two houses? If a golden meteorite fell from space and we decided to carve it up for distribution, should we really be indifferent between the needs of those who own two houses and those who own three? Sufficiency has an intuitive appeal but it doesn't necessarily trump considerations of distributive justice (whether prioritarian or egalitarian).

And while a strict egalitarianism may be vulnerable to the levelling-down argument, any pure, undiluted doctrine meets some objection when taken to its extremes. How many liberals or libertarians would *not* allow an innocent person to be locked up for five minutes if doing so would save millions of lives? Egalitarians need only claim that equality is *central* to justice, not that it exhausts the meaning of justice.

In short, there are many ways of extending and refining definitions 1, 2 and 3. The essential message of this chapter is that, just as we faced contrasting and competing versions of equality in Chapter 2, the same applies to liberty. Freedom is not just 'one thing'. Liberties sometimes conflict one another. Freedom for one individual may not be quite the same as freedom for another – recall Tawney's comment about the pike and the minnow. And the liberty I need in one part of my life may be unwanted, perhaps even threatening, in another part.

Recent Developments

Freedom as non-domination

We encounter republicanism in Chapter 4 but one element of it relates to our discussions here (Wall, 2003).

Many republicans believe that liberals make the mistake of confusing liberty with 'non-interference'. For Pettit (1997; Skinner, 1998) what matters is not simply the fact of non-interference but the *power* to resist interference. Imagine that you live in a benignly fascist society. The Fuhrer, SS and Gestapo exist, but they leave everyone alone. You and everyone else live out your lives of prosperity and happiness. Would this society be a free one? Not according to the republican. The *fact* that you were not interfered with matters less than the *power* the fascist authorities possessed to do so if they wished. Had they done so you would have been unable to prevent them. Therefore, a free society is one in which citizens are not subject (whether actually or potentially) to the arbitrary powers of others.

However, if I am only free when I am *never*, even potentially, subjected to the arbitrary power of another then this might be too utopian a stipulation, since such a condition may be impossible to realize. If, by contrast, some forms of arbitrariness are less acute (and therefore more tolerable) than others then republicans need to acknowledge this and potentially make room for a notion (liberal or otherwise) of non-interference. (For Hobbes's alternative approach, see Skinner (2008: ch. 5).) Thus, while interest in republicanism has recently revived, its contribution to debates about freedom remains uncertain.

Freedom as ambivalence

Originating with Blaise Pascal (1623–1662) and Soren Kierkegaard (1813–1855) there is an 'existential' tradition of thought which has wielded some influence on social policy by highlighting the ambiguities of freedom. Kierkegaard (1992) insisted that humans are faced with a series of choices throughout their lives, there being no courts of morality to which we can appeal to discover which option is best. We simply have to choice, make a 'leap into the dark', and live with those decisions for better or for worse. This means that freedom is permanently characterized by dread, anxiety and uncertainty.

Of course, we routinely appeal to a variety of courts: God, nature, the state, parents, tradition and custom, the law, etc.; but such appeals are inauthentic attempts to strip ourselves of a responsibility that we cannot ultimately avoid. Such attempts to flee from freedom and responsibility are what Jean-Paul Sartre (1905–1980) referred to as 'bad faith'. For Sartre (1958), our societies are founded upon bad faith attempts to be both free and not free at the same time: by adhering to rules, timetables and schedules, the bourgeois citizen is the model to which we are all encouraged to aspire.

Bauman (1993), too, focuses upon the ambiguities of liberty. The exhilaration of being free accompanies a profound anxiousness as to what we should do, but a simple appeal to moral systems is no longer possible. Rules of conduct can no longer be canonized or treated as unquestionable commandments: to be free is to be an adjudicator of what is right and wrong. Bauman (2005, 2007) favours the metaphor of liquidity. Liquid is a substance which is not solid, yet it can support us if we learn how to swim. A liquid society, though, is characterized by profound uncertainty – even skilful swimmers can drown – and our liquid lives are characterized by fears about being left behind, by worries about events which cannot be anticipated. Our lives become episodic and organized around short-term commitments and opportunities. Our desire for ontological security demands that we narrate those episodes into a meaningful whole; but the fragmenting, non-linear nature of modernity prevents us from doing so.

Bauman draws upon the philosophy of Emmanuel Levinas (1906–1995) to suggest that we have to recognize ourselves and others as free beings rather than as specimens of moral and theological systems. People tend to clothe each other in hierarchies and regulations, and it is only when these systems are 'unveiled' that people can properly recognize one another and their interdependent freedoms. This means disassociating freedom from a crude marketplace individualism. In fact, there are two ways in which we try to fly from freedom in contemporary society. We hand our freedom over to market forces and/or we live uncritically within some collective tradition, e.g. religion.

Bauman's analysis here accords with that of Giddens (1994) who agrees that neither of these options is available to us any longer. Giddens suggests that we now live in post-traditional societies, these being societies where we cannot avoid reflecting upon all customs, ways of life and traditions of thought if we wish to avoid falling into fundamentalisms of one sort or another. Our reflexive societies must therefore be 'beyond Left and Right' and this implies building systems of 'positive welfare' that are less concerned with the distribution of material resources and more concerned with counselling to the non-material sides of our nature (Giddens, 1998).

Bauman seems to agree with Giddens about the virtues of reflexivity as a means of coping with the ambiguities of freedom, but he retains a central place for redistributive welfare institutions as a way of building cooperative and egalitarian social relations. Universal and comprehensive welfare services are needed to reflect and express the 'commonality of fate' which is central to the human condition. For Bauman, then, freedom implies an irreducible inter-subjectivity and the welfare state represents not a flight from freedom but a means of easing the sources of insecurity, of pooling anxiety and of reflecting upon the conditions of our existence together rather than in the isolated cells of the marketplace.

Freedom as governmentality

Structuralism is the search for the underlying scaffold which underpins and shapes the 'surface' relations of society. Marxists have long believed that the scaffold is an economic one. With the 'linguistic turn' of the twentieth century, many theorists became more interested in language.

To be an agent is to be that which names and is named. To name is to confer meaning since without a name, the object or event we are referring to, cannot be understood. Indeed, some believe that what we call 'the world' is itself a construction of language. Structuralists searched for the structures of language in the relationship between sign and referent. Semioticians like Saussure (1857–1913) had said that a sign – the linguistic unit through which meaning is produced and circulated – consists of a signifier (a word, image or sound) and a signified (the concept which words, images and sounds signify) which connect the sign to its external referent (that which exists in the world, independently of mind and language). The sound uttered when I say 'tree' links to a mental picture of a typical tree that I have in my mind as well as the actual trees which exist in my garden.

Post-structuralism was the attempt to treat referents and signifieds as constructs within the stream of signification. I cannot comprehend the tree in my garden directly. I can only do so through interpreting 'tree' and 'garden'. For post-structuralism, the world is textual and discursive. Our task is to read the world in the same way that we read a book, a musical composition, a communication, or anything which involves the circulation of meaning. The world consists of signs, codes and programs which agents continually reinterpret and reconfigure. You and I meet through the words on this page and this meeting is every bit as significant and relevant as a face-to-face meeting. Indeed, the latter would also be a form of textual interpretation, with clothes, gestures and demeanour substituting for nouns and verbs. And if the signifier is dominant, then discourse consists of *difference*. Rather than being locked down, the signifier perpetually reconstructs its world. The meaning of 'tree' is never finalized; it changes because language is subject to permanent flux, instability and fluidity. The self is a dispersed and fragmented flow that constantly confronts that which is 'other' to itself. Understanding is always incomplete. There is no extra-textual frame of reference which allows us to understand everything. All we can do is to inhabit the fragments and flows of the text.

According to Foucault we should therefore focus upon the conditions through which knowledge and ideas are generated, i.e. discourses. When we make truth-claims (*x* is better than *y*), we reproduce relations of power (see pp.97–8). Therefore, instead of discovering 'the truth' social scientists should try to unmask the power which resides within all truth-claims. Much of his work therefore consists of genealogical analyses of the institutions through which discursive practices are woven: the prison, the asylum, the clinic, as well as the 'institutions' of sexual conduct.

For instance, Foucault (1967) traces the historical constructs of reason and madness. Madness was once treated theologically, as a sign either of divine grace or of infection by satanic forces. By the seventeenth and eighteenth centuries, with increasing secularization, madness was equated with the anti-social forces of the criminal and the pauper, and so silenced through incarceration. The Age of Reason needed the 'unreasonable' against which to define itself. In the nineteenth and twentieth centuries madness was medicalized, i.e. re-defined as mental illnesses that require specialized treatment rather than punishment. So whilst we may like to regard the psychiatric treatment of mental illness as a sign of our enlightenment, Foucault underscores the extent to which it is another form of confinement and incarceration, albeit one that is done in terms of the rights and welfare of the individuals concerned ('rights' and 'welfare' also being discursive constructions). The modern fear of 'madness' is a fear of our own possible descent into unreason.

Foucault regards the 'panopticon' as the essential metaphor for all modern institutions. The panopticon was Bentham's Utilitarian design for a prison. The underlying rationale was the need for as few prison officers as possible to survey as many prisoners as possible. Therefore, the officers would need to work with a central tower around which would be built many tiers of cells. The cells would be perfectly exposed, so that the prisoners would always be visible to those within the tower, but the officers would be invisible. The prisoners would not know when they were being observed and so would need to act as if they were under constant surveillance. Bentham's design was never actually built, but Foucault treats it as a metaphor for modern forms of discipline and normalization. Therefore a Foucauldian reading of social policy involves the application of this metaphor as a devise for interpreting welfare institutions and administrative practices.

Thus, while the prisoners knew they were in a prison, we both do and do not know that we inhabit a series of panoptic gazes. In the family, the school, the doctor's surgery, the workplace, etc. we freely govern ourselves in particular ways according to a subtle interplay of norms. Everything that we see, hear, read and experience subtly communicates to us a cognitive and perceptual 'map' of what should and should not be regarded as normal. I am the bearer of aesthetic and moral judgements that I have internalized in the attempt to appear and act as normal. We organize our lives in terms of certain norms and expect others to do the same: we strive to remain within a zone of normality and regard everything lurking outside that zone as unnatural and disorderly. It is not that the self pops into existence, recognizes social norms and gathers itself around them; instead, *the self is a physiological and psychological effect of normalization*. Foucault draws attention to the ways in which we are not only social constructions as traditionally understood, but *discursive* constructions: embodiments of normal/abnormal signs and differences, the products of normalization who reinsert its social practices into the social field.

Social practices, institutions and policies can, then, be interpreted as normalizing discourses: the means through which we are made as the signs of normality/abnormality. Donzelot (1979) accordingly examines the way in which the modern family is organized so that it both disconnects and reconnects the private and the public. The two must be kept separate in order to preserve the space of the private, economic actor (the individualistic workers and entrepreneurs of market societies). Yet the two must also be conjoined so that the family operates for, and in accordance with, social authority. Social policies are therefore the paradoxical techniques of disconnection and reconnection – the technologies of normalization – and Donzelot illustrates the way in which the modern family is produced through a barrage of medical, religious, legal, cultural and philanthropic 'interventions', effected by an endless queue of experts.[7]

The 'governmentality' literature has been inspired by such critiques (Rose, 1999a, 1999b; Dean, 1999). Its approach is one of analytics rather than normative evaluation (it diagnoses social conditions rather than assessing them as good or bad); and it adopts a post-realist stance, concerned with the operation of power rather than its 'inner essence'. So, while liberals say that freedom exists *here* and is threatened by force and domination over *there*, governmentality sees each as being implicit within the other. Freedom is an effect of power and power is a product of freedom. Unless we recognize the two as being reciprocally intertwined we neglect the extent to which liberal societies – and welfare states – are themselves dependent upon violence, regulation, policing, exclusions, authoritarianism and domination (Dean, 2007: 95–6, 114–6). We do not exercise freedom by liberating it *from* governance because governance (the conduct of conduct) is present everywhere. When my neighbour plays Mozart very loudly and I respond with some Throbbing Gristle, we are each shaping the other's space of behaviour, the horizons of possibility. Welfare systems can therefore be understood as contributions to the governance *of* the self *though* the self as one of a multitude of lines on a grid of power/freedom. Governmentality draws attention to how our subjectivities and the interstitial minutiae of our daily lives are administered (Rose, 2007).

So, post-structuralism potentially enables us to re-write the history of social policy and to understand welfare systems as regimes of knowledge/power that do not necessarily follow a steady incline of progress, liberation and empowerment. Fraser (1989) analyses needs not as 'atoms' of human nature but as constructions that emerge through a long series of discursive and social struggles. Needs do not precede politics, they are politicized through and through. Needs are contested spaces of discourse through which experts try to turn the body into objects of administrative knowledge, where oppositional movements challenge these disciplinary strategies and where 'privatizers' try to separate the sphere of private responsibility from that of public action. Therefore, post-structuralism does not offer prescriptions for welfare reform because it insists that all truth-claims are manifestations of, and articulated by, particular (non-universal) 'power interests'. Instead, post-structuralists are intellectual janitors, forever 'clearing the ground' by undermining accepted narratives and ensuring that new critiques, new claims and new struggles can emerge.

Many have argued, however, that this is all an unwelcome diversion from real world issues (cf. Watson, 2000). If post-structuralism rejects universal accounts of the good then what reason do we have to prefer one truth-claim over another? What is the point of 'clearing the ground' unless we are trying to build the *universal* foundations of human liberation? Political post-structuralists (Laclau & Mouffe, 1985) observe that social struggle is never-ending and that a final resting place, a post-political utopia, can never arrive. Yet, even if this were true, are not some struggles more just and less cataclysmic than others, and do we not need a universal reference-point if we are to identify them?

We have now almost completed our introductory tour of justice. We reviewed two definitions of liberty, as advanced by libertarians and economic liberals. We then offered a third definition, one which draws from the kind of egalitarian principles we explored in Chapter 2. Our overview of those definitions was capped by a discussion of negative and positive liberty. We then complicated matters somewhat by reviewing how those definitions can be rearranged and refined. And we ended by suggesting that, as old as it is, the concept of freedom is constantly being renewed and reinvented.

Our tour has at least one more stop to make. Many of the greatest controversies concerning social policies in recent years have revolved around the meaning and the application of citizenship. Yet we are citizens in so far as we are members of communities; communities which we create and which, to an extent argued over by liberals and non-liberals, *create us*.

Questions for Further Discussion

- When and why might forced slavery be justified? Discuss with particular reference to the political philosophy of Robert Nozick.
- So long as you do not harm others should you be free to do whatever you want to do?
- Is taxation theft?
- When is it justifiable to restrict my freedoms in order to enhance yours?

4

Citizenship and Community

- Citizenship Rights
- Marshall and Social Rights
- Social Obligations
- Four Ideals
- Challenges to Liberalism
- Recent Developments

Interest in citizenship revived in the 1980s (Kymlicka, 2002: ch.7). This was due, firstly, to corresponding debates concerning agency, class, social movements and identity and, secondly, as a response to the rise of economic liberalism with its emphasis upon commodified market values, consumerism, self-interest and populist authoritarianism. Furthermore, community and civil society came to be regarded as crucial sites of civic association and political participation.[1] To some extent these debates revitalized long-standing oppositions, with the Right emphasizing market liberties and socio-moral obligations against what they saw as the dominance of the 'big state'; and the Left stressing social equality, welfare entitlements and political rights against the new hegemony of market forces (the 'big market').

If anything, the concept of citizenship has become *more* important over time, particularly due to the accelerating pace of social change, technological developments (such as the Internet) and the new global contexts we explore in Chapter 10. Being a citizen means being rooted in something; but what are we citizens of, exactly? To be a citizen implies interacting with others; but how inclusive should such interaction be? Citizenship involves mutual participation; but what should we participate in and how? What communities are we members of and what do we want those communities to become?

This chapter introduces some recent debates, while revisiting some of the earlier discussions about wellbeing and justice (also Lister, 2010: ch.7). The basics of the debate are covered on pp. 66–70; then we explore a taxonomy which allows us to understand some of the central concepts at work and upon which some of the key perspectives can then be mapped; as in the previous two chapters we conclude by outlining some recent interesting developments.

Citizenship Rights

There are two conditions upon which citizenship can be said to depend. Firstly, the state must be pluralist and democratic, since dictatorial states do not have citizens, they have subjects. Secondly, civil society must be open and free. For citizenship to flourish, then, two extremes must be avoided. The state must not be allowed to absorb civil society, as happens in totalitarian nations where the attempt to engineer a perfectly ordered, regulated society strangles the spaces of creativity and disorderliness that citizens require. But nor should the state become merely one organization *within* civil society. Instead, the state is the ultimate guarantor of the rights and obligations of citizenship, e.g. through the rule of law.

In short, state and civil society must counterbalance one another. It is not always clear how this is to happen or where the borders of state and society should be drawn. Yet it is the very nature of a free society that this can never be entirely settled and free citizens are those who constantly renegotiate and redraw the relevant borders. Therefore, citizens are both the sovereigns and the subjects of the polity, i.e. they abide by the laws and procedures of which they are themselves – theoretically – the authors. The key concept at work here is that of rights.

Rights were originally defined as natural, i.e. as residing within and bestowed by 'natural law'. This implied that rights exist *prior* to the legal, political and social institutions through which we govern our lives. As the notion of natural rights fell from favour, one alternative was to regard rights as constructed, consensual or institutional. Rights were thought by some to be constructs *of* society: the means by which social beings agree to recognize one another as equal members of the same polity. Whichever account we prefer, rights are commonly held to imply the following.

Rights:

- are universal across time and space, belonging to all regardless of class, sex, race, nationality, etc.;
- are inalienable – they cannot be surrendered, stolen, sold or traded;
- imply autonomy, i.e. they confer upon people the liberty to determine desirable goals and to pursue those goals so long as others are not harmed;
- are possessed by individuals;
- protect and empower people against the illegitimate and arbitrary use of power by others, as in the doctrine of *habeus corpus* which prohibits non-judicial incarceration and ensures 'due process';
- enjoins public authorities to allocate resources and goods fairly to individuals;
- are legally enforceable;
- are attached to considerations of justice rather than charity, patronage or benevolence;

- imply duties;
- may be regarded either as foundational or as 'claims' (where a right is a claim to have one's fundamental needs and interests realized).

Yet, much of even this list can be disputed. Perhaps rights are western constructs that apply only to modern liberal democracies. Perhaps we should think of 'group' rather than individual rights. Perhaps animals possess rights. Perhaps we should first define a list of obligations and view rights in *that* context.

Although we cannot review each and every controversy, what follows is designed to capture some of the most important debates. For social policy students, the immediate and essential controversy centres around the concept of *social rights*. A key figure in this debate is T.H. Marshall.

Marshall and Social Rights

Marshall identifies three elements of citizenship (Marshall & Bottomore, 1992). *Civil rights* define the liberty to form contracts and own property (and so imply equality before the law) as well as freedom of assembly, speech and thought. These emerged in the eighteenth century with the development of the legal system. *Political rights* define the right to participate in the political process (to vote and to stand for election). These emerged in the nineteenth century with the development of democratic systems. *Social rights* define the right to experience minimum levels of economic and social wellbeing as participants in society's way of life. These emerged in the twentieth century with the development of welfare systems.

Marshall's chronology is a simplified narrative, he admits. In reality, the evolution of these civil, political and social components was much more complex. For instance, by the late nineteenth century, the modern industrial economy was emerging, the labour movement was gaining in influence, and therefore social rights, e.g. to education, began to develop *alongside* political rights.

Political and, in particular, social rights are arguably less compatible with a free market society than civil rights and this led to an important strain in modern society. On the one hand, we have markets with their propensity to create *inequalities*; on the other, we have political and social conceptions of citizenship that demand *equality*. This led, according to Marshall, to a 'hyphenated society' whose capitalist, democratic and welfarist elements exist side by side in an uneasy, though ultimately productive, tension. Marshall says that a hyphenated society is preferable either to one organized purely according to market forces or to one organized purely by the state. He himself believed that social policies should aim to eliminate not inequality per se but *unjust inequalities*, i.e. those deriving from undeserved advantages and disadvantages. They should prescribe a 'baseline' of equality, e.g. the equalization of educational opportunities, but nothing more radical. The welfare state's aim is to create a society based upon merit and social mobility rather than class divisions: a society of citizens.

Marshall continues to represent an important reference point for a wide series of debates (Barbalet, 1988; Turner, 1993; Bulmer & Rees, 1996; Reisman, 2005). Four criticisms are worth mentioning.

- Marshall tries to squeeze too much into his three categories. For instance, he treats industrial rights (to form trade unions, bargain collectively and strike) as a sub-set of civil rights, yet civil rights arguably strengthened the grip of employers over workers that distinct *industrial* rights began to loosen once they had been won by workers' organizations.
- Even a moderate class-based analysis therefore, allows for the possibility of forms of citizenship that go beyond Marshall's categorization. We could, for instance, define a set of *economic rights* that entitle workers to either the full or partial ownership of capital or productive property.
- Marshall's chronology has allowed critics of social rights to suggest that these do not constitute a *real* category of citizenship rights, e.g. because they demand a level of state intervention which is inconsistent with the limited government implied by both civil and political rights.
- Marshall has been accused both of being too anglocentric and of ignoring other dimensions of citizenship that have grown more and more prominent over the post-war period, e.g. gendered and racialized dimensions.

In short, Marshall perhaps adopts a simplistic model which might be accused of underestimating the extent to which a 'right' is an inherently contestable category defined by ongoing struggles over its meaning and implications. Arguably, the most prevalent controversy of recent years has concerned the relationship between social rights and obligations.

Social Obligations

Many on the Right have alleged that the concept of a 'social right' is incoherent (see Chapter 7). A right belongs to an individual. But social rights enhance the power of the state and (through excessive taxation, for instance) undermine private property and the space of personal freedom. We should therefore think of rights in terms of negative freedom and impose strict limitations on state activity. A related criticism is that social rights can be neither universal nor enforceable. Since the introduction of welfare systems requires a large degree of wealth, the effectiveness of social rights is conditional upon the degree of economic development, a condition that contradicts the entire purpose and rationale of rights.

Various counter-arguments can be made. It could be claimed that because rights can be potentially undermined by markets we need a set of social rights to protect us against the excesses of capitalism. Social rights 'decommodify' citizenship so that we do not define either ourselves or others in terms of prices, profits and other market values (Esping-Anderson, 1990). Citizenship must imply rights *against the market* and not just against the state. Furthermore, it can be claimed that the design and enforcement of *all* rights, not just social ones, requires some degree of economic development, because every right has to be embodied in an institution and this implies a substantial commitment of resources (Plant, 1993).

Nonetheless, the central allegation, that social rights eclipse the obligations that people owe to one another, has been massively influential, not only on the Right (Deacon, 2002). By concentrating upon entitlements, the accusation goes, the welfare state has produced a destructive, possessive and passive form of citizenship (Mead, 1986). As people become more dependent upon the state, they become less willing to look after, and do things for, themselves and others. At the bottom end of the income scale this generates a welfare dependency, where

- whole generations of families cut themselves off from the world of work;
- an underclass forms that has little respect for authority and the rule of law,
- single, never-married mothers effectively 'marry the state'; and
- biological fathers absent themselves from their children's lives.

By giving people a safety-net to jump onto, the state has only increased the likelihood (the 'moral hazard') of people doing so and thereby undermines the habits of work and independence. The social rights of the welfare state has produced a society of takers rather than of givers, of 'free-riders' who accept the benefits of social cooperation but are unwilling to contribute.

Social rights can be defended from such attacks in several ways. Firstly, it can be pointed out that the likes of Tawney, Beveridge and Marshall did not fail to emphasize the importance of duties and responsibilities, as even a casual reading of their key publications reveals. Secondly, we can remember that social rights were often promoted by social democrats and socialists who believed that a welfare state was the stepping-stone to a new form of society. Social rights already imply solidarity, cooperation and mutuality. True, in an environment of social injustice and market insecurity, social rights *per se* may become less effective as a means of individual empowerment, *but it is free market capitalism which is ultimately to blame for this state of affairs* (Schram, 2006: Ch.6). Finally, it can be claimed that the Right-wing critique is based upon a crude individualism which unfairly disregards the many undeserved advantages and disadvantages that people face (see pp. 51–5). To insist that what is wrong with society is that people, especially the poorest, have *too many rights*, is to overlook the effects that systemic inequalities of socioeconomic power have upon our talents and opportunities. It could be said that duties correlate not to rights but to powers, i.e. one's ownership of resources and property (Fitzpatrick, 2003: 42–6). A right is merely a claim; it is the actual power those claims do or do not confer which really counts.

Nevertheless, the view that social obligations are as, if not more, important than social rights, became highly influential on policy-makers (Clarke et al., 2007). We explore some of the political debates in Chapter 7. For now, I want to pursue a more philosophical exploration of some key questions:

- How should we conceive the relationship between rights and duties?
- To what extent should people be coerced into performing social obligations?

On pp.75–81 we review various perspectives which have been adopted regarding these questions. Beforehand, we sketch a taxonomy which should enable us to map those perspectives by framing the relevant concepts.

Four Ideals

Figure 4.1 cross-references two axes: a Left–Right axis running horizontally and a liberty–community axis running vertically. We might locate Rawls in quadrant 1 and Nozick in quadrant 3. Each is concerned with liberty, but Rawls' concern with end-state distributions which favour the least advantaged places him on the Left and Nozick's emphasis upon procedural entitlements

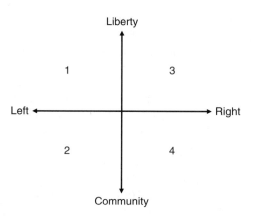

Figure 4.1 Four perspectives on community

that are indifferent to inequalities places him on the Right. So, the quadrants might be characterized as follows:

1. This ideal-type includes liberal rights and liberties and an emphasis upon social justice. This quadrant belongs to the 'liberal Left'.
2. This quadrant also supports social justice. However, the emphasis here is upon solidarity, belonging, shared traditions, mutual obligations and the common good. We will see why on pp.75–80. This zone belongs to the 'non-liberal Left'.[2]
3. This ideal-type associates liberal rights and liberties with free markets and/or the libertarian, minimal state. This zone belongs to the 'liberal Right'.
4. Like quadrant 2, the fourth quadrant also emphasizes solidarities, duties, etc. However, here there is a conservative emphasis upon moral desert. This quadrant belongs to the 'non-liberal Right'.

What separates theorists into different zones? How can we judge between them? There are many ways of coming at such questions and the next section will illustrate why. For now, I want to propose that the following headings represent vital areas of disagreement.

Reciprocity

At a philosophical level, it is obvious that rights and duties tend to go together. If I have a right to remain uninjured, then you have a duty not to harm me. It is facile, however, to infer that everyone thereby possesses rights and duties in equal amounts and equal types. A baby has rights, but what duties do you expect her to perform? An individual may have an obligation not to harm his pet, but that doesn't necessarily mean that the animal has rights against him. So, although there may be some kind of *society-wide* reciprocity between rights and duties, there are any number of ways of fitting rights and duties together for any particular citizen (cf. Fitzpatrick, 2005: 53–6; Taylor-Gooby, 2009: 73–9). Take the following four examples.

(a) Unbalanced Reciprocity

This implies that the balance between rights and duties is tipped heavily in favour of one or the other. There are therefore two sets of unbalanced reciprocity.

(i) We might prefer to make rights fundamental. If we are on the liberal Left we might argue that, depending on how equal our society is, more duties should fall upon the privileged than upon the disadvantaged. To suggest that all citizens should possess rights and duties in equal measure is tantamount to arguing that market inequalities do not matter. Conversely, the liberal Right might argue that duties only derive from the exercise of rights within a market place. To be a citizen is to be a market actor who only bears responsibilities that he has freely contracted to bear.

(ii) We might prefer to make duties fundamental. The non-liberal Left could argue that rights do not exist in a social vacuum but derive from communal participation. Inequalities of power and privilege are certainly unjust but egalitarian objectives can only be met if everyone pulls in the same direction according to a moral-cultural ethos of mutuality and solidarity. The non-liberal Right might argue that rights only derive from the exercise of social obligations, e.g. within families, neighbourhoods, civil associations, charities, churches, etc. We are therefore entitled to take only if we have substantially demonstrated our propensity to contribute.

(b) Balanced Reciprocity

This means that rights and duties balance more evenly. There are two sets of balanced reciprocity.

(i) There is *specific reciprocity* where rights and duties reciprocate at the level of the act. By making a claim on the basis of an entitlement, I simultaneously agree to perform the corresponding duty. For example, if I claim the right to live in a peaceful neighbourhood, then I cannot myself disturb that neighbourhood. Or, if I make use of publicly provided services, I cannot refuse to pay the taxes which pay for them. Specific reciprocity is therefore contractual. Just as my purchase of a drink requires me to pay some money, so my claiming a right or performing a duty requires my possession of reciprocal duties and rights.

Specific reciprocity can take many different forms. For egalitarians, citizenship rights and duties feed into one another as we progress towards the goal of social justice. For economic liberals, free markets allow 'citizens' and 'consumers' to become indistinguishable. For familial conservatives, the family is the nursery of communal citizenship; I learn to be a constructive, social participant through observing my long-term commitment to family members.

(ii) There is also *generalized reciprocity* where rights and duties balance out at a more generic level. By claiming an entitlement, I am not necessarily subjected to a corresponding and immediate obligation. My right to live in a peaceful neighbourhood may still allow me to disturb that neighbourhood from time to time, e.g. by throwing a party, so long as I am a good neighbour overall. My taxes fund the public good rather than merely my own entitlements. So, generalized reciprocity establishes a 'looser' equilibrium between rights and duties. As with specific reciprocity, generalized reciprocity can also take many different forms.

Coercion

The enforcement of certain duties is *always* justified. In any society there will need to be some means of enforcing the observation of basic 'negative' duties, especially the duty not to harm others. The controversy arises when we consider more 'positive' duties, i.e. to participate in one's social way of life. It would take too long to examine all positive duties, but we acquire some idea of the debate's terrain by focusing upon an important question for social policy: should unemployed claimants be required to work and/or train for their benefits?

The liberal Left will usually oppose such 'workfare' measures. Since one of our basic needs is the need for a minimum income and since we have a right to have those basic needs fulfilled, then attaching conditions to benefit receipt is unwarranted. The non-liberal Left, however, may well advocate workfare measures on the grounds that social justice requires both a needs-based redistribution and a society-wide mutuality of effort, e.g. whilst taxpayers have an obligation to assist the least advantages, claimants must reciprocally do all they can to contribute to society (for useful discussions see Deacon, 2002 and White, 2003).

The liberal Right are usually ambiguous towards workfare. On the one hand, an individualist-entitlement version of citizenship is likely not to support a state benefit system in the first place; on the other, where a benefit system operates the degree of state intervention required to run a workfare scheme is probably not justifiable.[3] The non-liberal Right gives unequivocal backing to the workfare principle as embodying a set of responsibilities that we owe to the community and as a means of proving that we deserve the community's help. Without welfare conditions to reintegrate them back into society, those such as benefit claimants are simply free-riders.

So, the ideal-types offer distinct responses to the above question: duty-based approaches tend to favour the workfare proposal, whereas rights-based ones do not. The issue becomes more complex, though, when we introduce reciprocity arguments into the picture.

If we support an unbalanced reciprocity based upon the prioritizing of rights, workfare will not be to our liking. Egalitarians might argue that workfare is anti-redistributive in that what it gives with one hand (benefits), it takes with the other (benefit conditions). Entitlement theorists, as noted above, will disapprove of the state's coercion of free individuals. However, those who prefer an unbalanced reciprocity that is based upon duties are likely to be split. Inegalitarians will support workfare on the grounds that benefits are entitlements that must first be earned. But egalitarians may well feel that workfare is an obligation too far, i.e. that although a communitarian approach correctly emphasizes duties, these should fall most heavily upon the employed and the most affluent. Those preferring specific reciprocity will probably support workfare, although, as before, some egalitarians and anti-statists may well dissent, albeit for different reasons. Those preferring generalized reciprocity will probably dislike workfare although, this time, it is those wedded to a civic/familial ethos who may well dissent.

In conclusion, the liberal Right and Left will probably *not* support attaching conditions to the receipt of benefits (although the former may be more split on the issue than the latter) whereas the non-liberal Right will do so. The non-liberal Left will also be somewhat split. A strong vein of duty and reciprocity runs through the non-liberal Left's view of citizenship; though, many will agree with Arneson (1997) that attaching strong conditions to claimants is a harmful diversion from more radical issues. In short, there are numerous positions that can and have been taken regarding the relationship between right and duties and the extent to which people can be coerced into performing the latter.

Exclusions and inclusions

Citizenship is a badge of belonging, of inclusion within a political community, and it is this sense of belonging which acts as a source of identity. Yet 'inclusion' only has meaning as the opposing term to 'exclusion'. An inside implies an outside. Therefore, citizens are political members in that they are distinguished from those who are excluded from membership. Recall Chapter 3, when I noted that in ancient Athens women, slaves and foreigners were defined neither as free nor, therefore, as citizens. Yet it can be observed that *any* form of citizenship must arguably contain some exclusive components. Even global citizenship (see pp. 82–3 and Chapter 10) might imply treating some as strangers rather than compatriots.

This exclusive aspect of citizenship has become more problematic the closer our societies have moved to the ideals of liberty, equality and democracy. We cannot consistently proclaim the rights and freedoms of all whilst maintaining systems of subordination and social repression. Therefore, how is it possible for citizenship to be in some way exclusive without this leading to oppressive forms of injustice? Many of the philosophers we mention on pp. 75–85 are wrestling with this difficult problem.

A key question for social policy students to consider is this: can second-class citizenship be abolished or is this too idealistic an aspiration? Those on the Left and the liberal Right are all likely, though to varying degrees and for different reasons, to suggest that citizenship can become a truly universal category. For the liberal Right the market is the arena within which this will occur as everyone becomes a citizen-consumer; but according to the Left social justice is needed if social exclusion is to be abolished. We return to such disputes in Chapter 5. The non-liberal Right, by contrast, suggest that since citizenship refers to the demonstrable membership of, and active practices within, particular communities we should *welcome* its exclusionary implications. Compatriots can only be valued as such if there are others who, as members of other communities and cultural contexts, are non-compatriots. The non-liberal Left, too, recognize the importance of cultural boundaries and so may be sceptical towards things like multiculturalism and mass migration because these are seen to threaten the solidarities upon which people's sense of justice depends.

Challenges to Liberalism

We are now able to map some key schools of thought onto Figure 4.1.

Conservatism

Conservatism is that branch of right-wing thought which gives a strong emphasis to traditions, customs and authority (see Chapter 7) and so belongs to quadrant 4. Conservatives view citizens as 'duty-bearers' who are characterized in terms of what they owe *to* their community rather than any rights that they may receive *from* it. Desert is more important than either needs or entitlements. State welfare systems are only justified if they enforce responsibilities and shore up familial and civic forms of mutual assistance. Conservatives therefore exemplify what we have been calling the non-liberal Right.

Communitarianism

This term is now less prevalent than it was in the 1980s and 1990s but continues to possess some salience (Dagger, 2009). With the waning of Marxism and socialism, some worried that liberal ideas (and errors) would dominate political thinking. As such, a series of challenges to liberalism emerged in the early-to-mid 1980s by those who would come to be called communitarians (though not all of them accepted the label) (Macintyre, 1981, 1987; Sandel, 1982; Taylor, 1989; Etzioni, 1994).

According to Kymlicka (2002: ch.6), liberalism is based upon two premises. The first relates to the 'good life' with liberals insisting that individuals should be able to decide for themselves what is and is not the good life. For some, it implies caring for people, for others it implies making lots of money, for others it implies being creative and artistic, and so on. The point is that there are many possible versions of 'the good' and individuals should be free to choose between them.

But communitarians disagree. There are, they say, only a limited number of versions because the good derives from already-existing communal traditions and cultures. To live a good life involves discovering those contexts, recognizing the hold they have on you as the bearer of such traditions and cultures and so living your life according to their demands. Therefore, the good is not to be understood individualistically; the good is always a *common good*. It is this common good that makes freedom possible and actions are virtuous or otherwise in terms of their contribution to the common good. According to communitarians, belonging to a community of the good (whatever community that might be) is more important than the right of individual choice.

The second premise of liberalism is that the individual self is unencumbered, or distinguishable from the ends that the individual chooses to pursue. I may become a businessman, a caregiver or an artist, but these are contingent identities that I can potentially change at some future date. It is the capacity to choose that defines me rather than the particular choices that I make, meaning that the self is conceptually distinct from its ends. But the communitarian alleges that this is an empty interpretation. The self consists of social roles, the performance of which makes me who I am. My ends are constitutive identities rather than contingent ones. The self is not an abstract, free floating entity, but something that is shaped and defined by the goals of an individual's life, goals that have in turn been formed by the community of the good within which I am immersed or embedded.

This debate is important because it relates to the fact that citizenship has both passive and active elements. The passive aspects correspond to what Habermas (1994) calls 'received membership'. Here, a citizen is a bearer of a prescribed legal status and the individual contributes relatively little to the institutions, relations and practices that ensure the maintenance of that status. The active elements correspond to what Habermas calls 'achieved membership' where citizenship implies active participation by, and integration of, individuals into the societies that constitute their identities. Citizenship represents a combination of received and achieved membership, but liberals tend to emphasize the former and communitarians the latter. To gain some idea why, let us concentrate upon liberal and communitarian views of the state (see Chapter 5 also).

Liberals believe that, by and large, the state should be neutral between the various conceptions of the good that are on offer to its citizens (B. Barry, 1995). If some people wish to pursue a religious life and some do not then the state should be neutral between the two. If the state forces religion upon its citizens then it discriminates against the non-religious; if it prevents the formation of churches then it discriminates against the religious. A neutral state is that which permits religion, but is dissociated from the church. It is impossible to define a 'common good' since anything which is good for absolutely everyone is likely to be fairly meaningless. It is dictatorial to demand that the state enforce a common good because humans are diverse and cannot be slotted into the same square peg without damage being done to that diversity.

However, other liberals argue that the state cannot be based upon neutrality (e.g. Kymlicka, 1995: ch.5). Firstly, because this is too idealistic an aspiration (as the state is run by those who hold certain beliefs and are likely to favour those beliefs in the making of policy); secondly, because the state must reproduce the conditions of its own existence it cannot do so without preferring some versions of the good over others. Therefore, the liberal state should not aim at neutrality *per se* but should aim at fostering the autonomy of its citizens, i.e. their capacity to be self-determining.

Communitarians, as we have seen, demand that the state should embody and sustain the common good. For example, where a society has historically held to Christian principles the state is perfectly justified in promoting the culture and the practices of Christianity.

It is not difficult to see where social policy fits into the picture (Rothstein, 1998: 30–55). If the state should be purely neutral then so should social policies. In terms of education, this could require a system that exposed pupils to the greatest number of ways of life without any bias on the part of teachers or the curriculum. If the state should foster autonomy, then the education system should teach its pupils to cultivate their powers of self-will and self-governance, while respecting others. But if the state should embody and promote a common good (as communitarians demand) then so must social policies. Here, education should imply an induction into the way of life of the community within which that education system operates, as well as instruction about the nature of the common good as it is interpreted by that community.

Liberalism favours rights and entitlements, then. If individuals are defined as free beings, if being a citizen means having to choose between competing conceptions of the good, and if the state should be neutral and/or prefer autonomous ways of life, then citizenship must be grounded in individual rights. This does not necessarily mean ignoring duties: it means that rights are more fundamental. Communitarianism favours duties and obligations. If individuals are defined as communal beings, if being a citizen means identifying with the good of one's community, and if the state should embody and aim to promote the common good, then citizenship must be grounded in communal duties. This does not necessarily mean ignoring rights, it means that duties are more fundamental.

Over time, it became clear that many liberals acknowledge the importance of communal values and identities while many communitarians were seeking to steer liberalism in those directions rather than advocate something completely alien to liberal principles (Walzer, 1983, 2004, 2007; Dagger, 1997; cf. Etzioni, 2004). Communitarianism stretches across quadrants 2 and 4 in Figure 4.1, therefore. However, liberal communitarians (or communitarian liberals?) are those who are comfortable with aspects of zones 1 & 3 also.

Republicanism

Some who challenged liberalism often drew from traditions of thought that were republican (Oldfield, 1990). As the sound and fury concerning communitarianism faded, so republicanism has come to the fore (Sandel, 1996, 2009: chs. 8–10). Chapter 3 outlined the republican notion of freedom as non-domination. More broadly, republicanism is concerned with participation in a *public* and *political* community. So whereas a communitarian says that a community itself has value, a republican focuses specifically upon the means by which social affairs are organized and run. It has been claimed that republicans are concerned with the 'liberties of the ancients' (participation in political governance) rather than liberals' emphasis upon the 'liberties of the moderns' (personal attachments and projects) (see Arendt, 1958).

Republicans believe that citizenship is an active and interactive form of membership which is concerned with the 'public good' and civic virtue rather than private interest (Fitzpatrick, 2005: 13–15). We are not just private individuals. Principles such as equality and liberty cannot be realized without a strong sense of community and solidarity among citizens. Such principles are rendered meaningless and impractical unless an ethos of reciprocity binds together those being defined as equal and/or free. The state and other civic associations must therefore be based upon and foster this ethos of mutual participation. Left republicans believe that unjust inequalities make participative and democratic citizenship less easy to practice (Richardson, 2002: chs. 2–6); indeed, it could be argued that a republican emphasis lies at the heart of socialism and egalitarianism (Gaus, 2003). Right-wing republicans focus more upon the responsibilities that a commitment to communal belongingness and public activity is said to require.

In truth, the distinction between communitarianism and republicanism is not always easy to draw. Take debates about social capital, for instance (Fitzpatrick, 2005: ch. 3). Social capital refers to the connections and networks which bind individuals together and which possess social value because they establish and represent enduring relations of trust, reciprocity and interdependence (Putnam, 2000: 18–26). Social capital is concerned with social obligations and civic engagement, then. Measures to improve social capital therefore draw upon both communitarianism and republicanism. In the latter context, the expectation is that greater social capital would turn us away from a political culture in which electorates are largely treated – and treat themselves – as the self-interested, passive consumers of electoral politics and into a participative system in which individuals become the co-sovereigns of their political environments.

Because it is not always easy to distinguish between communitarianism and republicanism, many of the above critiques apply to the latter also, although republicans are arguably better disposed towards liberal justifications of rights and freedoms. Republicanism therefore occupies a central position in Figure 4.1, touching upon aspects of each quadrant, though republicans will obviously differ in their priorities and emphases.

Deliberative democracy

This emphasis upon civic engagement and political renewal is also characteristic of deliberative democracy (sometimes known as 'radical democracy') (Dryzek, 2000; Fishkin & Laslett, 2003; Gutmann & Thompson, 2004; Cohen, J., 2009). For deliberative democrats, the problem with liberal individualism is that it has either led to, or failed to prevent, the ascendency of a consumerist politics. Dominated by top-heavy political parties and remote, detached legislatures, this is where people are required to do little more than place a cross on a ballot paper every few years. Democracy has been reduced to pandering for, and counting the preferences, of voters who – aided by a manipulative media – are assumed to be primarily self-interested beings. Questions such as 'what kind of society is good?' and 'why prefer this principle to that?' barely register anymore.

Deliberative democrats wish to revitalize participation in politics and political decision-making. Although there are interesting examples of political engagement outside the party system, e.g. single-issue campaigns, these alone are insufficient. Rather than delegating responsibility to distant officials, they say, we need wider institutional reform based around deliberation. This implies reasoning with others in a public forum to improve the process of decision-making. Instead of leaving something to technocratic experts, experts and laypeople come together in formal settings. The model here is that of a jury which is expected to deliberate rationally and discursively about the evidence and arguments with which it has been presented. Citizens' juries, citizens' parliaments and 'deliberation days' have all been tried as means to kick-start a change in our political culture (Ackerman & Fishkin, 2005). Athenian democracy and the Roman Republic were participative (at least among those defined as citizens) and deliberative democrats wish to revive those older traditions in order to disperse political power, promote justice and improve social interdependencies.

Critics allege that deliberation cannot become a model for institutional reform because it is too impractical. We can improve representative democracy but not replace it (Goodin, 2003). Another criticism concerns power. Firstly, unless we equalize the social conditions of political participants then some – as now – will inevitably wield more influence over the political process than others (Fitzpatrick, 2002). Secondly, even if conditions are equalized in a socioeconomic sense, power operates across many more dimensions than this. The deliberative ideal is where 'the force of the better argument prevails' (Habermas, 1990: 158–9); but this emphasis upon 'voice' potentially neglects those whose voices have traditionally been suppressed and culturally marginalized. The danger is that deliberative democracy is another model which would subtly prefer the interests and assumptions of white, western, middle-class males.

In terms of Figure 4.1, deliberative democracy shares the communitarian emphasis upon community (deliberation requires mutual communication) and the republic emphasis upon public participation. Arguably, though, it leans slightly more towards zones 1 & 2, with many on the liberal Left giving it their support.

Differentiated citizenship

The argument that power operates across multiple dimensions is one we have already discussed. On pp. 61–4 we saw that power is not so much that affects agents, but that through which agency is produced and configured. As promised, we will revisit such ideas in future chapters. In the context of citizenship, one key influence has been that of Iris Young (1949–2006). Young (2000: 36–51), for instance, criticized the deliberative emphasis upon speech, arguing that communication and the circulation of social meanings are often non-discursive. This derived in turn from Young's (1990) long-standing, postmodern emphasis upon 'difference'.

For entirely well-intentioned reasons we often say that people are 'basically the same underneath', i.e. beneath the surface differences of gender, ethnicity, nationality, etc. we are all human. But this potentially obscures the extent to which we are also *different*. If a person is someone who has been socialized into a way of life then they will bear the imprint of that culture throughout their lives in the form of accents, habits, assumptions, and so forth. Indeed, the very way in which we perceive and mentally apprehend the world around us is cultural and therefore differential: the eighteenth century Native American did not see the world the same way that you do. Therefore, we are members of diverse social groupings with complex identities. Concepts like justice, citizenship and equality should therefore encompass the category of difference and challenge those political philosophies which emphasize 'sameness' and so are potentially oppressive to those who do not conform to mainstream perceptions of normality. Given the dissimilar histories and life-opportunities between black and white people it is misguided and insulting to imagine that these differences can be subsumed under, and by, a banner of equal citizenship (see Chapter 8). Young was an exponent of 'group rights', believing that new group-based forms of political representation and democratic participation were a necessary condition of empowerment.

Liberals are therefore accused by postmodernists like Young of merely 'tolerating' differences. Liberal tolerance implies agreeing to endure that which you dislike or feel indifferent towards. But for Young this is represents another form of oppression because it effectively 'privatizes' human difference by treating differences as a personal matter. But what this ignores is the value which differences bring to a public, democratic culture. Instead of simply tolerating them we ought to afford them 'recognition' as matters of justice and even celebrate them as helping to keep our societies free, open and diverse. If gays and lesbians are effectively denied the freedom to act and dress as they wish in public, because of moral-cultural disapprovals that such liberals refuse to challenge because they are not obviously discriminatory, then such liberal tolerance really contributes to subtle forms of oppression.

Differential citizenship is therefore based upon disparity and divergence rather than the essentialisms of sameness and identity. One potential problem is that this approach may homogenize and fetishize 'the group'. Even as members of groups our identities stretch and disperse along multiple lines of affiliation. Billy and I are both white men. But Billy is a 70-year old rural farmer from Australia who has 11 grandchildren and lost his leg to diabetes. To what extent, then, are Billy and I members of the same group? We are and yet we aren't. An emphasis upon groups may actually *contradict* a commitment to difference, ghettoizing individuals in boxes by over-emphasizing just one aspect of their identity. Paradoxically perhaps, and when taken to its extreme, an emphasis upon difference can actually lead back to an homogenized sameness and inspire the exclusion of others who are different. It may inspire us to abandon universal categories and understanding in favour of the local and the particular (if we are all different then there is no common human denominator) which seems to contradict what citizenship is about in the first place.

Furthermore, if our identities are multiple then perhaps the liberal stress upon the rational self, rather than the encumbrances of our cultural membership, is the right one after all. If we are so 'different' that we are effectively locked into our identities then such ideas only invoke a strong, non-liberal communitarianism. But if all we require is to be aware of the role played by cultural identities then it is unclear how much of a challenge is being made to liberalism after all.

Therefore, differentiated citizenship may be located across quadrants 1 & 2 in Figure 4.1. We will revisit such ideas again in Chapter 8.

Recent Developments

Global citizenship

For those like Marshall, citizenship rights developed, and were intimately associated, with the rise of the nation-state. For Marshall, citizenship implied national membership. However, if we have entered a world in which the role of the nation-state is shrinking then what happens to citizenship rights and obligations? Do we cease to be *citizens* in this globalized environment and become something else entirely – what would that be? Or do we become *global citizens*? But what does it mean to say that we have global rights and responsibilities? Do you have a right to ensure that the Great Barrier Reef is protected or that Internet Service Providers in Russia do not threaten your child's wellbeing? Do you have obligations to each one of the near 7 billion inhabitants of Earth?

We review the possibilities at greater length in Chapter 10. For now we can observe how some argue that the concept of justice breaks down in a global context (Nagel, 2005). Rights and obligations have to be enforceable and that implies authorities who able to do the enforcing and coercing. Since such authorities are bound to be local and national in scope, and since we can hardly abandon the notion of rights and duties, then any global issues are inevitably filtered down and through the local and the national. We should help the globally poor as matters of humanitarianism, not as matters of justice between global citizens.

Others propose that citizenship is being spread and moulded across multi-layers of governance and regulation (Held, 2010). Imagine an office building with several floors. Like a busy manager who has to constantly move between floors, so a global citizens is one who possesses, and has to navigate among, numerous levels. Our sense of who we are and what we owe to others is increasingly being pulled and stretched along multiple, intersecting and sometimes indistinguishable planes: the global, the regional, the national, the local, the neighbourhood. The analogy is slightly misleading. It is not so much that agents move *between* the floors; it is more that the floors constitute the stages *out of which* a globally-oriented agency is being formed.

Think of the environment. The widespread recognition of global warming exemplifies an understanding that national boundaries are more porous than they once were. Rising sea waters don't care what nationality you are. But when we say that problems are global, we don't mean that they operate in some far, abstract space; we mean that they exist – or are capable or existing – everywhere. Thus, global warming may impact upon your elderly neighbour during increasingly hot summers and therefore upon your obligation to be a good neighbour. Such global problems require global solutions. This doesn't mean leaving things to international agencies and organizations, it means that responsibilities synchronize as the global and the local conjoin.

We are, to say the least, at the beginning of a long period of transition during which our expectations, assumptions and very identities are shifting. In the mid-1990s the idea that a child in her bedroom could be the victim of online bullies or sexual predators was simply fantastical. Yet such risks have become part of the landscape of our understanding. Debates about global citizenship do not necessarily contain an answer for the metamorphosing nature of social relationships, but they do capture the widely held suspicion that something profound *is* happening. Therefore, hard-headed decisions about how to regulate and apportion responsibilities are difficult matters of case-by-case negotiation. In social policy terms, the difficulty is multiplied. We can just about grasp the notion of global civil and political rights, but what about *global social rights*?

Cultural citizenship

We have already encountered something of what this means. For instance, those who stress the importance of relational equality are highlighting the role played by culture within systems of human wellbeing and justice. In this chapter the idea that citizenship is about identity, rather than merely about formal, legalistic rights and responsibilities, emerges out of the same territory.

Culture refers to the social meanings, traditions, identities and values which constitute a particular way of life and sense of belonging. Agents help to shape and define their cultures but are also sites of cultural reconfiguration. We are constructed by, and assemble ourselves through, our cultural relations. Cultural citizenship therefore implies being attuned to the diverse influences upon social membership and political participation (Stevenson, 2003). Citizenship is not just about the institutions which govern our lives, it concerns the everyday characteristics of the lives which are governed. Justice cannot exist unless it resides within our everyday interaction and our very individualities. Thus, both citizenship and justice should be understood as felt, experienced parts of civil society. We inhabit the cultures that inhabit us. Just as a fish relies upon water to maintain its life, so we breathe and move through the civic cultures upon which we rely. This means having shared interests, understandings and concerns. It does not mean consensus and facile conformity but agreeing about how to live with disagreements – something republicans and deliberative democrats are concerned with. Therefore, cultural citizenship demands the flourishing of something intangible. It means having public spaces and goods (parks, streets, town squares) that integrate and nourish us.

But that very intangibility also introduces something uncertain and anxious into the picture. We need to behave in ways that will nurture the sources of cultural citizenship, but what is that exactly? Our anxiety may lead us to try and codify a set of entitlements and duties. Perhaps we could introduce surveillance technology, monetary incentives and criminal penalties to ensure that public spaces are preserved. Yet if we go too far in that direction, then we may destroy whatever it is we need to save. For a culture is a living, dynamic, messy form of integration and self-organization. A 'way of life' has to be allowed to meander across a vast, if not unlimited, plane; if you try and run it along rigid tracks then you may deprive it of the fuel it needs to go anywhere.

In more practical terms, there are debates about national belonging. How many cultures can a 'cultural citizenship' encompass? How much diversity is *too much* diversity? To what extent can distinct cultures (linguistic, political, religious, etc) be accommodated before the overarching cultural umbrella begins to snap and dissolve? Cultures may well require what Putnam (2000: 22–4) called 'bonding capital' where too much cross-fertilization may erode a culture. Yet, if we push too far in that direction then we may be left with cultural separatism, where the ghettoized cultures we mentioned above appear and become oppressive to their least powerful members. Therefore, we are faced with the difficult task of trying to nurture 'bridging capital'. That is, of trying to maintain a delicate balance of cultural distinctiveness within a pluralistic environment of cultural interaction and mutual evolution. This has implications for minority cultures (Kymlicka, 1995a, 1995b), for practices of social inclusion and exclusion and for how we live together on a globalized but finite planet when there so many – and so many conflicting – ways of life to accommodate.

We have now completed what, in effect, is the first part of this book. pp. 65–70 laid the groundwork by demonstrating that what is contentious about citizenship is the question of how rights and duties relate to one another. For students of social policy the problem is then deciding about when we are justified in coercing people into performing moral and socially useful acts, and what forms of coercion might be called for. pp. 70–5 offered a taxonomy for understanding some of the key issues and points of contention. This was then used to map some influential schools of thought on p. 75–85. We concluded by reviewing some recent developments.

The last three chapters have endeavoured to show that a Left–Right political division explains much, though by no means all, of the controversy that the concepts of equality, liberty and citizenship generate. Equality and liberty are undoubtedly the opposite sides of the same coin, but this is a coin that can be spun in any number of ideological and theoretical directions. The metaphor is apt, since citizenship might be thought of as a currency which can take a number of forms depending upon how the coin is spun. In this chapter we saw that citizenship debates both intersect with those earlier discussions while striking out in new directions, some of which will be picked up later in the book. There is little doubt that these controversies will continue into the far future, establishing new lines of thought and argument that can be barely anticipated here.

As such, it is time for us to move on and examine, in the next two chapters, a series of concepts that lie at the political and sociological heart of social policy. We begin by examining some important political debates.

Questions for Further Discussion

- To what extent can social justice be promoted by enforcing the social obligations of citizenship?
- Should an account of the 'common good' incorporate the concept of social rights?
- Has T. H. Marshall's expectation that class society would become a society of citizens been fulfilled?
- Can communitarianism adequately recognize, support and promote moral and cultural diversity, e.g. of families and nations?

5

State, Power and Poverty

- The State
- Power

- Poverty and
  Social Exclusion

In this chapter and the next we investigate the political and social 'spaces' within which justice, and injustice, operates; the arenas which make concepts of equality, liberty, citizenship and community an actual reality for people. Chapter 5 deals with the origins, means and ends of government. On pp. 86–93 we examine justifications of the state and political authority. What is the relationship between government and state? What is the nature of the state's power? pp. 93–8 then ask, what is power? How does the state shape the lives of its citizens? Finally, on pp.98–104, we draw upon these critiques when exploring debates about poverty and social exclusion. These questions are to some degree dependent upon, and so lead us towards, Chapter 6 where we examine theories of structure and agency, class and other forms of social association.

The State

Theorizing the state

Our interpretation of the state derives from the most fundamental questions of what it means to be a social being. Is the state the product of individuals choosing to associate together for their mutual benefit? Or, is the state inscribed within those social processes through which individuals are themselves constructed? Do we make state and society or do they make us?

There are two senses of 'the political' at work here. If individuals make state and society, then we might regard the political as the means by which our 'pre-political' interests become articulated and reconciled. If you want our tribe to become farmers while I want us to remain hunter-gatherers, then perhaps we should create a governing assembly to decide the matter. Conversely, if there can be no such thing as a 'pre-political individual', then the political is the means by which our interests and identities are formed and configured. The idea of a governing assembly appeals to us because we are already social agents who have been shaped by, and within, the requisite traditions and customs.

Such distinctions speak to distinct ways of understanding the nature of society, state and agency (cf. Chambers & Kopstein, 2006; Jessop, 2008: 2–11). 'Individualists' interpret the state as the end-product of individuals deliberating and acting together. A Utilitarian, for instance, might say that the state exists in order to promote utility. And although they reject Utilitarianism, 'social contract' theorists agree that the state is, in some way, there to serve individuals.

Social contract theory says the following: when individuals choose to enter into formal agreements with others they incur obligations which mirror and enforce that agreement. Political authority, legitimacy and obligation can be understood in similar ways. When you and I chose to enter into a joint association, we have an obligation to share both the benefits and the burdens of said membership. That political association is a 'polity' overseen by the state, whose job it is to hold the polity together. To be a citizen is to owe a 'political debt' to other citizens.

Of course, social contract philosophers disagree about important details. For Hobbes (1973), obedience to the sovereign is owed because only through the protections guaranteed by an all-powerful 'leviathan', can you experience freedom in the first place. For Locke (1960), Hobbes opened the door to absolutism and dictatorship. Much better, Locke thought, to base political authority upon a doctrine of natural rights. Government should be limited because when entering into social associations people give up only some of their freedoms in order to *enhance* their freedoms overall. This implies a political system of checks and balances, based upon what Montesquieu (1689–1755) called a 'separation of powers', in order to ensure that the state remains within its legitimate boundaries (Montesquieu, 1989). Rousseau (1973) agreed with Hobbes that the sovereign – or what he called the 'general will' – has dominion over everything, but effectively agreed with Locke that it secures legitimacy by facilitating individuality. Rather than curtailing the 'particular wills' of its members, the general will raises them to a higher level of social being. It was such ideas that Rawls drew upon in his thought experiment of the original position.

It is important to understand that none of the above regards the social contract as an historical reality. People didn't walk out of the primeval savannah and declare 'hey, why don't we form a government!' Instead, the social contract is a means of comprehending how and why people manage to live together in relative harmony. That said, there are occasional examples where the will of 'the people' is formed under conditions resembling a contract. The events of 1774–1789, which led to the formation of the U.S. Constitution, is one possible example.

None of which is persuasive, according to those who possess a more 'solidaristic' or 'organic' interpretation of state and society (de Jasay, 2004). It does not make sense to pretend that individuals *precede* the state. To be an individual is to be someone who is already woven into the subtle webs of social interaction. People don't grow up in a vacuum. They are able to communicate and cooperate precisely because they were socialized by and into a cultural mesh of social meanings. Society gave birth to them, not the other way around. Political authority, legitimacy and obligation do not flow from us. *We* flow from them. Only within a bounded horizon of interpretative meaning can we become social agents capable of recognizing other beings as persons deserving of respect. Hegel (1967) articulates this way of thinking. Social contract ideas capture only one, relatively brief moment of social development, he insists. State and society are not machines which require political engineers; they are more like gardens whose roots have to be nurtured by those who possess the requisite skills. The state is the soil which binds the roots together.

Many of us might struggle to place ourselves exclusively within either the individualistic or the solidaristic camp. If so, we can take comfort from other philosophers. Marxism draws upon both, for instance. Marx criticized Hegel's notion that the state stood over and above civil society, unifying its disparate parts. However, he agreed that social contract ideas have taken one phase of social development – the rise of 'economic man' in the form of the bourgeois property-owner – and mistaken it for an enduring, universal reality.

According to Marx (1977: 27–30; Jessop, 2008: 56–61), the nature of the state derives from the nature of the economy which underpins it: a feudal state is different to a capitalist state because the economies of these systems are different. In a capitalist society, the capitalist state is itself a player in the struggle of class against class, constantly favouring property-owners over the property-less. Originally, Marx held a simplistic view of the state as an organizing committee for the bourgeoisie; he subsequently refined this view, but nevertheless maintained that capitalist states act *in general* in the interests of the ruling class to maintain the accumulative cycles of the capitalist economy. It is unclear what, for Marx, a communist state would resemble – or even whether there would be one. Marxists have sometimes made cryptic reference to the 'administration of things' rather than of people, though after the experience of Soviet absolutism there is more to be said for a liberal constitution of codified rights, of checks and balances, than simplistic calls for 'social and not just political emancipation' might have realized.

Max Weber (1864–1920), in turn, criticized Marx's economic determinism. He famously defined the state as that which holds a monopoly on the use of legitimate violence within a given territory (Weber, 1991: 77–8). Social power is more than mere economic power. The rational-legal authority of the state derives from the formation and application of impersonal rules within hierarchical structures of decision-making.[1] The state is therefore the closest approximation we have to a pure bureaucracy – regardless of whether we are talking about a capitalist, democratic, authoritarian, socialist or communist state – and so its growth is perhaps the most important manifestation of the increasing 'bureaucratization' and 'disenchantment' of the modern world: the confinement of the spirit within an 'iron cage' of impersonal and spiritless rationality.

These debates have been rediscovered and reinvented down the intervening generations. The idea that the state's influence was becoming ubiquitous in the modern world helped to promote the further and not unrelated idea that the state could be used as a means of advancing individual and social wellbeing. That is, it could be a humane tool of progress and not just a bureaucratic instrument of impersonal rationality. Justifications for a welfare state proceed from that point on.

The welfare state

By the 'welfare state', we sometimes refer to the overarching goals of the modern state and sometimes to the functions of distinct institutions – social security, healthcare, education, social services, etc. – which inhabit its various branches: a legislature (which makes the laws), an executive (which applies the laws) and a judiciary (which interprets and upholds the laws). In Britain, the Houses of Parliament are the legislature, the government is the executive, the courts are the judiciary, with the crown or the monarch as the head of state. Theoretically, then, the legislature should be the dominant partner, though since the mid-nineteenth century, the executive has taken over many of its powers and functions. This easily leads to confusion. Often, 'the government' is used as a proxy for parliament or sometimes for that political party which holds the most seats. Strictly speaking, the government consists of those several dozen ministers who command the respect of, and so are accountable to, the legislature. In any event, the government of welfare services became a central occupation of the state from the late nineteenth century onwards.

Two key justifications for state welfare traditionally dominated political debates.

One is essentially economic. John Maynard Keynes (1883–1946) argued that the state can and should secure the conditions for stable economic growth (Keynes, 1954; Skidelsky, 2003: ch. 38). Prior to the 1930s, mainstream economists held that the state should not normally intervene in the economy, as this would be damaging and counter-productive. The invisible hand of the market was thought of as the best means of creating wealth and innovation, satisfying preferences and providing opportunities. So when critics condemned high levels of unemployment as examples of market failure, the defenders of laissez faire capitalism argued that unemployment was actually the result of workers pricing themselves out of jobs by asking for wages higher than employers could afford to pay. Therefore, the solution to unemployment was for workers to reduce their wage demands. If I hire four workers at £5 per hour each, I pay out £20 every hour. But if those workers reduce their wages to £4 per hour I can then afford to take on another person. If this happens across the economy, unemployment will be 'soaked up'. By contrast, state interference only upsets the invisible hand. If, for instance, people know their incomes will be protected should they become unemployed they will have little incentive to reduce their wages.

Keynes accepted that unrestrained markets could balance themselves out in the long run. The trouble, he argued, was that in the long run we are all dead! By the time market supply and demand has corrected itself the social consequences of falling wages and might well have been devastating. Some degree of state interference is therefore justified. If the government prints money in order to build a hospital then this creates jobs and much-needed services. The money does not just get spent once. It goes into wallets and purses, helping to stimulate the rest of the economy too. This is known as the 'multiplier effect'. After WW2, the Keynesian approach implied a mixed economy (the public ownership of major industries and utilities to shield them from market forces) and the state management of demand. This implied lowering taxes, printing money or creating jobs through public works programmes, in the expectation that the beneficial effects of doing so will reinvigorate an ailing economy. Keynes therefore believed that an economy could be run at or near full employment so long as the correct monetary and fiscal policies were pursued.

So, Keynes articulates what became a central economic justification for the post-war welfare state: *to save capitalism from itself.* Without state intervention, market capitalism and liberal democracy would be unstable, especially during economic crises. By manipulating demand, the state could apply its foot to the accelerator or brake, as circumstances required. The welfare state would educate and train its future workers and, through healthcare and social insurance, reduce people's vulnerability to capitalism's risks and hazards, offering a series of safety-nets that would cushion them during periods of economic downturn. Keynes did not originate these ideas, but he offered their greatest justification.

Keynesian economics became widely accepted for a third of a century after his death. But with rising inflation and unemployment in the 1970s, coupled with a new era of floating exchange rates, offshore havens and financial deregulation, arguments for Keynesianism began to falter. The radical Right was able to diagnose these developments more persuasively than the Left so that, by the early 1980s, Keynesian recommendations no longer appeared persuasive. The goal of full employment appeared dead. This did not lead to a dismantling of state welfare, but even the most social democratic nations began to restructure and rethink their systems (Plant, 2009). If the 'classic welfare state' was designed for a capitalism that would be less reliant upon free markets, the post-classic welfare state has had to cope with the return of a *laissez faire* emphasis upon privatization, deregulation, reduced expenditure and self-help individualism.

From that point on, a second major justification for state welfare became even more important than before. This *moral justification* invokes the debates about justice which we have reviewed in previous chapters.

For social liberals – like Keynes – the value of the welfare state lies in its capacity to counterbalance the economic power of the wealthy, creating opportunities, fairness and upward social mobility. In a democracy, everyone has a vote and every vote counts equally. Power percolates downward and one consequence of this is the creation of a 'social wage': individuals' incomes are effectively boosted by having access to services for which they do not have to pay at the point of use. State education counteracts, to some extent, the advantages conferred by private education. Ideally, then, state welfare parallels the democratization which occurs within the polity.

For egalitarians, the moral justification resides in the extent to which state welfare enables egalitarian goals to be realized. This may be about raising the social wage or countering discrimination. But there is also what might be called an 'egalitarian iteration'. State welfare feeds upon the tax revenues generated by high levels of employment, but is also a means of creating the very employment it needs, e.g. through public sector expansion. And public sector jobs in nursing and teaching are more likely to be taken by women, thus aiding the goal of gender equality.

Communitarians are more concerned with the common good and cultural unities. The classic welfare state appealed to a strong sense of national value and identity. The idea of people across social ranks pulling together for a common purpose may have been crystallized by World War Two, but it denotes a communal, collectivist ethos long articulated by the labour movement. If the welfare state does not nurture that sense of justice, or even erodes it, the system undermines its own moral legitimacy. Note that this potentially conflicts with liberal assumptions. Marshall, for example, argued that 'class' association should be replaced by that of 'citizenship'. But if welfare state values owe much to class-specific solidarities then a meritocratic society of classless citizens might empty state welfare of its moral ballast, setting it adrift of distinct communal needs and responsibilities.

The potential strength of state welfare, then, is that it can be many things to many people. Liberals, egalitarians and communitarians can all find something they like; a basis for agreement which reduces the toxicity of any disagreements. The same logic applies to our earlier discussion. Individualists can reasonably view the welfare state as a means by which individuals enter into a mutually beneficial system to protect each other against common risks and dangers. Solidaristic interpretations focus upon the welfare state's ability to bind social groups and economic classes together. In these terms it can be seen to provide a coherence and integrity to the miscellany of civil society, bringing the family, the workplace, the church and the voluntary sector together under the tutelage and authority of the statutory sphere.

Of course, there is no such thing as *the* welfare state. Some systems are liberal (USA, Australia), some are conservative (Germany, France) and others are social democratic (Sweden, Norway), in the famous classification of Esping-Anderson (1990). But, in more general terms, justifications for state welfare tend to be eclectic yet also robust, offering philosophical stabilizers which have kept the basic idea of the welfare state afloat during periods of ideological assault and economic turmoil.

Governance

If the age of the classical welfare state is over, then what has replaced it? A greater emphasis upon free markets, to be sure, but state welfare services and justifications have remained remarkably buoyant. Even so, many suspect that we can no longer quite speak of state, government and society using a vocabulary that assumes stable, predictable and enduring boundaries between the relevant actors, sectors and institutions. Over recent decades, a whole series of shocks and developments have complicated the picture. Thus, new vocabularies have become prevalent as a means of trying to capture what is going on (Cochrane, 2004).

'Governance' is now a popular term of reference (Bevir, 2010). The concept implies that the central agencies of the state can no longer deal with others – or with each other – simply and directly. To take one example, in 2007 there were approximately 100,000 non-governmental organizations around the world, many of which are truly global in membership and influence. A government either has to ignore or engage with such NGOs. If it ignores them, this might only create future problems since, as societies have become more individualized, with people experiencing a greater sense of entitlement and expectation, government ignores voices and demands at its peril. Yet if it engages with relevant NGOs, this makes the business of designing and implementing policy that much harder. In short, government becomes a multidirectional and multilevel series of processes and partnerships which is highly complex to manage and contain. The term 'governance' is meant to express that complexity. At-a-distance forms of administration begin to replace more immediate, hands-on types of regulation and management. Welfare states now correspond less to the top-down, command-and-control model than used to be the case.

This conceptualization overlaps with another: governmentality (Hindess, 1996: 131–6). We encountered this in Chapter 3. Let me offer a personal example. Recently, my university circulated an email stating that portable heaters would no longer be allowed in offices because they alter local temperatures, interfering with the heating systems of buildings. They were to be confiscated, therefore. Now, since I have an unnatural affection for my heater I locked it in a drawer and felt pleased with myself for protecting it from the 'office appliance kidnappers'. However, I am not aware of *any* heaters being confiscated! After all, why waste time, effort and staff loyalty by actually impounding equipment when you only have to threaten to do so, trusting that idiots like me will behave exactly as expected, helping to resolve the problem you wanted to resolve anyway? Thus, governance-at-a-distance actually intensifies the panoptic gaze where we are regulated, and regulate ourselves, through our freedoms.

For Foucault (1980: 121), this process represents the decapitation of sovereignty. Centuries past, the king would dispense justice either directly or through proxies – judges, for instance – who made decisions under the authority of the king. What we have done, according to Foucault, is 'cut the head off the king' and so changed the way in which power operates. Power no longer plunges downwards from a Hobbesian leviathan; instead, like liquid it flows sideways, flooding every crevice and fissure across the social landscape. We might be overwhelmed by the majesty of Parliament or Congress, we might be awed as outsiders, by their obscure symbols and rituals. But for Foucault this is a mirage or, to shift metaphors, the equivalent of an amputee imaging that his limb is still there. The state exists but it is decentralized, operating throughout the interstices and capillaries of the social body.

This perspective blows apart those we have reviewed above. The welfare state is not that which is concerned with the welfare of autonomous citizens residing within civil society. It is instead a convenient description, a sign which summarizes the discursive disciplines that construct the very subjects who experience levels of welfare in the first place. The 'welfare state' is therefore something of a misnomer and what we should analyse instead is how 'technologies of power' operate through the imaginary limbs of society. We return to these ideas below.

Power

What appears to be at stake here is the character, operation and distribution of power. Power can mean the power *to do* something (recall the discussion of positive freedom on pp. 54–5). Power can also mean having power or sovereignty *over* something or someone. Some theorists focus upon 'power to' and others upon 'power over'. For example, for liberals power resides in political democracy with the state acting as an 'honest broker' between plural and competing interests; but for Marxists, power is fundamentally about the ownership of economic resources with the state defending its concentration in the hands of the wealthiest. This section, then, outlines the main positions which have been adopted vis-a-vis the nature of power (Scott, 2001; Haugaard, 2002).[2]

Power as force

For Bertrand Russell (1872–1970) power implied the 'production of intended effects', while for Robert Dahl *A* has power over *B* to the extent that *A* can get *B* to do something that *B* would not otherwise do (Lukes, 1986). Steven Lukes (2005) is attracted to the notion that power basically implies a capacity to change one's environment in some way. This capacity implies having 'power over' something, whether this be another person, an object, an event or, of course, oneself. Analyses of political power as force dominated the debate for decades and can be sorted into three categories: pluralist, elitist and radical.

A pluralist theory basically says that political power is and should be distributed amongst a plurality of actors, agencies and groups in society (Dahl, 1961; cf. Dahl, 1985). Because power is a threat to our freedoms, we have developed ways of dispersing power. So, through mechanisms of political representation and participation, everyone has the opportunity to contribute to important decision-making processes. An election is the most obvious example. This does not mean that the specific outcome of decision-making processes will satisfy everyone; individuals and groups conflict about the right way to do things. The point is that political resources are dispersed so that political conflict and debate is not dominated, either exclusively or permanently, by one side. This means that the state should be interpreted as a neutral umpire of the political game, facilitating that competition but not intervening in favour of any one team. Of course, crude and sophisticated versions of pluralism exist. Crude versions propose the perfect dispersal of political power, the perfect equality of social actors and the perfect neutrality of the state. Sophisticated versions treat pluralism as an ideal to be aimed for but one which, admittedly, we often fail to attain.

According to a pluralist reading, then, we can say two things about the welfare state. Firstly, the particular social institutions of the welfare state could be thought of as the outcome of past and ongoing political conflicts between competing interest-groups, e.g. capital and labour. Secondly, the welfare state, in a more general sense, could be interpreted as a neutral arbiter, refereeing conflicts over the production and distribution of social resources without favouring one outcome over another.

The advantage of pluralism is that it proposes an optimistic evaluation of politics, one which acknowledges the complexity of policy-making processes. The disadvantage is that it may well offer an *over*-optimistic appraisal of political power, downplaying the significance of systemic inequalities and failing to analyse processes that take place 'behind-the-scenes' of surface social phenomena. To understand what this means, let us explore elitist theories.

Elitism states that political power is nowhere near as decentralized as pluralists seem to imagine (Mills, 1956). The mechanisms that pluralists treat as open and undominated are, in fact, skewed in favour of already-powerful actors, groups and agencies. Elections and lobbying are both dominated by the interests of those – the wealthy – who can afford to buy influence from parties, governments and the media. The idea that decision-making processes are open to everyone is naïve since the powerful invariably set the agenda and effectively devalue the interests and voices of the less powerful. In a conflict over the building of an out-of-town hypermarket whose interests are most likely to prevail: the corporation with an annual turnover of millions or the local protestors whose financial resources are modest? According to elitism, the state is itself a player in the political game, intervening on behalf of the elites to the detriment of the others. As with pluralism, crude and sophisticated versions of elitism can be imagined.[3] Crude versions regard the interests of elites as always being dominant, whereas sophisticated versions acknowledge the complexity of political power, e.g. once in a while the state *will* favour the arguments of the local protestors. Elitism and pluralism are not always so sharply distinguished.

An elitist reading of the welfare state suggests that it favours one particular form of production and distribution. However, whether it is capital that is favoured or labour depends largely upon your ideological stance. The Left may see the welfare state largely as a pro-capitalist institution: something that helps the market economy to run more efficiently, forestalling the likelihood of riot, social dissent and anti-capitalist revolution. The Right may view it as a gravy train for the undeserving and for giving unearned social benefits to shirkers which the economy cannot afford.

The strength of elitism is that it offers a structural reading of society that understands the extent to which political power operates 'behind our backs', as a strategy which favours the interests of privileged groups and individuals. It suggests that policy-making is as much about what is omitted from consideration as what is included. However, elitism can be accused of promoting a pessimistic approach to politics. If a minority of elites dominates the process, then why bother engaging with it? It can also be accused of being resistant to empirical analysis. If elites rely upon subterfuge, dissimulation and secrecy for their power then how can we ever really identify and study it?

A radical interpretation of political power agrees with elitism on key points but there are two main differences (Lukes, 2005). Firstly, the radical interpretation detaches 'power' from 'politics' and tends to identify a dominant ideology within a wider assemblage of social practices. Marxists argue that in a capitalist society elites are always *capitalist elites*. Some versions of feminism also buy into the radical view, offering a gendered interpretation that regards the dominant elites as patriarchal. Secondly, the radical interpretation proposes not only that the interests of non-elites are pushed down the political agenda, but that non-elites are kept in ignorance of their interests in the first place. According to Marxism, capitalism keeps workers in a state of 'false consciousness' where they barely even recognize the extent to which they are exploited.

On these grounds the welfare state can be thought of as a means by which a dominant elite maintains itself in a position of power by preventing non-elites from recognizing their real needs and interests. For instance, a long-term aim of the socialist movement has been the freeing of workers from the source of their enslavement, i.e. the wage contract. Yet the welfare state ensures that paid work continues to be valued over all other forms of participative activity, locking people into their role of wage-slaves through a series of ideological and disciplinary measures.

The strength of the radical explanation is that it offers a 'grand narrative' of social reality. Instead of a simple elite/non-elite contrast, it sets out to explain why some elites will habitually prevail over others. However, radical theories are potentially guilty of over-simplifying the complexity of society, of similarly treating power in reductive, simplistic terms and of not being able to explain how social systems endure when the 'non-elites' are victorious in their struggles. This interpretation hovers on the edge of functionalism, reading social progress as just another form of power exerted against the ignorant, weak and disadvantaged.

Power as authority

Hindess (1996; cf. Morriss, 2002) warns against the danger of ignoring an older tradition in political theory. This rests upon the notion of consent and so draws a distinction between legitimate and illegitimate uses of power. So, whereas 'power as force' regards power almost as a wild animal to be tamed, 'power as authority' focuses upon the power to do x through systems of authority and legitimacy. This notion dovetails with aspects of pluralism, but is concerned not only with how power operates but with the normative question of how legitimacy can be ensured.

Think of the following. On one level, lecturers obviously have power over students to set and mark assessments and award degree grades. And yet it would be mistaken to interpret this power simply as a force A wields over B. Why? Because in this example B – the students – have *chosen* to submit themselves to the academic standards and practices of higher education. The power that lecturers possess, therefore, is an authority which flows from the power students have to determine the direction of their own lives. The power of lecturers exists only in so far as students consent to recognize it and abide by the judgement of those teaching them. 'Power over' derives from 'power to'.

Therefore, while we might be receptive to the observations of elitists and radicals when they tell us that power is skewed towards the powerful, both make a mistake if they then imagine that questions of consent are chimerical and irrelevant. Marxists, for instance, have frequently been too dismissive of liberal justifications for representative democracy. Indeed, it is by focusing upon consent and authority that we may help to overthrow illegitimate inequalities of power. So far as the welfare state is concerned this notion of power offers a necessary corrective to those theories, proposed by both Left and Right, that take a deterministic view of the development of state welfare. An emphasis upon consent reminds us that the welfare state is, to whatever extent, consented to by those who are its clients, customers and citizens.

Power as production

Chapter 3 gave a preliminary sketch of Foucault's ideas and we added to this above. We have noted how Foucault considers the self to be formed in and through practices and discourses of normalization. Freedom, governance and power are therefore intertwined as a kind of 'discursive technology' (Brown, 2006). To treat power as either force or authority involves clinging to a simplified 'monarchical' notion of power as external to the self. By, metaphorically speaking, cut the sovereign's head off we will be able to recognize the real nature of power.

But what is this exactly? Traditionally, power has been thought of in negative terms, as something that distorts, deceives, represses, controls and oppresses. Yet, Foucault (1984: 61) insists that this is too narrow and myopic a view:

> If power were never anything but repressive, if it never did anything but to say no, do you really think one would be brought to obey it? What makes power hold good, what makes it accepted, is the fact that it doesn't only weigh on us as a force that says no, but that it traverses and produces things, it induces pleasure, forms knowledge, produces discourse. It needs to be considered as a productive network which runs through the whole social body...

Sexuality, for instance, is a discourse concerned both with control of the population, e.g. through family planning strategies, and the libidinal instincts of the human body. Therefore, this discourse is not simply repressive but also *productive*. Suppression and control always leads to resistances. Attempts to prohibit and criminalize same-sex relationships shaped the liberatory and celebratory politics of today's gay and lesbian movements.

For Foucault, then, power is everywhere. It has to be understood as a micro-practice, something which perpetually occupies the minute capillaries of everyday life. Power is 'biopower', an intimate set of habits through which social fields are wrapped onto the body and through which the body expands into and patterns its environment. Power is that which makes us make ourselves as agents, or, in an oft-cited phrase, power involves the 'conduct of conduct'.

Another personal example. In a classroom, students often occupy the same tables and chairs week after week. In one sense, this is hierarchical. Individuals classify and arrange themselves into an order which suggests a regimented, predictable, obedient receptivity to the teacher's dominance. It signals a willingness to be commanded. Yet it is also a means of influencing and, indeed, *producing* the educational environment. By zeroing in on their familiar, favoured spot in the classroom, a student shapes the behavioural possibilities of those around her. Do I as a teacher accept the students' expectations or should I try and subvert them? This to-and-fro, where we shape and are shaped, is continuous and often unconscious. We make ourselves not through the grand narratives of ideological principle but in the mundane infinities of the ordinary and everyday.

Thus, Foucault weaves together 'power over' and 'power to' in imaginative ways. Power is not some mysterious force 'out there'. It is here and now. Power as production is the self acting upon the self. It is you and me. We are the constant re-manifestations of power. Thus, we cannot understand consent unless we appreciate the discursive construction of the self who does the consenting.

The potential problem with this idea of power as production, though, is that it *devalues* power as a useful concept, rendering redundant the distinction between its legitimate and illegitimate uses. The power that I have to make you read the footnote at the end of this sentence (go on, what have you got to lose?) is hardly the same as the power which in a patriarchal society, say, men wield over women.[4] If truth and freedom are nothing more than 'regimes of power', they become just another form of discourse and cease to have normative authority. If power is everywhere then, in a sense, power is nowhere. Power may occupy the tiniest droplets of micro-history, but unless these are viewed within a larger account of grand social forces and historical movements then studying them leads nowhere. If the historical or social scientist is allowed no access to 'grand narratives', then these disciplines become little more than mirrors for the self-admiring historian and social scientist. Social theorists need telescopes as well as microscopes. Despite his claim that power always implies resistance, critics have questioned whether Foucault offers much to a progressive politics.

Poverty and Social Exclusion

We are still, then, left with the question, what is power *for*? How can we make it a servant rather than a master? How can we transform the injustices of power into the power of justice? These are crucial questions for social policy. It could be claimed that the central rationale for state welfare concerns the fight against poverty. The economic and moral justifications we explored above both have poverty at their heart. We save capitalism from itself by reducing levels of poverty and so improving the moral legitimacy of our social institutions. Therefore, when we place debates about state and power together we are led, as welfare theorists, towards considerations of poverty and its younger cousin, social exclusion.

Definitions

At its simplest, poverty denotes a lack of even a minimum level of subsistence: food, safe drinking water, shelter, physical and mental health. This 'absolute' definition is largely applicable to developing nations. According to the United Nations Development Programme (2007: 25), by 2004 there were about 1 billion people living 'at the margins of survival on less than US$1 a day, with 2.6 billion – 40 percent of the world's population – living on less than US$2 a day' and 10 million children dying every year from poverty and malnutrition. Absolute definitions have traditionally been contrasted with relative ones, where someone is defined as poor relative to the standard of living of those around them. It is here that the term social exclusion began to gain purchase in Europe in the 1980s. Many on the Right had long resisted the concept of relative poverty, for how could it be possible for someone to own a TV and other consumer goods and yet still be defined as being relatively poor? No, 'relative poverty' confused deprivation with mere inequality and inequality, for the radical Right anyway, was regarded as a social *good*.

The term 'social exclusion' undercut such arguments (Byrne, 2005). It reemphasized the idea that deprivation is about an enforced exclusion from what most people take for granted, a marginalization from society's way of life. What makes life worth living is not just income and possessions, but a level of respect, participation, self-worth and dignity that those at the social periphery are less likely to attain. Inequality matters because systemic, structural inequalities represent a pernicious form of socioeconomic and cultural segregation, one which raises the status of some at the expense of others.

More recently, the idea of there being a 'poverty of capabilities' has reinforced this stance. As we have seen, capabilities are that which enable people to be and to do. But the capabilities necessary to live a fulfilling life will differ from place to place – lack of access to mobile technology will typically matter more in London than in Lagos. Therefore, a 'poverty of capabilities' encompasses both absolute and relative definitions: poverty implies a lack of access but the kind of access which counts will vary with the social context.

Social exclusion does complicate things. It is possible to be poor but not social excluded. Students, for example, may have low incomes but also considerable access to networks and clubs. It is also possible to be socially excluded but not poor. An elderly disabled person might be asset-rich but fairly lonely and isolated. By and large, though, the literature treats poverty and social exclusion as complementary.

As such, social research now employs both static and dynamic indicators (Flaherty et al., 2004: ch. 1; Gordon, 2006), though we should avoid identifying 'poverty' with the former and 'social exclusion' with the latter. Poverty statistics have traditionally offered a snapshot of distributions in income and wealth which can distort even as they clarify. Where we should draw poverty lines is contentious, and in any event relatively few people remain in poverty permanently, it being more common for households to oscillate above and below the poverty line periodically. Research all too easily becomes a technical, statistical exercise. Yet poverty research can also capture the sheer physical and emotional grind of coping, day in and day out, with disadvantage. Social exclusion tries to capture the complex and multidimensional processes of deprivation, but it too has its 'static' characteristics. The post-1997 UK government came up with 59 indicators allowing it to measure progress on social exclusion and inclusion. It should also be observed that if you define justice as a matter of inclusion rather than inequalities – implying that an inclusive society is one which can still contain massive inequalities – then you shift the political terrain away from that upon which anti-poverty researchers have traditionally fought (Levitas, 2005).

To understand why, we need to appreciate some prominent explanations of poverty and exclusion.

Explanations and solutions

Poverty and exclusion may be injustices but, because considerable disagreements exist about how justice should be theorized, there are inevitable disagreements about the causes of and solutions to them. Four key perspectives are outlined below (also Alcock, 2006: 35–46).

The first belongs to those on the Right for whom poverty is behavioural or pathological (Murray, 1984). This can mean either that the poor are deliberately lazy and indolent, or that they are genetically predisposed to being poor, or a bit of both. Either way, this is an explanation where the sources of poverty are located squarely within poor individuals themselves. The solution is to force the poor out of their indigence, though policies of enforcement and punishment, or to counteract genetic dispositions (if it is assumed that addiction is heritable then one remedy is to prevent or discourage the 'genetically inferior' from having children).

The notion that the poor are poor because they are lazy is very old and underpins the centuries-old distinction between the deserving and undeserving poor, with the former being regarded as virtuous, e.g. people disabled from birth, and the latter as immoral. The 'undeserving poor' is a category appealing to rational choice liberals on the Right. If being a social agent means responding rationally to external stimuli then it is no surprise that some will try to attain the most they can through the least effort. The idea that the poor are biologically and genetically inferior is more recent. For Herrnstein and Murray (1994), low intelligence and poverty are not simply correlated: the former *causes* the latter.

There is a tension between these two pathological accounts, for one seems to be claiming that the poor are responsible for their situation whereas the other attributes social positions to biological inheritance. Murray (2000) tries to weave these accounts together. By choosing to be poor people pass on inferior genes to their offspring; over time, there is a deterioration in the genome of the poor. It should be noted that the scientific evidence for this is zero.

In short, the disadvantage of pathological explanations is that they ignore the numerous causal factors of poverty. They single out one factor and magnify its significance. Thus, many of us may know someone who is deprived and yet indolent. But this captures only one part of the reality of social life. If ethnic minorities are more likely to be poor, which is the case across the world, should we attribute this to some inherent laziness? What about the effects of racial discriminations or historic injustice? The importance of our social environments in shaping our identities and our social status is too well documented for such individualistic and biological explanations to take us very far.

The second explanation is also conservative, though it does make room for environmental factors. The 'cycle of deprivation' argument recognizes the importance of socialization but adds that if the social environment is dysfunctional in any way then children will grow up accordingly. So if, as a child, my family and immediate community are lacking in social and moral disciplines (hard work, civic participation, etc.) then I am likely to grow up with similar values and expectations. Consequently, my habits, values and attitudes will leave me poor too. This explanation identifies a 'culture of poverty' which is inherited from one generation to the next. Mead (1986) argues that a dysfunctional environment is one of the effects of the welfare state which first helps to create poverty and then perpetuates it by engendering a 'culture of dependency' where people lose the habits of work, responsibility and self-help. It is such arguments that underpin the underclass debate.

Though it has its counterparts on the Left, e.g. Marx's category of the lumpenproletariat, it was really the American Right who popularized the term within their anti-welfare state politics (Deacon, 2002: 34–9, 51–3). Murray (1984) alleged that over-generous benefits in America had led to the emergence of a significant underclass of several million people. By encouraging neither marriage nor independence within the labour market, assistance benefits had created a generation of unemployed and unemployable black youths, as well as a generation of lone mothers who expected to be 'married to the state'. For those such as Murray, therefore, the term 'underclass' does not refer to an extreme of poverty, i.e. the poorest of the poor, but to a different *type* of poverty: the value-system (the culture) possessed by those who expect society and the state to do everything for them without having to contribute anything in return. These kinds of arguments have given a theoretical justification for the expansion of disciplinary workfare programmes where claimants are compelled to work or train in return for their benefits, in order to re-motivate the habits that they have allegedly lost.

However, the cycle of deprivation argument betrays a number of weaknesses. Although, it acknowledges the importance of social environments it then falls back on something resembling the pathological explanation. Mead, for instance, rejects any suggestion that unequal distributions of social resources matter. He separates 'values' from 'socioeconomic inequalities', insisting that contemporary poverty is a kind of cultural deprivation in which the poor – buoyed by the liberal Left – have excluded themselves from moral norms and social virtues.[5] Once again, therefore, we are invited to ignore the structural, strategic forces which distribute people, from birth, across the social hierarchies of advantage and disadvantage. Research suggests that there is no general culture of dependency. Dean and Taylor-Gooby (1992) concluded that terms such as 'underclass' and 'dependency culture' are not so much objective phenomena 'out there' as symbolic and discursive constructions which indicate a widespread tendency to blame the victims for the very disadvantages which have been perpetrated against them.

This kind of research implies that we ought to focus upon the social, political and discursive constructions of poverty (Fraser, 1989: 144–83). Deprivation may be a measurable reality – a lack of sufficient nutrition, poor health, etc. – but is also a categorization, a partitioning, a string of signifiers, codes and symbols that we, as social scientists, pride ourselves on comprehending. Conservative terms like the 'underclass' are guilty of blaming the victim. But is may be that anti-poverty campaigners are guilty also. After all, few of those classified as poor are willing to describe themselves as such. Is this a coping mechanism, a kind of false consciousness, or is it a reaction against another category which is just as distorting and as patronizing? By constructing and labelling people as 'the poor' perhaps we are 'othering' them as strange, inadequate, abnormal and aberrant, denying them their voice (Sennett, 2003: Lister, 2004). In short, poverty discourse is a form of 'production' in the sense we used on pp. 97–8. When we talk about social exclusions we may be helping, through the very vocabulary we use, to perpetuate the disadvantages which we see ourselves as trying to solve.

The third explanation focuses upon the failures of government and collective action. It is the policies and institutions set up to eliminate deprivation which have failed (to whatever degree) and may even have made the problem worse in some respects.

There are many possible reasons for a failure of collective action. It may be that radical and effective strategies are just difficult to implement. If the causes of poverty and exclusion are multiple, complex and reinforcing then successful interventions demand an investment of time, effort, patience and, yes, money that many governments – the prisoners of electoral cycles – are unwilling to commit.

Another possible reason involves 'path dependency'. This is the idea that what we do now is fundamentally shaped by how things have been done in the past. This QWERTY keyboard I am using is frustrating, but it is practically ubiquitous because of decisions taken many decades ago. Similarly, institutional cultures are like tankers: difficult to turn round. We may praise Scandinavian countries for their low rates of poverty without also appreciating the long-term consensus and effort it required. In short, what we do here constrains what can be done elsewhere. If you introduce in-work benefits to eliminate the unemployment trap then you may displace rather than resolve the problem, creating other forms of trap (poverty trap, savings trap) elsewhere in the policy chain.

But this 'policy failure' explanation is vulnerable on two fronts. Many on the Right would still insist that policies fail when they do not take account of the failings of the poor. By distributing entitlement-based hand-outs, we are encouraging the poor to define themselves as passive, and as having rights but not obligations. Many on the Left insist that policies fail when they do not take account of certain structural constraints. The welfare state redistributes (mainly horizontally) a certain amount of income but leaves untouched the vastly unequal system of capital ownership. Drawing upon the more cultural ideas we just encountered, we might add that a focus upon policy neglects the fact that governments are themselves woven into the process through which the 'poor' and 'non-poor' are discursively constructed. The inadequacies of our collective actions may originate in the inadequacies of our language and cultural representations.

The fourth explanation, focusing upon 'structural constraints', belongs more to socialists and egalitarians (see Elster, 1985: 319–44; Wright, 2010: 311–36). This says that society is largely determined by forces beyond individual control and even beyond many forms of collective control. Imagine that a radical government comes to power and announces that it is going to eliminate poverty by raising public spending, instituting a maximum wage, making taxation fully redistributive and socializing the means of production. International investors and multinational companies would run a mile, financial markets would withdraw credit, the currency would sink, and economic meltdown would loom. In other words, socialist islands in capitalist oceans are vulnerable to economic tsunamis. They either have to isolate themselves, form partnerships with like-minded countries or compromise so much with the imperatives of global capital that their principles erode (for an alternative view see Bowles, 2006). Capitalism keeps democracy on a short leash. Since even sympathetic electorates know this implicitly, few such governments ever come to power in the first place. Therefore, poverty is a result not just of the failures of collective action *but of its very limitations*.

Marxist socialists not only articulate this view, they go even further by insisting that poverty is functional for capitalism (Jones & Novak, 1999). What capitalism needs is a 'reserve army of labour'. Wealth derives ultimately from the exploitation of labour; paying people much less than they are worth.

Without a pool of labour – out of which employers can draw during periods of economic growth and back into which workers can be thrown during periods of economic contraction – profits are undermined and capitalist accumulation begins to stutter. Furthermore, poverty disciplines the rest of us. Because it is such an undesirable condition, the non-poor are effectively required to adapt themselves (their beliefs and values, their behavior and appearance, their very identities) to the imperatives of capitalism. In short, poverty is *strategic*, a means by which privileged elites exert power over the disadvantaged, distributing just enough to the middle-classes to keep them fat and content. Poverty and capitalism are conjoined.

The disadvantage of this perspective is it might encourage passivity and fatalism. If capitalism places very narrow limits on collective action, then can we ever really change anything? Is anything short of a full-scale socialist transformation not worth fighting for? Are even Scandinavian social democracies to be condemned? The danger is that we underestimate the positive impact which collective action has already had – in the form of a welfare state – and leave ourselves with no clear way forward or policy agenda. It is easier to blame poverty on the evils of capitalism than to devise realistic, if imperfect, alternatives.

We can see why questions of state, power and poverty are vital to social policy. What is the state? What is the welfare state? What power does the state wield? To what extent is the state itself a product of the economic and discursive powers which shape the social field? And if the job of the welfare state is to assist the powerless then what does this imply? What are the causes of poverty and social exclusion and how should be try to solve these social problems?

These are questions which initiate a potentially endless journey and we have not even finished asking them yet. I began by claiming that the debates of Chapter 5 are interlinked with those of Chapter 6. We have here looked at the more political aspects of social organization and interaction. In Chapter 6 we turn to more sociological ones.

Questions for Further Discussion

- To what extent can we understand 'the state' by analysing the 'welfare state'?
- Identify the main kind of power operated by welfare institutions.
- Is it credible to equate 'poverty' to 'social exclusion'?

6
Society and Class

- Agents and Structures
- Class

- After Class

The contrasts of the last chapter reoccur here in individualist and organic accounts of society. All welfare systems operate within some kind of a class structure and all welfare systems have altered the characteristics of social classes to varying extents. The impact of social policy has therefore shaped those questions that are central to modern societies:

- To what extent do we live in a class society?
- How much of our politics is – and should be – a politics of class?
- What influence has state welfare had on class relations?
- Is class being superseded by other social categories?

Our task here is to review some of the key debates. We begin by exploring structure and agency (pp. 105–12), before moving on to class (pp.113–21) and asking whether class is still a crucial category of social understanding (pp.121–5).

Agents and Structures

Society can be understood atomistically or holistically.

The atomistic perspective states that to comprehend 'the social' we have to disassemble it into its most basic parts. We understand society by understanding its components, its individuals. A society is the sum of its parts; a table upon which billiard balls frequently collide. A holistic (or organic, solidaristic or collectivist) perspective says that society is more than the sum of its parts; it is a *whole* whose identity cannot be reduced to its atoms, to the identities of its individual members. Its parts are interdependent rather than, like the billiard balls, discrete units.

These 'binary paradigms' are ideal-types, of course. Few philosophers belong to one camp entirely. Nor should you confuse this with an ideological distinction (Fitzpatrick, 2005: 50–3). Theorists from across the political spectrum can be atomists, holists or a bit of both. Within sociology this contrast reappears in a number of guises, chief among which has been the structure-agency debate.

Imagine that a bridge needs refurbishment. We cannot close the bridge because it is an important transport route, so we decide to renovate it gradually. On January 1, we remove the first of the bridge's 365 bricks and replace it with a new one. On January 2, we swap another new brick for an old one... and so forth. On December 31, we replace the last of the old bricks. *Voila!* But is the bridge after December 31, the same as the bridge we had before January 1?

Structuralists and holists would say yes. The bridge occupies the same place, performs the same function and the organization of its material – the relations between the bricks – has not changed. What matters is the whole, the totality. But atomists (and individualists) insist that the bridge is different. You cannot alter the materials, the parts, the bits and pieces, without changing the nature of the bridge.

Most of us would probably say that the bridge *has and has not* changed. The structure matters, yes, but then so do the parts. Can we reasonably define the bridge with exclusive reference to one and not the other? Perhaps not, but does that get us off the hook of deciding which is the most important element: the parts or the whole, the atoms or the totality, the agents on the structure.

Is society the sum of its parts or is it more than its basic components? In truth, the structure-agency debate no longer attracts the attention it once did because a variety of theorists claim to have either resolved or transcended it.

Tony Giddens and Pierre Bourdieu (1930–2002) each propose sociological frameworks that weave agency and structure together. According to Giddens's (1984: ch.1) 'structuration theory', society is activated by its agents, but individuals are those who – sometimes consciously and deliberately, sometimes not – reproduce social structures. Actions are structured while structures are the products of agentive practices (recurring actions – routines – that accumulate into enduring institutions and systems). Structures persist but they also evolve. They constrain actors while also enabling them; we are ruled by rules which we can and do change.

For Bourdieu (1984: 466–84; cf. Bennett et al., 2009), society can be understood as a social field consisting of relations, lines and grids of power. We inhabit that field but are also inhabited by it. *Habitus* expresses the mutuality (this occupying-that-which-occupies-us) of being both a subject and object of power. It is that through which hierarchical differentiations become manifest and are reproduced. Since those with more economic capital will typically possess more 'cultural capital' (taste, education, travel experience, familiarity with the arts, linguistic skills, e.g. being articulate and possessing the right accent) inequalities are maintained not only through material exploitation but also 'symbolic' domination and violence. To be poor is to be marked not only by physical deprivation but the signs of what is widely assumed to be cultural and aesthetic inferiority. We sense our place in the social scheme of things and differentiate ourselves from others accordingly. A *habitus* involves the disposition to know where class distinctions lie and which boundaries we can and cannot cross.

However, it is difficult to see the structure-agency duality fading away altogether. Marx (1977: 300) long ago observed that, 'Men make their own history, but they...do not make it under circumstances chosen by themselves, but under circumstances directly encountered, given, and transmitted from the past'. Archer (1995) proposes that while it is not a question of *either* 'agency' *or* 'structure', nor should we collapse these terms together and so lose what is informative and distinctive about each. An axis needs its north and south poles. Let's illustrate this point using the example of agency.

Being human

Is there such a thing as 'human nature'? For a long time social philosophers assumed so. Many thought that Darwinian evolution proved that humans are essentially just advanced animals; though whether this vindicated a politics of competitive self-interest – as in the case of Mandeville and Spencer (see Chapter 3) – or the cooperative, communal anarchism of those like Kropotkin (1842–1921), depends upon your understanding of nature (Kropotkin, 2009). But other social theorists also worried that 'biology' was just an excuse for oppression. When people say 'greed is natural' or 'homosexuality is unnatural', aren't they constructing nature as justification for their all-too-social prejudices? Social constructionists said that the 'natural' is really just a projection of social assumptions and conventions. More recently, debates in behavioural neuroscience and environmental politics has complicated the picture. We are social animals, for sure, but also living beings rooted together, and to other species, through nature.

Take food, for instance. We all need to eat food. It is a physiological drive necessary for life. Yet the *kind* of food we eat is a cultural formation. Most of us stick closely to the meals we became familiar with as children. National stereotypes or not, which countries do the following foods suggest to you? Frog legs, hamburgers, sauerkraut, fish and chips. True, culinary tastes are more globally cross-cultural than they used to be, but this does not invalidate the basic point.

In short, food sits at the intersection of biological needs and social constructions. We are, somewhat paradoxically, both natural and social beings. Thinking through the philosophical and social ramifications of this is proving to be one of the biggest challenges of the twenty-first century.

There are considerable intellectual disagreements, first of all. The debate that Foucault once had on television with Noam Chomsky is instructive (Foucault, 1984: 3–7). Chomsky argued that there *is* such a thing as a human nature, for if there were not then scientific understanding would be impossible and political critiques could not be formulated (if there is no human nature to be repressed then we have no grounds upon which to criticize repression). Foucault, though, insisted that we should not ask questions about human nature *per se*, the existence of which he doubted, but investigate how the concept of 'human nature' has emerged, developed and operated within discursive regimes. Chomsky asks the question 'why?' (why does injustice persist?) and concludes that without some notion of a human nature we have *no* reason to fight for justice. Foucault asks the question 'how?' (how does power operate?) and concludes that by ignoring this question we risk perpetuating what we call injustice.

Alternatively, perhaps we can simply say that 'human nature' encompasses two levels. There are universal biological needs which lead us to form kinship units, tribes and eventually civilizations. Thus, communication is both a natural fact and a universal need (without it, other needs cannot be fulfilled). But communication is also a social practice which in some way 'makes' the agent who does the communicating; George Steiner (2002: 119–27) was fond of quoting Heidegger's observation to the effect that language speaks *us*. Language is a tool which uses the user. Human nature thus immerses us in the social which then alters the configuration of our natural impulses. Humans may be rooted in nature but they are much more than the natural, making it redundant to ask what humans are *essentially*. Individuals are as good or as bad as the socio-political systems they establish to govern their lives.

This leads to a key question for social policy (Goodin, 1988: 113–18): are humans self-interested or altruistic? Social democrats and socialists have traditionally thought that humans are, or have the capacity to become, altruistic (Page, 1996). Titmuss (1970) famously argued that a blood donation service based upon altruistic gift-giving is more reliable and welfare-enhancing than one based upon monetary exchange. Self-interest loosens the informal bonds of cooperation, creating distrust and disunity. By contrast, many on the radical Right view humans as essentially self-interested (cf. Mack, 2009). This is often the basis of their support for *laissez faire* market economics (where the invisible hand transforms individual acts of self-interest into public benefits) and/or moral conservatism (so that ethical constraints are imposed upon choice and behaviour). Too much altruism makes the tribe vulnerable to free riders.

In Le Grand's (2003) formulation, the Left sees humans either as *knights* or as possessing knight-like capacities that the appropriate social environment can allow to flourish. Yet the Left's paternalistic streak also leads it to see many people as *pawns* who need guidance by unselfish elites. The Right see people as *knaves* and so advocate either market-based or authoritarian societies (or both) in order that knavish instincts can be controlled and harnessed. For economic liberals, a market society is ideally populated by *queens*, i.e.

responsible consumers capable of maximizing their preferences. This is a neat formulation and some agree that by focusing too much on class structures the Left has lacked a proper account of agency (Deacon & Mann, 1998). However, some counter that such accounts simplify the complexity of the Left's political philosophy and so misread its critique of the post-war welfare state (Fitzpatrick, 2005: 50–6; also Todd, 2008).

Le Grand also argues that social policies should not assume that people are one thing or another and have to be robust enough to appeal to all 'types'. In my 'two-level explanation' this means that social context always matters. A pre-social core of biological needs, e.g. the consumption of food, can drive us to compete or cooperate. If there is not enough of this dead wildebeest carcass to go around, then we are going to have to fight over it. But if by cooperating we can collectively catch more wildebeest than we could each catch individually then perhaps 'enlightened self-interest' is preferable.[1] Furthermore, Darwin (2004: 134–40) was insistent that our sense of altruism – helping others at cost to oneself with no (or little) personal benefit – and moral duty was about more than self-interest and group-preservation.

Such explanations have widespread relevance. A medical model may search for the causes of mental illness through neuro-physiological understandings of brain-body chemistry. At the other extreme, recall Foucault's critique of madness on p. 62. This inspired the 'anti-psychiatry movement' of the 1960s, which interpreted mental ill-health as an understandable and even a beneficial response to a sick society (Laing, 1970). Medical practices are not responses to a natural condition, they are further attempts to de-normalize and abuse society's victims.

A two-level explanation rejects both approaches. Medicalists who ignore social context are equivalent to those who believe that counselling and therapy are adequate solutions to unhappiness (see Chapter 1). But those for whom mental illness is nothing more than an oppressive discourse are so afraid of 'the natural' as a tool of analysis that they only end up confirming the bigot's view that nature is essentially harsh and exploitative.

How, why and when the 'natural core' is activated, depends ultimately upon the character of our social systems. A two-level explanation preserves the poles (nature and society) through an axis which connects them without collapsing them together. So, deciding *how* we ought to live does not derive automatically from debates about *what* we are. Questions about the ethical dimensions of social life require an understanding of the social dimensions of our ethics (see Fitzpatrick, 2008a).

Revisiting needs

All of which relates to a concept we have already encountered. The needs with which social policy is concerned are first and foremost *basic* needs, including those natural needs whose lack of fulfilment means that human life cannot flourish nor perhaps even survive. However, social policy also takes an interest in basic *social* needs, such as the need to be recognized as a valuable social participant. And once we consider social needs then the distinction between basic and non-basic needs begins to blur.

Abraham Maslow's (1908–1970) ideas have been massively influential here. Maslow (1954) defined a hierarchy of needs:

1. At the bottom are the physiological needs whose fulfilment we require for sheer survival.
2. Next are needs related to physical safety and security.
3. Then needs concerned with our relationships with others (especially ones of emotional and sexual bonding).
4. Coming next is the need for self-esteem.
5. While at the top of the hierarchy is the need for creativity and self-actualization.

Maslow believed that once each level of need has been fulfilled, the next level up the hierarchy then becomes important.

Maslow's hierarchy is attractive because it suggests that the basic needs can be determined scientifically and objectively. We can work out the daily intake of food and water that the human body requires and so define as being in need, those who are not achieving this intake. Such a method allows us to determine the level of deprivation that has to be present for someone to experience absolute poverty. When asked about what the state does and does not have a responsibility to ensure, my students often reply that the state should guarantee that no-one goes hungry, and so forth, but that it cannot be expected to guarantee self-esteem.

Yet students also appreciate that Maslow's hierarchy is simplified. The levels are not as discrete as they first seem. Physical security may be necessary for self-esteem, yet the reverse may also be true. Without the confidence and self-assurance which come through social participation, our sense of security may be undermined. Physical security implies more than walls, ceilings and locks. So, if the state does have a responsibility to guarantee healthcare and education, etc. we cannot necessarily class this as a guarantee of *basic needs* because – even in Maslow's model – it is not necessarily easy to distinguish the basic from the non-basic.

In short, we need to do two things. Firstly, understand the extent to which our poles (natural/social, basic/non-basic) are linked and interdependent. Secondly, appreciate that each term nonetheless fulfils an important role and should not simply be dispensed with. Dichotomies, binary paradigms and ideal-types can be useful instruments of analysis.

But there is another dimension at work here. If natural needs are activated as and through social constructions, we are left with the question of power.

Construction is about the 'who' as well as the 'how'. A radical view of power suggests that disadvantaged, discriminated and exploited people are often unable to control the means by which their needs are represented and delivered within institutional settings. For Fraser (1989: 171–83), policy struggles (over who defines what is and is not recognized as a legitimate need) are central to what she calls a 'politics of need interpretation'.

In other words, we cannot simply state that needs are both natural and social and leave it at that. Some constructions may be better than others and *politics* is the name we give to the struggle over the sources of power which shape the constructions which define a society's way of life and its distribution of material and cultural resources. If politics is both about how *we make* the world and how the world *makes us* then state welfare systems are of essential importance to this process.

This leads us on to theories of class.

Constructing realities

Beforehand, let us summarize what is at stake in the above discussion.[2] What is social reality?

It is tempting to dismiss the question. Reality is that which is revealed to your senses. Sure, we can be fooled from time to time, e.g. due to illness or delirium, but our experiences during such incidents are unreal precisely because they are exceptional. Realists argue that the world exists independently of mind and language, the contents of which more or less accurately reflect the world which is out there.

But is this the end of the story? Food exists out there in a real world, yet its *social meaning* is culturally relative. A slice of bread may simply relieve hunger, but may also be a sign of religious significance (as symbolic of Christ's body). Since meaning is a mental and discursive category, then perhaps our minds and languages reach into the world to an extent that naive forms of realism fail to appreciate. To say that something is a social construct is not to deny its reality; rather, it is to establish that the world appears to us as it does through social frameworks, cultures, classifications and structures.

A famous example was proposed by Kuhn (1970: 116). When the Earth was thought to be the centre of the universe, it was assumed that perfection and purity characterized the heavens (the realm of God), whilst corruption and flaws were properties of the human world. So when astronomers occasionally saw black spots in that part of the sky occupied by the sun they did not perceive these spots as existing *on* the sun itself. The sun belonged to the divine heavens! No, sunspots must be an atmospheric occurrence. Only with the passing of this geocentric model did scientists realize that sunspots really are a *solar* phenomenon.

Or take Berger and Luckmann's (1966: 211) claim that sociology should study 'society as part of a human world, made by men, inhabited by men, and, in turn, making men, in an ongoing historical process'. In the course of defending 'the social construction of reality' they themselves use 'men' as a proxy for 'human'. Unwittingly, they underscore the extent to which gender is a social construct.

Social constructionism has three basic forms (Hacking, 1999). Firstly, there is the *social making* of something. We can talk of something being made real through social causes, processes and forces. Women are more likely than men to remove body hair not because of genetic predispositions, but because our cultural practices identify women with femininity, femininity with attractiveness and attractiveness with smoothness and softness. Secondly, there is the *making of meaning*, of our sense of reality. Reality is filtered by our brains, emotions, instincts and expectations. What we *see* is what we *want to see* based upon what we have *seen before*. Freud famously disregarded the reports of sexual child abuse that his patients were reporting and formulated 'seduction theory' instead (Masson, 1992). (Consequently, it took longer for child abuse to become a recognized social problem.) Finally, there is an anti-realist sense in which nothing is real that is not also a construction. Recall the anti-psychiatry movement's insistence that 'madness' denotes the assumptions of those with the power to label others as deviant and dysfunctional.

Social policy relates to these debates not only because it is a branch of social research and theory, but because what we see, and do not see, as a social problem is to some extent a reflection of prevailing social constructions (Lister, 2010: ch. 5; also Spicker, 2011; McKay, 2011; Fitzpatrick, 2011b). Europeans are much more likely than Americans to regard poverty as a trap and luck as a factor in determining levels of income (Alesina & Glaeser, 2005: 183–4).

Schram challenges liberal and realist accounts of social policies on the grounds that by downplaying the role of culture they subtly legitimate existing distributions of power (Schram & Caterino, 2006). By making the world *as it is* appear to be the world *as it must be* liberal realism allows existing realities to appear natural and inevitable. All too often we are mesmerized by appearances. An unemployed person who stays at home all day must be unemployed because they are lazy! But if the social world is a construct then existing distributions are contingent and can be radically revised.

Schram's approach risks pushing beyond realism towards a philosophical idealism. For idealists, reality is itself a manifestation of mind and language. But if we go down this road the danger is that we forget the extent to which reality is *non*-constructed, e.g. where *a* causes *b*, regardless of our social and cognitive categories. For *critical* realists, social contexts help to make and make sense of reality, but reality itself is anchored outside the scope of mind and language (Lopez & Potter, 2005).

Class

Theories of class

While debates have moved on, the theoretical approaches of Marx and Weber continue to dominate both conceptual and empirical analyses of class (Crompton, 2008: chs. 3 and 4).

Marx (1977: 222–31) claimed that history is the history of class struggle between those who oppress and those who are oppressed. In the Feudal era, the former were those who owned the land (lords) and the latter were those who did not (serfs). Each historical epoch is characterized by a series of exploitations and conflicts between these two camps, one epoch giving way to another when the existing inequalities of property ownership can no longer sustain the ongoing development of technology, industry and knowledge. The basic hierarchy between oppressor and oppressed remains, though the class character of these social categories evolves. In the capitalist era, the essential conflict is between those who own capital (the bourgeoisie) and those who do not (the proletariat). Marx was certainly aware that there were a wider variety of classes, and other social groups, but he anticipated that the *industrial* conflict between bourgeoisie and proletariat was becoming the main driving force of *social* conflict.

Key to this approach is the base/superstructure model. The base consists of 'productive forces' and 'production relations'. The forces (tools, technology, skills/knowledge) establish our connection to and gradual mastery of nature. The relations denote the system of property ownership which places machinery, industry, etc. into a socioeconomic context. A machine lying idle in a desert is scrap. What makes it a productive force is its location in a property system. I own the machine. Therefore, you must work for me by operating it, or else starve. The superstructure consists of those domains (politics, law, culture, family) whose characteristics are largely determined by the base. Families in capitalist societies serve and reflect a system of economic domination. The superstructure legitimizes and preserves the base.

Marx distinguishes between a class-in-itself – the objective conditions of the base – and a class-for-itself – the subjective consciousness of the members. Workers who believe that capitalism is in the best interests of the working class are guilty of false consciousness and have not attained the 'for-itself'. Only when workers recognize the need to revolutionize the base, will they become fully conscious of their role in history. A properly organized labour movement will be the gravediggers not only of capitalism but of all class struggle.

Therefore, Marxists theorize class as bearing both objective and subjective components. The proletariat need to develop a class consciousness through both ideological emancipation and practical organization (a combination known as 'praxis'). The eventual victory of the working class would also be a victory for *all* humanity since it would place capital under common ownership and so eliminate the basis of all class oppression. For Marx, a class society is any society based upon the unequal ownership of productive property and a classless society therefore requires the establishment of common ownership, first through socialism (the state control of capital) and then communism (where the state withers away because society becomes self-organizing).

The strength of this analysis is that it underscores the socioeconomic features of class. Rather than regarding class merely as a sign of status, class is a politicized strategy wielded by the powerful against the powerless. This is an insight that we have been at risk of forgetting in recent decades.

But Marx's analysis requires an uneasy balance between determinism and non-determinism. Recall the quote on p. 107 about 'men making their history'. Should we assume a 50/50 balance between 'men' and 'their circumstances', or should we tip towards one end of the spectrum? Marx sometimes wants to have it both ways. If social progress is inevitable, why should any one individual organize for the revolution when the revolution is coming anyway? If it is not then, again, why should any one individual bother when it seems more realistic to create just and humane forms of capitalism? The problem for Marxism resembles that at the heart of all sociological and political theories: how can we reconcile structural, socioeconomic determinisms with human agency?

Just as he opposed Marx's theory of the state (see Chapter 5) so Weber (1991: ch.7) also proffered an alternative account of class. He argued that the economic dimension of production and ownership was only one aspect of the inequalities in social power. In addition to class (the economic), 'status' (the social) and 'party' (the political) are important additional elements of stratification. So far as class is concerned, Weber agreed that a major influence at work was the ownership of property and that each person's class position coincides with their position in the social hierarchy. However, he did not believe that the social and the political could be reduced to the economic, nor that class was simply about property. Instead, class position is also about the market capacities we do or do not possess, i.e. the skills and education each of us has attained. Our class position can alter even when our ownership of property remains the same! Marx is also accused of neglecting the importance to class of consumption and lifestyle (see below) and of homogenizing the concept. Weber believes that the intermediate classes lying between and among the bourgeoisie and proletariat are significant and he draws attention to important divisions and distinctions within each class itself. For Weber, classes are less historically and politically important than Marx believed, being only one of a number of sources of social identity and interaction.

As such, Weber claims that social status is crucial. What we consume and how we live are related, but not reducible, to our economic position, meaning that an individual's self-image and standing in the eyes of others are also an essential source of their social identity. Status is, then, as important as class in shaping a person's 'life chances'. Weber also treated political power as an important form of stratification that could not be reduced to economic class. For instance, when Centre-Left parties form a government their members are thereby able to wield power over those who may own more economic resources. In Weberian terms, state welfare could be interpreted as one such form of power.

Therefore, Weber did not talk of a class society *per se*, but of modern societies as being stratified along a number of dimensions. The advantage of this analysis is that it chimes more harmoniously than Marx's theory with our contemporary experiences. The emphasis upon status and consumption offers a multifaceted reading of social developments that treats social actors as *agents* and not the passive recipients of oppressive and exploitative strategies.

However, Weber is also something of a pessimist who regarded the stifling bureaucratization of modern society as irreversible. While recognizing the pluralism of class divisions, status groups and political alignments he downplays the social dynamics that can drive progress and emancipation forward. Critical and humanist schools of Marxism have sometimes out-Webered Weber in their openness to the possibility of social change and emancipation (Habermas, 1987a: 303–31).

For a long time, Marxists and Weberians warred against one another for intellectual dominance. But as class *politics* has faded (see below), a rapprochement has taken place. Yet many within academia also turned away from class at the very time (the 1980s onwards) when we seemed to need class analyses more than ever. How can we explain this paradox?

Social changes and mobilities

It could be argued there *is* no paradox. Firstly, capitalism itself has evolved. Perhaps the conditions which Marxists and Weberians were trying to understand have faded. Secondly, might political changes have worked a similar effect? There has been a relative 'disaggregation' of class-party allegiance, a dis-alignment in voting behaviour and the appearance of new political identities and alliances (see below and Chapter 8). Finally, new intellectual fashions have come and gone. With Marxism being dominant in the 1960s–70s the subsequent rejection of it was, to some degree, also a rejection of class analysis *per se*. In particular, the 'cultural turn' was a rebuff to materialistic and economistic theories (Skeggs, 2004; Devine & Savage, 2005).

Yet those leaping on the bandwagons of 'identity politics', 'postmodernism', 'post-structuralism' and so forth, were often too quick to dismiss the value of what they were racing away from. More recently, some driving the cultural turn have looked over their shoulders and reversed course back towards class; in part, because of the continued political dominance of free market liberalism.

For it is this which explains the paradox just mentioned. Free markets have intensified class inequalities but, by reflecting and promoting an ethos of individualistic self-interest, have also made class-specific alliances less attractive and more difficult to organize. To some extent, this is not surprising. Since the 1980s, rates of poverty and social exclusion have risen most sharply under governments of economic liberalism (Dorling, 2010: 272–91); and the poor often have more things to worry about than political mobilization. But there has also been an ideological component to the paradox. In a post-communist age, the Centre-Left has struggled to renew itself, sometimes accepting large swathes of economic liberal thinking. People have jumped onto a bandwagon often in the hope that this would be the 'next big thing'. Without a language of collectivism, cooperation and social ownership, philosophies and politics of class have failed to reactivate (Meiksins-Wood, 1985). It has been much easier to diagnose the sickness than to prescribe a remedy.

The diagnosis is clear (Heath & Payne, 2000; Goldthorpe & Jackson, 2007; Hills, 2009: 319–26; National Equality Panel, 2010). *Absolute* social mobility in the UK has improved during the post-WW2 period due to occupational changes which have created more opportunities for working-class children. The decline in manufacturing was counterbalanced by more white-collar jobs. However, *relative* social mobility has stalled and possibly declined. The expansion of higher education, clerical, professional and managerial jobs may have opened up more 'room at the top' but has disproportionately benefitted middle-class families. The *opportunities* for upward mobility have enlarged but the *distribution* of those opportunities across the classes has remained pretty much the same. Those children coming from the salariat (the middle classes) are five to six times more likely to achieve salariat jobs than are their peers in working-class homes. So

- by the late 1990s, 46% of sons from social class 1 households (the higher professionals) had also grown up to occupy social class 1, compared to 9% of sons from social class 7 households (the lower working class);
- by 1997, 75% of children from working-class households would grow up to be working-class adults;
- by the late 1990s, 47% of people from the richest fifth families attended university, compared to 9% from the poorest fifth (a rise from 3% in the 1940s and 1950s);
- life expectancy for the poorest is seven years shorter, on average, than that for the wealthiest (Marmot Review, 2010);
- poor children are 5 times more likely to die in an accident and 15 times more likely to die in a fire; and
- the Marmot Review also found that on average poorer men will experience declining health from the age of 49, compared to 66 years for the wealthiest men.

The literature thus suggests that where income inequality is high, social mobility is low. This contradicts the radical Right claim that increased inequality acts as an incentive to individual effort and aspiration. In reality, the greater the distance between the rungs the harder it is to climb the ladder. If you want more social mobility, a society where socioeconomic position is more likely to reflect individual merit, you actually need greater social *equality*. Of course, many people support the *principle* of social mobility – how else to explain their own affluence? – though largely once their own children's futures are secured. Politicians know this instinctively. Is class politics is alive and well and thriving in middle class households?

This is what makes prescribing a remedy difficult. Those who proclaim the 'death of class' have a point (Clark & Lipset, 2000). According to some commentators, while social stratification matters, this no longer equates to *class* stratification (Cannadine, 2000). We are much less troubled by class society and structures than we used to be. Individuals are told, and tell themselves, that their destinies are in their own hands. No-one dictates where they can or cannot shop. Isn't it then equally clear that where they work, how hard they work and how much they end up earning, spending and saving is also in their hands? People from poorer backgrounds still have the same access to education as the rest of us. If relative social mobility has stalled, then maybe they are just not trying hard enough! Besides, even if justice demands social equality this takes considerable time and effort. Therefore, while I sympathize with your political aims my principal duty is to myself and my family. Sorry!

We therefore have our paradox: social class matters but we are now less likely to *think* it matters. Social policies have struggled to cope with this tension.

Class and state welfare

Five questions illustrate why (cf. Lavalette & Mooney, 2000).

Firstly, how has class influenced the welfare state's development? We might answer this in terms of social structure. For instance, a functionalist believes that x is explained by the function it performs within the system of which x is a part. Capitalism needs class stratifications and the latter need social policies which will service the basic needs of workers without redistributing enough power to overturn the capitalist system. Parsons (1961) argues that the function of schools is to instil in their pupils the values and capacities that they will require as working adults. The education system inserts individuals into the roles upon which society is structured and so has to be explained in terms of the wider social division of labour. The problem with this reading is that it potentially overlooks the inconsistencies and self-contradictions of the education system, e.g. the way in which it foments rebellion and social conflict. (At this point, strict functionalists interpret rebellion as functionally necessary for society!) Functionalism can only offer neat explanations of social phenomena by homogenizing the objects of its analysis.

An alternative, agency-based account of state welfare attributes it to struggle and conflict between relevant actors. Welfare services represent a victory against those who believe that market forces should dictate the distribution of social goods. Korpi's (1983) 'power resources model' says that political power requires the mobilization of collective interests and so is more than a simple reproduction of economic power. The welfare state was the culmination of a battle to organize the political and public sphere around the interests of the working class and rebalance the relationship between labour and capital. Unlike 'structural-functionalism', the power resources model focuses upon the cracks and fissures of the social system. However, it may overlook the extent to which state welfare was the result of a contingent series of unintended consequences, one which serves multifarious needs and interests (Przeworski, 1985). The political is kept tethered to the powerful interests which dominate the economy.

Secondly, which of these explanations is most convincing? Both have their appeal. Take gender, for example. A structure-based account says that the gender-bias of welfare systems is due to the wider bias of a productivist capitalism whose primary purpose is to accumulate profit. During the agricultural and industrial ages, women were generally less productive than men. If women have made advances recently, this is because technology now requires intelligence and social skills rather than sheer physical labour. But an agency-based explanation might simply observe that the women's movement lagged behind a male-dominated labour movement by several decades. Recent advances have occurred across many sectors – job markets, political representation, welfare services – because women have spent several decades fighting for them.

Whichever explanation we prefer, we already have some idea how to answer our third question: how has state welfare altered class relations (Esping-Andersen, 1993)? To some extent the effect has been gendered. Many welfare state jobs have been 'occupationally segregated', e.g. teaching, nursing, clerical/administrative, so that the expansion of the public sector brought with it greater (if limiting) opportunities for women. Furthermore, state welfare is often thought to be a key factor behind the growth of the 'new middle class'. Though there are many perspectives on this (Crompton, 2008: 103–9), the term basically denotes divisions within the middle class, e.g. between public sector professionals and their counterparts within the private sector. With the former more dependent upon high levels of government spending than the latter, public/private splits within the middle class matter most whenever resources are scarce, as in the wake of the 2008 financial crisis, and contribute to the shifting political alliances about the future of public services (see Chapter 9).

Of course, the presence of public sector professionals is no guarantee that class inequalities will be significantly reduced. Social democratic countries have formed cross-class constituencies around pro-welfare, universalist and redistributive socioeconomic policies. But in other national contexts, such constituencies have been weaker and less effective. Indeed, it may well be class stratifications are *reinforced* by middle-class producers who are paternalistically happy to deliver services but, in trying to defend their jobs and status, less happy about handing real power over to service users.

Our fourth question, then, is: what role does state welfare play in *maintaining* class inequalities? On the one hand, it seems necessary to keep the middle classes locked into systems of state welfare because, if they bolt for private provision instead, the residual services left for the poor will be poor services (see Chapter 2). On the other, the need to keep the middle classes happy may reduce the resources available for vertical redistribution and perpetuate myths of meritocracy and desert. Such myths neglect the egalitarian critique, which points to the role played in social distributions by undeserved advantages (where the wealthy are members of the 'lucky sperm club'), and so make egalitarian solutions less easy to implement. Consider education.

For some, it is clear that social background is the determining influence upon educational success or failure (Bourdieu & Passeron, 1977). Others insist that a well-functioning system of education can help to correct any imbalances in the social environment by providing an equality of opportunity (see Halsey et al., 1997). What we have here is another stand-off between Left and Right.

Those on the Left (Devine, 2004) cite the importance of the following:

- Economic resources – private education, private tutors, books and computers, geographical segregation (with housing markets excluding poorer children from the best public schools);
- Social resources – access to privileged friends, networks and contacts;
- Cultural resources – higher expectations regarding universities and occupations, organization of family time, e.g. foreign holidays, educational toys and play.

It is thus simply unreasonable to expect state welfare to resolve the poverty that capitalism creates.

The Right point to things such as the relative powerless of parents (compared to teachers and unions), the misguided egalitarianism of state-run education, the naturalness of such inequalities (the poor are not uneducated and therefore unintelligent because they are in a lower class, they are in a lower class because they are unintelligent). If poverty and social problems are pathological and behavioural we can condemn state welfare for trapping the deprived within a moral vacuum and then encouraging them to remain there (Saunders, 1996).

The prescriptions which follow on from these competing interpretations are therefore at odds. The Left focuses upon school structures, collective resources and *social* context. This is to prescribe an egalitarian policy within a universalist system where schools act as social institutions with redistributive responsibilities. This implies support for comprehensive, non-selective education. The Right focuses upon educational standards, personal responsibility and *family* context (Tooley, 1999). This view prescribes a private system of education where parents are empowered as consumers, purchasing (and perhaps even organizing) services on behalf of their children. Schools are not tools of egalitarian engineering.

What seems clear is that state welfare, when properly organized and funded, *can* reduce poverty levels. More people would be living in poverty if the welfare state did not exist (Kenworthy, 2004; Scruggs & Allan, 2006). This might suggest that state welfare ameliorates class inequalities but does not – and perhaps cannot – abolish them.

This leads to a final question which returns us to the paradox we encountered above: to what extent has state welfare contributed to an individualization of society?

Welfare institutions are often contrasted with the dynamic freedoms of the market. Over here we have profitable, responsive, flexible companies ready to satisfy every consumerist whim. Over there we have slow, unaccountable, bureaucratic public services which insist they know best. Now, there is an element of truth to this. In trying to fulfil many different values, not all of which sit well together, welfare services occupy multiple roles. A hospital repairs wounds but also engages with the entirety of an individual's health and lifestyle. A school educates children but also has wider communal responsibilities. Social workers offer advice but also intervene into long-standing, family complexities. Local government empties your bins but is also a source of democratic legitimacy. Therefore, just as the shop selling your new iPad doesn't care about you beyond the contractual obligations of a monetary exchange, so public services look at you as more than just customers, which may mean that they are sometimes less *consumer*-friendly than the High Street's indifferent, have-a-nice-day ethos.

Yet, to some extent, state welfare has *contributed* to individualization (Offe, 1987; Inglehart, 1990). By promoting equal opportunities, the welfare state may have encouraged meritocratic attitudes. If everyone – the reasoning goes – now has an equal start in life, then surely where you end up is a result of your own efforts! By reducing poverty, the pull of class background seems to matter less. By offering job opportunities to women, class identities and the ideological, collectivist narratives of old have faded. By guaranteeing everyone's basic needs it has entrenched popular perceptions of the distinction between the deserving and undeserving. By saving capitalism from itself and promoting growth, state welfare helped give birth to generations of citizen-consumers who have outgrown it.

In short, state welfare has not been a collectivist citadel holding out while the surrounding countryside transformed itself into hordes of possessive consumers. Individualization has in part been driven by the welfare state itself. Thus, when we remind ourselves of our earlier paradox – social class matters but we are now less likely to *think* it matters – we are dealing not only with what has happened *to* the welfare state but with the social effects of state welfare itself.

More than ever, then, the contemporary welfare state has to reconcile divergent moral trajectories. There are the raised expectations of a consumerist 'me-now' society. Any faults and errors are quickly seized on by a corporate media slathering over the potential for profits that public sectors keep locked away from private providers. But there are also the traditional aims – redistribution, public service, universalism, solidarity – which can often seem passé in our here-today-gone-tomorrow cultures. The strategy of the 'new social democrats' (see Chapter 7) was to inject private sector methods and values into the public sector while trying to renew the values of the latter. But, whatever the path taken in the future, in trying to satisfy these tensions the form the welfare state takes in this century will depend upon how it responds not only to the 'outside world' but to itself, to the ongoing effects of previous generations of social policies.

This takes us to our final discussion.

After Class

The claim that 'class is dead' is advanced not only by those eager to propose that free markets liberate everyone, but by theorists seeking to overturn what they saw as intellectual rigidities of social science and philosophy. This shift away from class was therefore due to a bizarre alignment of the economic Right and many (but not all) on the cultural Left. 'Identity politics' and 'individualization' captured the level of the biographical; while 'networks', 'flows' and 'movements' related more to the associative.

Post-class theorists often oppose concepts and theoretical assumptions which they view as stifling. They promote the concept of 'individualization' because 'collectivism' is seen as rigid and static. The 'communal' and the 'post-social' are similarly regarded as preferable to 'society'. The 'cultural' – discourse, consumption, lifestyle, status, symbols, differences, identities – is seen as a refreshing alternative to materialistic social science with its focus on economic factors like income and occupation. 'Fluidity' seems a better metaphor for a globalizing, post-industrial, post-imperial world than 'structures' and 'hierarchies'. And so forth. Overall, the perception that we had reached an epochal, paradigm shift in human affairs, and so needed a radically new social vocabulary, has been widespread.

We will explore some of the most influential ideas in the chapters to come. In Chapter 8 we will take a look at identity politics and Chapter 9 will explore post-national flows and networks. Yet it is worth observing here that those promoting the 'cultural turn' often remain indebted to the concepts and methods which they claim to oppose. Take the 'risk society' thesis.

Risk society

According to Beck (1992; Beck & Beck-Gernsheim, 2002: ch. 3, 48–9), we have entered a second modernity. The first modernity was an age of industrial progress in a world that was taken to be stable, knowable and scientifically cal-culable. The second modernity that emerged in the latter period of the twen-tieth century is a risk society characterized by the attempt to limit, manage and navigate through a series of 'bads', hazards, anxieties, uncertainties and incalculable dangers. Beck had been struck by the worldwide consequences of the Chernobyl and Bhopal disasters, and the way in which invisible but deadly contagion had crossed spatial borders (national boundaries) and temporal ones (since the effects will be felt for generations) without any respect for the tidy assumptions of industrial modernity. Post-industrial pollution does not respect class or national boundaries. It is not necessarily that the world has become more dangerous: it is that risks are now the unintended consequences of our centuries-old attempt to pacify and control that world. The second modernity is therefore the first modernity turned in on itself in a process of 'reflexive modernization' (Beck et al., 1994).

Two concepts are crucial. 'Reflexivity' expresses the notion of self-interaction. Events within one part of the social field can have drastic and unpredicted effects elsewhere: actions become reactions to other reactions. Cause and effect become confused as each site within the field becomes one of multiple causes and multiple effects. Positivist social science becomes redundant. But we are also called on to *reflect* upon this shift (Archer, 2007). Institutions must become learning institutions that reinvent themselves in response to ever-changing circumstances. Traditions, communities and authorities must become open and self-reflexive if they are not to ossify into fundamentalist forms of power (Giddens, 1991, 1994).

The second concept, 'individualization', captures the notion that our identities are no longer just inherited. Instead, your identity is fluid and diverse, that which you give to yourself through your association with others. Groups and communities matter but they matter in so far as we construct them as part of our individualized biographies. Who you were, who you are and who you will be, are never finalized and fixed. They are always subject to new imaginings and negotiations. You belong to many networks which also constitute and configure *you*; you are inside them just as they are inside you. The biographical and the associative are enmeshed (Touraine, 2000).

For social policy, the implication is that the welfare state becomes both a source of, and a response to, new social risks (Bonoli, 2005; Holzman, 2006; Taylor-Gooby, 2007). The collectivization of risks through social insurance was suited to an industrial era of patriarchal families and steady employment. But social insurance came to seem less relevant to labour markets of part-time and occasional work, especially for women juggling earning and caring. Means-tested benefits, in-work benefits and tax credits seemed to offer a flexible alternative but these, in turn, exacerbate risks and anxieties by creating poverty traps, savings traps and caring traps. We could privatize everything but this, surely, would aggravate the inequalities and social problems that state welfare was designed to counter. In short, whatever we try to do to secure against insecurity rebounds upon us, creating new insecurities and the need for new solutions (which will also be imperfect and subject to further revision). Giddens (1998) proposed that there are no ideal welfare solutions. Instead, through an ethic of 'positive welfare' people should be armed with the cognitive and moral tools, and the equal opportunities, to construct their own social biographies without reliance upon either the state or the unregulated market.

Such ideas can make this seem an exciting, always changing, new world. Dangers lurk but, if handled properly, they can be thrilling and enabling. The problem is that 'class' becomes lost. Beck did not deny the existence of poverty and inequality, he denied that a class analysis is appropriate to understanding them. 'Class' becomes a zombie category, both dead and alive (Beck, 2007). Giddens (1998: 64–5) defines equality in terms of social inclusion.

Now, there were undoubtedly reductive, economistic approaches to class which deserve rejection. But those who abandon class only manage to invert the earlier either/or logic. Philosopher *A* explains everything in terms of class and is rightly criticized. But if his critic, Philosopher *B*, claims the opposite – that *nothing* can be explained in terms of class – how is this an improvement?

Thus, over the last decade, class has been rediscovered and its importance reasserted. Some believe that class analyses should fully accommodate the cultural turn so that class is seen as a multiplicity of cultural identities (Savage, 2000; Bottero, 2005); others want to incorporate elements of the turn without abandoning what was valuable about traditional social science, even if this means retaining distinctions, e.g. between agents and structures, that others would collapse (Phillips, 1999; Crompton, 2008; also Aronowitz, 1992). Whichever approach is taken, the claim that class is dead is less persuasive than it once seemed (Sayer, 2005).

Social movements

A similar view can be taken towards another post-class thesis.

Marxist and socialist analyses of social change often felt stagnant. Whatever workers did the tendency was to interpret such actions in terms of their contribution – or lack of – to a revolutionary process of historical development. Such interpretations often focused upon labour to the neglect of other social movements, missing their significance and specific identities. Therefore, social movement theorists may remain interested in class but arguably apply a wider analytical lens (Della Porta & Diani, 2006; Lister, 2010: 256–66).

A social movement is a *process of collective action*, which can encompass the very large (revolutions, nationalisms, social conflict and disintegration) and the very small (mobs, gangs). It can be a formal, semi-formal or informal network of interrelated actors who share similar values, identities and objectives in a given socio-historical context. Social movements are often taken to be concerned with the following:

- Particular issues that are often conceptually broadened out into universalistic values and concerns.
- Civil society, culture and lifestyle rather than state institutions and political power.
- Openness and flexibility rather than with forming rule-governed hierarchies.

Interest in social movements goes back a long way but gathered speed in the 1960s when a host of new, non-class-specific movements emerged. The civil rights/liberties movement, the women's movement, the students movement, the gay and lesbian movement, the Green movement, the peace/anti-war movement and the anti-nuclear movement all signalled an evolution in political consciousness and organization that did not fit neatly into the sociological categories of the time. More recently the global justice, anti-racist, nationalist, religious, global terrorist and indigenous peoples movements have confirmed such developments.

However, whether this signals the death of class depends upon who you read. It may be that class-specific identities *have* declined in importance, in which case the 'new social movements' represent a vital category for understanding contemporary society. Or, it may be social science which has changed. Perhaps we once underappreciated the place social movements have occupied within modern societies. Thus, Tilly (2004) traces the history of social movements back to the eighteenth century and Annetts et al. (2009) have explored the extent to which social movements inspired the ideologies and practices of the welfare state. Class retains its role as a key sociological concept, however.

There are two main ways of theorizing social movements (cf. Annetts et al. 2009: ch. 3): resource mobilization theory (RMT) and new social movement theory (NSMT).

RMT originated within the American academy and leans towards liberal individualism (Zald & McCarthy, 1987, 1988). Its premise is that collective behaviour must be explained in terms of the motivations and decisions of individual actors, e.g. how do leaders mobilize participants and how are resources (money, media attention, public support) mobilized? Classes and class activities *may* be an outcome of such mobilizations, but not necessarily. Therefore, class should not be treated as a social category in its own right. RMT shares many assumptions with the RCT that we outlined in Chapter 1 and can be criticized on many of the same grounds. It was partly in order to avoid such criticisms that RMT expanded in the 1980s, becoming more interested in the cultural environments of collective action.

NSMT originated within Europe and relates social movements to wider socio-historical developments. Whereas the labour movement had tried to effect change through the state and electoral politics, and had been eventually co-opted into the institutions of bureaucratic capitalism, the new social movements were concerned more with the values to be found within civil society (Touraine, 1981, 2000: Ch.3; Melucci, 1989). This signifies that the key struggle no longer takes place between capitalist and proletariat over the means of production but between technocrats and new social movements over the conditions of representation and self-determination. The new social movements are therefore drawn from a multiplicity of class positions and defined by a cultural politics and identity politics that constructs new meanings and forms of identification with which to challenge dominant power relations.

Chapters 5 and 6 have contrasted two ways of looking at the political and social worlds, one dealing with parts and the other with wholes. Although they do not align exactly, this distinction runs through a vast series of debates, a few of which we sampled above. What does it means to be an agent, a social being? How is our perception of social reality constructed? How should we understand class? What role has class played in social developments? Do we now live in a post-class society? And throughout our journey we have kept the influence of social policies always in mind.

Indeed, throughout Chapters 1–6 we have been presented with a series of contrasts between the 'old' and the 'new'. To this we must now add another question: to what extent do we now live in post-ideological times? We have sometimes made use of the Left–Right spectrum on the grounds that this continues to frame many – but certainly not all – of the social philosophical debates relevant to social policy. It is now time to specify the principal features of that ideological map and consider their continued relevance.

Questions for Further Discussion

- Who provides the most convincing critique of the welfare state, Marxists or Weberians?
- How and why do analyses of state welfare inspired by new social movement theory differ from those inspired by theories of class?
- To what extent is class equality compatible with gender equality?

7

Ideologies

- Radical Right
- Conservatism
- Social Democracy

- Marxism
- Feminism

A full understanding of philosophical ideas and debates cannot be reduced to a series of ideological positions, though we have found it impossible to discuss concepts like wellbeing, equality, etc. without political ideologies entering the picture (George & Wilding, 1994; George & Page, 1995; Taylor, 2007; Lister, 2010: ch. 2). This chapter assumes simply that an ideology offers a critique of existing society, a vision of a better one and a strategy for getting from here to there (Ball & Dagger, 1991; cf. Freeden, 1996: chs. 1–3). We begin on the Right and work our way Left (see Schumaker, 2008).

Radical Right[1]

The radical Right argue that freedom creates, justifies and is guaranteed by capitalist markets, private property and a minimal state (N. Barry, 1987, 1999; Saad-Filho & Johnston, 2004). However, there are crucial differences of emphasis here. Right libertarians (see Chapter 3) defend freedom from *all* forms of coercion and interference, which typically leads to support for free markets. But market conservatives think that economic liberalism requires an additional social and moral ethos based around family values, respect for and obedience to authority (cultural institutions, national identity, laws, customs and traditions, religious practices, a strong work ethic). The state should be small, but is still allowed to promote certain ways of life over others. Free markets will not, by themselves, create responsible families and individuals.

Both wings of radical Right thinking identify a contradiction between the promises and the outcomes of state welfare (Shapiro, 2007; cf. Jackson, 2010). The promises have included: the maintenance of full employment, high levels of redistributive equality, the fulfilment of basic needs through legally-guaranteed entitlements, an ever-expanding public sector, state control of the macro-economy, corporatist arrangements between workers and management. Yet, in trying to fulfil these promises, post-war governments gradually undermined the ability of the economy to finance them. By raising public spending to unsustainable levels, by crowding out private investment and entrepreneurialism and by taxing people excessively, the welfare state only undermined its own moral and financial conditions. Consequently, these contradictions had to be removed by the radical Right in the 1980s. Since then, the emphasis has been upon: low inflation, supply-side reforms, e.g. creating competitive workers (rather than jobs), social inequalities, monetary incentives, responsibilities, an entrepreneurial and risk-taking private sector, deregulation and privatization, labour market flexibility, the rights of managers and shareholders, consumer choice. Some would go further and abolish state welfare completely (McGee, 2002), though others would leave a minimal income guarantee in place (Murray, 2006).

The specific criticisms that the radical Right makes of the welfare state can be summarized as follows (cf. C. Pierson, 2006: 149–55). Firstly, state welfare is held to undermine the disciplines of the market by reducing the rewards for success and lightening the burdens of failure. Capital has little incentive to invest due to high levels of taxation and regulation; people have little incentive to work hard because they will be taxed heavily while, if they don't work, they will receive generous benefits from the state anyway. The welfare state therefore undermines competition and innovation, inviting (in the 1970s) a depressed and stagnant economy of high unemployment and high inflation. It also encourages people to be lazy, to expect the state to do everything for them. An ethos of self help and of personal and civic responsibility is gradually eroded leading to higher levels of crime and antisocial behaviour and to a general lack of respect and decent behaviour. As such, free market inequalities are good. They encourage people to better themselves, reflecting and rewarding individuals' merits, efforts and hard work.

Secondly, the larger the public sector, the more the private sector is squeezed out. This means that entrepreneurialism is undermined and the economy is left with too many non-producers taking wealth out and too few producers left to create that wealth. Some allege that post-war reforms always made it likely that the growth in social expenditure would outstrip the economy's ability to finance such growth (Barnett, 1986). Governments attempted to generate high levels of growth in an attempt to plug this gap, but this only had the effect of creating damaging inflation.

Thirdly, the welfare state holds a monopoly on the delivery of welfare services. But whereas monopolies in the marketplace can always be challenged, state monopolies cannot; leading to distortions within the market, a neglect of consumer choice and widespread inefficiencies. Public sector leaders have all of the 'voice' while, subject to high rates of taxation, consumers have little freedom to exit and purchase non-state forms of welfare provision. According to public choice theory (Thompson, 2008) political parties have an interest in expanding the public sector and raising social expenditure, in order to buy the votes of the electorate and appease special-interest groups. This leads to an overloaded and ailing welfare system where the state is incapable of adequately performing the many tasks it gives itself.

Fourthly, the defenders of state welfare misidentify the nature and the causes of poverty, by confusing this with inequality and attributing it to abstract, structural phenomena (see pp. 103–4). Instead, we should focus upon the culture of the poor, their beliefs, values and behaviour. The welfare state generates a 'dependency culture' where people are encouraged to throw themselves onto the over-generous and comfortable safety-nets on offer. State welfare creates an underclass of the 'undeserving poor', the irresponsible who exclude themselves from mainstream society (Murray, 1984, 1990).

Fifthly, collectivism and paternalism produce a nanny state which insists it knows what is good for us more than we do ourselves. At worst, the welfare state can lead us down the 'road to serfdom' toward an autocratic society (Hayek, 1944). Either way, an egalitarian politics of the common good causes the space of individual freedom and self-determination to shrink. The spaces of autonomy shrink as civil society becomes subsumed within the public sphere, with citizens subject to the diktats of the centralized, top-heavy, authoritarian state. By contrast, market reform implies rolling back the borders of the coercive state, allowing the entrepreneurial spirit to be unleashed.

Finally, the welfare state stresses rights and entitlements rather than the duties and responsibilities, needs rather than desert. It embodies a something-for-nothing attitude that then pervades society, undermining moral, cultural and social authority (Mead, 1986). The ethics of community, mutual responsibility and desert are weakened because the welfare state does not ask enough of us: the affluent think that paying their taxes is all that making a social contribution requires, while the poor sit back and wait for their benefit cheque. Collectivism encourages a generalized dependency where we expect the state to do things for us and we no longer look to the family or community organizations as sources of wellbeing. The ties of family and of civic association begin to unravel as people are no longer held to account for the consequences of their actions.

Criticisms

Four criticisms seem particularly important (e.g. Honderich, 2005; Harvey, 2005).

Firstly, there is a potential contradiction between free markets and the conservative emphasis upon tradition, authority and family. For Right libertarians this is not a problem, since free choice demands the availability of anything which is consistent with voluntary action: hard drugs, prostitution, a market in transplant organs, extreme pornography, etc. However, relatively few libertarians adopt a complete 'anything goes' philosophy. It is more common to see the defenders of free markets arguing against Centre-Left measures while subtly sneaking in their own rules and conventions designed to shape market processes and outcomes. So, Hayek (1960: 226–32) sees market monopolies as always preferable to public ones (Hayek, 1960: 226–32). Socialist engineering is pernicious but forcing free market systems on people, reengineering them as consumers, is fine (Lazzarato, 2009). The undeserving poor need discipline, but we shouldn't be too concerned with the undeserving rich (Mead, 2005).

Such compromises are inevitable. Moral conservatives are aware that unrestrained markets create the very insecurities which threaten an ordered, stable society: civility, trust, mutual respect and common goods (Gray, 1993). It is difficult to appeal to a citizenship of active solidarity and then insist that people do whatever market forces require them to do. Family life, for instance, implies a degree of solidity (of geographical rootedness and emotional connection) which is incompatible with market mobilities. But in trying to reconcile market imperatives with conservative ones, the radical Right tie themselves up in knots in order to conceal an essential truth: there *is* no such thing as a *free* market. All markets come with a price. The real question is, who pays the price and why?

Secondly, inequality is not only bad for the disadvantaged, it is bad for everyone else too, including the affluent (see Chapter 2). Low social expenditure intensifies those social problems which lower everyone's quality of life, e.g. rising crime rates, reduced consumption, unemployment, threadbare public goods and services (plus an impoverished sense of public space) and a generalized insecurity (Marquand, 2004). Nor do inequalities incentivize people to work harder. Instead, by lengthening the distance between the rungs of the wealth and income ladder, they make it more likely that existing positions become entrenched. Those at the top don't have to try as much; those at the bottom figure 'why bother?'; while those in the middle can feel embattled from both sides. But in an effort to deny this, social problems are attributed to 'problem people'. The welfare state's war on poverty is thus transformed into a war on the poor (King, 1999). The radical Right cause a deterioration in the social position of the poorest and then set about blaming the victims of their policies for the resulting social problems.

Thirdly, the radical Right often assert a simplistic dichotomy between markets and states: the more we have of one, the less we can have of the other. But this view can be challenged. Historically, capitalism has depended upon a large degree of state control and intervention without which free markets could not have developed in the first place (Polanyi, 1944). Politically and philosophically, there is the Keynesian point that capitalism risks imploding without institutional support; a pure free market economy would collapse very quickly.

Finally, the radical Right concentrate upon certain forms of dependency only. They obsess about benefit dependency, but ignore the extent to which the job markets inhabited by 'hard-working taxpayers' require a 'reserve army' of casualized labour which can be easily hired and fired. The low, infrequent pay, inadequate benefits and deprived circumstances upon which millions of the underprivileged depend, indicates a skewed distribution of social resources towards the better-off. Those the radical Right complain are being exploited ('the taxpayer') thus owe much of their wealth not to hard work but to a fundamental, structural unfairness in the distribution of property, opportunity and wealth. The radical Right therefore invert reality, insisting that it is the poor who exploit the rich because what counts is motivation and effort, rather than class structure and socioeconomic circumstances. They therefore identify freedom with 'market freedom' and dependency with 'state dependency', capturing only a minor dimension of the way in which our freedoms and dependencies interlink.

In short, the radical Right can be accused of *undermining* social obligations. When relations of community and reciprocity become subservient to the profit motive and self-interest, people lose the habits of caring about, or identifying with, others. By exacerbating inequalities, the ethical and cultural links between 'winners' and 'losers' begin to unravel, leading to a reduced sense of common space and purpose through growing feelings of distrust, alienation and insecurity.

Conservatism[2]

Other conservatives, though, are less enamoured with free markets, competitive capitalism, profit motives, self-interest and the consequences of what Thomas Carlyle (1795–1881) condemned as the 'cash-nexus' (Carlyle, 1971: 276–81). Some even agree with the Left that markets should be regulated, making way for other social and moral values. However, conservatives' attachment to tradition, cultural inheritance and hierarchical authority – and hostility to egalitarian redistributions – is what positions them on the political Right (Kirk, 1985; Kekes, 1998; Nisbet, 2001). In fact, there are many conservatisms and it is not always easy to tell where one ends and another begins.

Philosophical conservatism

This derives ultimately from Edmund Burke's (1968) warnings against abstract reason. By this he meant reasoning that tries to discern first principles and derive from them all rules of method and behaviour. For Burke, the practitioners of abstract reason ignored the extent to which reason is a matter of socio-cultural habit and conditioning. By trying to remake society, the French revolutionaries only unleashed the self-destructive and violent impulses which characterize humans and which an ordered society uses social customs and mores to confine and control. More recently, Michael Oakeshott (1901–1990) distinguished between two forms of knowledge: 'rational knowledge' is technical and abstract whereas 'concrete knowledge' is acquired through experience and practice (Oakeshott, 1962). When learning how to drive a car, rational knowledge is gained by reading a book entitled *How to Drive*, while concrete knowledge is acquired by actually getting behind the wheel and learning through trial and error. If you tried to drive from rational knowledge alone you would – like the French revolutionaries – only crash.

Ideological thinking is, then, the equivalent of trying to understand society by abstracting ourselves from actual practices and experiences. Conservatives insist that we can learn how to *do* by attending to the ways in which they are *already done*. We ought to see ourselves as gardeners, who inherit the work of previous generations and bequeath that legacy to the future, rather than engineers who try to design and repair societies from scratch. History and culture are stores of implicit knowledge and guidance that have been accumulated over many generations. Conservatives, in other words, emphasize the historical and cultural continuity of tradition and derived authority. Institutions should be allowed to evolve organically and slowly, for if we start major reforms without being guided by traditional institutions then the social repercussions can be disastrous. Social change is only ever successful when it emerges out of existing social relations; revolutions and rapid transformations easily lead to dictatorship or anarchy.

Conservatism, therefore, is a philosophy of limits and restraint (N Barry, 1997). If human nature is inherently flawed, then so is human society. Consequently, avoiding harm must be our first and overwhelming moral and political priority. We should not so much ask the question 'what is the best society?' as 'what is the least worst society?'. Conservatives focus upon the fragility and vulnerability of human life: hence Oakeshott's depiction of society as resembling a rudderless ship on a harbour-less ocean. If this is the case, then the most important thing to do is to avoid rocking the boat. Injustice can be corrected only if we are certain that doing so will not upset the established stability and equilibrium of the social order.

What exactly should be conserved, though? Conservatives treat the past's store of knowledge as if there is a single store, a unified past which all can recognize and to which all can appeal. They therefore emphasize the virtues of continuity only by neglecting the realities of conflict and complexity. If, for instance, different social classes generate different forms of knowledge and understanding, which type of knowledge should the conservative favour? In short, conservatives cannot disassociate themselves from the imperatives of abstract reasoning to the extent that they imagine.

The dilemma for conservatives is that, on the one hand, they emphasize respect for social practices and cultural inheritances which have been continuous across time; while, on the other, they often end up favouring privileged interests over those of the disadvantaged. Scruton (2006: 23–5, 98–101, 117, 138–45) values national culture and loyalty, while constantly downplaying, misrepresenting and denigrating contributions and influences to it made by the Left. Perhaps, then, my culture and my image of the nation isn't quite the same as yours, making simplified appeals to 'culture' and 'loyalty' misleading. Conservatives typically acknowledge plurality, diversity and conflict only up to the point where they can roll everything back into one big homogenized ball.

This criticism is especially relevant when we consider the welfare state. Those who denounce it tend to side with the radical Right desire to recreate the market conditions of the nineteenth century. But, by favouring the distant past over the more recent past, this contradicts the conservative preference for continuity and institutional knowledge. By contrast, *social* conservatives have welcomed the welfare state and so have tended to side with a politics of social democracy with its preference for universal provision and humane capitalism.

Social conservatism

This support has a number of origins. Of particular importance is the fact that conservatives tend to regard the nation as perhaps the most obvious haven for traditions and social order, a source of identity and solidarity. Benjamin Disraeli (1804–1881) famously described nineteenth century Britain as two nations and so the notion of 'one-nation conservatism', committed to national unity and class consensus, was born. Post-Disraeli conservatism began to make at least some room for working-class interests. Family values have also been crucial with social conservatives being prominent supporters of state education as a means of supporting families and ensuring that children were being properly raised. Social conservatives have always been aware of the extent to which free markets destabilize and disrupt the social order.

British social conservatism really derives from the experiences of the 1930–1940s. Mass unemployment, followed by the Churchillian sacrifices of war, convinced many conservatives that the state had a substantial role to play in avoiding a repetition of the 1930s depression and in embodying the common interests of the British people. Harold Macmillan (1894–1986) advocated a 'middle way' between free market liberalism and centralized socialism, and proposed that only conservatives could oversee this middle way effectively (Macmillan, 1938). As Prime Minister (1957–1963) Macmillan was to preside over the economic and social environment he had championed decades earlier: full employment, a mixed economy and universal provision for basic social needs. As free market ideas took a back seat, social conservatism was the ruling philosophy of the British conservatives for at least 30 years. In other countries, such as France and Germany, a distinct social conservatism continues to thrive, offering an additional defence against the wilder fantasies of free market ideology.

Criticisms

The radical Right accuse social conservatives of being as hostile as the Left to the value and virtues of the marketplace. Certainly, the marketplace might encourage a debased, mechanistic form of politics. Hayek (1960: 193–5, 502–3) always resisted the idea that economic doctrine was enough and despaired at those who thought that some magic formulae, like monetary policy, was enough to create a free society. Yet, an unthinking pragmatism was no better than an unthinking economism, he argued. By bending in whatever direction the political wind was blowing, conservatives surrendered their political ethics to circumstance, e.g. by supporting the collectivist ethic and institutions of the welfare state. Those who favour the regulation of capitalism, whether they conservative or socialist, do not understand how and why the invisible hand (or the 'spontaneous order') improves social and individual wellbeing. The conservative suspicion of market capitalism is therefore as misguided as the socialist one because individuals' capacity and right to choose their own package of goods and benefits from the marketplace is what drives humanity forward.

The Left are also critical of social conservatism. Firstly, because it may be more contented than the principle of social justice allows with the levels of poverty and inequality that prevail even under welfare state capitalism. Conservatives are concerned with order, inclusion and stability rather than justice *per se*. Secondly, the Left has always preferred a politics of internationalism while supplements, and may even override, local considerations and affiliations. By contrast, even social conservatism lends itself to the kinds of patriotic sentiments of 'blood and belonging' that keep humanity trapped within its national walls. Conservatism is therefore unprepared for an era where global problems require global solutions (see Chapters 9 and 10).

Finally, feminism has critiqued conservatism's defence of the traditional family, i.e. child-rearing within a heterosexual marriage (Gornick & Meyers, 2009). Feminists argue that the traditional family locked women into the roles of wife and mother, facilitating their economic, political and cultural oppression and sheltering the violence and sexism of gender relations. And in a society where many types of family now exist what should conservatives do? If they resist developments of stable (but non-married) partnerships, including gay/lesbian marriages (Scruton, 2006: 100–1), they could be accused of *undermining* family values. Or, if conservatives welcome such developments they have to recognize the virtues of individual choice and socio-cultural diversity, a recognition that apparently contradicts the conservative commitment to preserving inherited values and practices.

Social Democracy

In a broad alliance with social conservatism, social democracy was *the* ideology of the classic welfare state.[3] It can be thought of as a combination of two perspectives.

Social liberalism

We have already reviewed key aspects of social liberalism, in Chapters 2–6, in its commitment to

- equality of opportunity and social mobility,
- redistribution to help the least well-off,
- market reforms, e.g. through Keynesian economics,
- some notion of the common good,
- universal citizenship and social rights.

Social liberalism's starting-point is the freedom of the individual to determine the path of his or her own life. Individual autonomy, does not exist in a social vacuum, though; a market economy is a necessary but not a sufficient condition of freedom. Some social equality is required to correct the inequities of social background and an enabling, redistributive, managerial state is required to bring this about. The state's primary task is to create high levels of employment and to ensure that national wealth is distributed fairly. Citizenship therefore implies a strong dimension of social rights and entitlements.

Welfare services help to strengthen liberal democratic society. For Marshall, social rights completed and bolstered the revolutions in civil and political rights of earlier centuries. So while conservatives wish to ameliorate whatever threatens order and stability, social liberals are genuinely concerned with social justice. Consequently, they are more likely to identify a link between extremes of wealth and poverty and so to favour policies that assail privileged interests. It is the needs of the individual that count rather than the needs of history, tradition or established authority. Social liberals therefore support the formation of collectivist provision where this is shown to enhance individual liberty.

However, social liberals are less concerned than the Left with inequality *per se* and class structures. Capitalist inequalities which are consistent with basic principles of justice are potentially acceptable, compared to those on the Left who believe that capitalism must be abolished; crucial values – such as communal participation – are to thrive (Cohen, 2008). So, whereas socialists believe in the eventual abolition of class, social liberals are more likely to defend the welfare state as assisting us toward a meritocratic society that requires differential rewards for differential effort and desert. They are therefore likely to be prioritarians who defend high levels of *minimal* provision, i.e. raising the floor rather than lowering their ceiling. Social rights are mainly rights *within* the market economy, not rights *against* it; equality means equality of opportunity, not outcome; and although the state has a central role to play, mixed forms of welfare provision need to be preserved and encouraged.

From the radical Right comes the familiar criticism that only a *free market* liberalism can protect the rights and capacities of individuals. Social conservatives allege that the solidarities which social liberals support cannot survive in an individualistic society, since the selfishness to which individuals are drawn easily leads to social fragmentation. Cultural solidarity must emanate from, and in turn nourish, the nation's communal way of life.

Feminists allege that social liberalism downplays the importance of gender, treating it merely as another product of individuals' interactions rather than as that which configures social agency and interrelationships. Social liberalism offers a level playing field without acknowledging that the rules of the game to be played have been written over many centuries by privileged white men. Minimal provision and equal opportunities, do not begin to overturn the deep socioeconomic and cultural, symbolic injustices implied by gender inequalities.

For socialists and egalitarians, because social liberals do not recognize the extent to which individuals' fates are determined by their social environment, they neglect the level of social transformation that is necessary for social justice to prevail. Capitalism allows itself to be humanized only so long as the profits of wealthy elites are not threatened; equality of opportunity is meaningless and ineffective unless accompanied by a substantial equalization of outcomes. Even social rights are merely formal unless the correct economic conditions are in place, and the state has to be viewed as a countervailing force to the inequities of capitalist markets.

Democratic socialism

Democratic socialism passed through three stages in the twentieth century (cf. Sassoon, 2010).

The first period saw it rising in influence due to intellectuals such as Cole (1920), Tawney (1964) and Laski (1935), and the actions of European labour movements. Democratic socialists sought a middle way between capitalism and communism, concurring with liberals that the constitutional and electoral procedures of liberal democracy ought to be followed, but agreeing with Marxist socialists that a long-term transformation of society was both possible and desirable. This vision of a socialist democracy therefore offered a 'gradualist' alternative both to a capitalism that created mass poverty and to a communistic command economy that disdained democracy and civic freedoms.

In the 1930s to 1940s – with the Great Depression and the rise of fascism – democratic socialism entered its second phase. Through the medium of Centre-Left governments, and in alliance with many social liberals, democratic socialists began to wield a practical influence on western societies (Miller, 2003). It was as a rising star within the British Labour Party that Crosland (1956) gave what remains one of the most influential accounts of democratic socialist thought.

Firstly, socialism objects to the origins, the nature and the extent of the inequality produced by capitalism. By placing profits ahead of people, capitalism tends to generate large pockets of poverty and deprivation. Secondly, socialism is concerned with social justice and welfare, with the fulfilment of universal basic needs and with the particular needs of the disadvantaged and underprivileged. Equality of opportunity is insufficient since a meritocracy would still contain social inequalities and undeserved advantages; inequalities also have a habit of ossifying into rigid, cross-generational structures. Real freedom demands the abolition of class. Thirdly, socialism protests against class exploitation. A classless egalitarianism is therefore the goal that democratic socialism tries to achieve by advancing and representing the interests of the working class. Fourthly, socialism prefers cooperation to competition as a means of organizing societies and economies. Finally, socialism argues that capitalism is inefficient and wasteful: the human waste of unemployment and the material waste of overproduction. Socialist planning can set a more efficient and less anarchic framework for economic activity and so achieve generally higher levels of growth.

The Crosland of the 1950s believed that post-war reforms had irreversibly shifted the balance of power away from the capitalist class. By achieving *political* power, Centre-Left parties had wrestled *economic* power away from capitalists and handed it to a new class of business leaders and public sector managers who, through control of nationalized industries and utilities, would organize society for the good of all. The welfare state had replaced free market capitalism with a mixed economy that served socialist aims, representing a victory for the poor and for workers. Democracy makes Marxist revolution unnecessary. Markets are fine so long they are put in their place; and market values should certainly not be allowed to define and dominate social values.

Unfortunately, like Marshall, Crosland overestimated the political success and durability of the Keynesian welfare state, interpreting as irrevocable trends that were confined to the 1950s–1960s. By misreading the extent to which there had been a shift in the locus of power, social democracy revealed its underlying weakness. Firstly, it did not prepare for the possibility of major economic crises, and so failed to control the economic shocks of the 1970s; secondly, it left itself theoretically exhausted, old-fashioned and so vulnerable to the resurrection of the radical Right.

And as social democracy retreated, so democratic socialism entered its third phase, during the 1980s, with its ideals and proposals seeming ever less relevant and realistic. Whether a fourth phase awaits is something considered below.

What are the main critiques of democratic socialism?

We can accuse it of being too impractical in its hopes for a post-capitalist society. Democratic socialist programmes have only occasionally received more than a minority of votes from western electorates. Perhaps democratic socialists have set themselves too ambitious a task, enjoying their greatest achievements when they have moderated their demands and worked in alliance with non-socialist parties. This might suggest that democratic socialism has little to offer in and of itself and is more of a corrective to other political ideals.

The radical Right regard democratic socialists as naïve for believing that cooperation can ever become the principal means of organizing an economy. People can be altruistic, fraternal and communal, of course, but these impulses are short-lived and particular (reserved for friends, associates and compatriots). By ignoring this, socialists invariably end up placing too much faith in the state, treating it as the 'comrade writ large' and handing power over to bureaucrats and administrators who are ultimately far more self-serving, unaccountable, incompetent and autocratic than private sector managers, owners and shareholders.

Conservatives, too, regard socialism as utopian, rationalistic and as leading to the kind of social engineering that destroys social unity and stability. Social liberals regard the collectivism of socialists as unnecessary and undesirable. Many feminists object to the socialist emphasis upon class and economic stratification which, they allege, neglects the importance of other forms of social division, exploitation and domination. And Marxists argue that we cannot create socialism through gradualism and party politics. The democratic process can never deliver more than marginal reforms to a capitalist society for, as we have seen over the last 30 years, even marginal victories (such as a welfare state) are vulnerable to counter-attack by ruling elites.

A new social democracy?

Where does this leave democratic socialism? Nowhere, according to the proponents of the 'new social democracy' (Giddens, 1998; see Finlayson, 2003; Driver & Martell, 2006; Page, 2007). New social democrats seek a 'third way' between democratic socialism (the 'old Left') and the radical Right. Some aspects of the former are worth preserving, especially its emphasis upon moral values; but any hint of social ownership and egalitarian redistribution is rejected as old fashioned. Instead, we have to adapt to most of the transformations fashioned by the radical Right. Free markets are here to stay, material inequalities are less important than social inclusion, public services should be opened up to competitive pressures and the moral conservative emphasis upon obligation, respect, discipline, hard work, the common good and national identity should be welcomed. The state must become a 'social investment state', more concerned with improving the 'human capital' of the nation's workforce than with idealistic visions of social perfection.

It is accurate to define this new social democracy as a realignment of social liberalism and social conservatism, so long as we remember that in the course of this realignment both are reconfigured and redefined. Some elements of the above social liberalism is accepted (e.g. equality of opportunity and meritocracy) but any hint of Keynesianism is rejected. Similarly, the social conservative attachment to social cohesion and national identity is valued, but not its association with post-war collectivization, nationalization and hands-on management. Ultimately, the new social democracy has been a vocabulary of governance rather than a distinct political philosophy, one designed to forge disparate constituencies together (Fitzpatrick, 2003; Levitas, 2005).

Which is not to imagine that it abandoned familiar social democrat goals. In the UK, New Labour set out to tackle child poverty. Its prospects have waned, however (Fudge & Williams, 2006; Jordan, 2010). By appealing to moralistic, almost righteous forms of identity, behaviour and self-justification, ones which stigmatized outsiders and 'the undeserving', it only managed to stoke prejudices which can never be satiated and which eventually return to consume those who once fed them. Furthermore, without a critique of capitalism the new social democracy left itself vulnerable to capitalism's worst crisis for 80 years (see Chapter 9), coming to be seen as part of the problem rather than the solution.

Where this leaves democratic socialism is far from clear. Ideas and analyses continue to appear (Unger, 2005), largely unconnected to a mass political movement. Only in Latin America have there been recent signs of life.

Marxism

Although its influence upon western social policies has been marginal, Marxists have offered some interesting critiques (Kymlicka, 2002: Ch.5).

The base/superstructure model (pp. 113–4) essentially implies that the state is a product of that society's economic system. The state reflects, embodies and enables the perpetuation of private property in, and the unequal distribution of, the capitalist means of production. In effect, the capitalist state is an organizing committee of the ruling class. At its crudest, this implies that the state has no autonomy, designed to enable the exploitation of the poor, the concealment of the real nature of socioeconomic power and the suppression (through physical force when necessary) of working-class struggles. A subtler interpretation suggests that the state possesses a 'relative autonomy', meaning that it has some freedom of movement but only within the parameters dictated by the needs of capital to make profits. Geras (1989) likened this to a dog that is chained to a post and can move about within the circumference of the chain, but cannot go any further.

One implication is that whereas state welfare can *sometimes* alter the rules of capitalism it cannot change the basic nature of the game itself (Gough, 1979; Ginsburg, 1979). Some welfare states are better than others at reducing poverty levels, but since capitalism is based upon exploitation – wages are worth less than the value of the labour provided by workers – then all capitalist societies depend upon low wages and the unemployment needed to drive wages down. Poverty is also a source of discipline, a useful reminder of what can happen to you if you don't toe the line. Education and employment policies perpetuate the myth that an individual's social position is due to his efforts. And although social work, healthcare and family policies may look humanitarian – and those employed within such services are invariably well-intentioned – they help to drive an economic system where everything is judged according to its market value ('commodification'). Social workers are rarely appointed to affluent families; instead, they require dysfunctioning 'worker-consumers' to become socially efficient again. Healthcare systems deal largely with the costs of inequality to personal and social wellbeing, rather than a system of wage-slavery which exhausts individuals' mental, physical and emotional energies. Domestic labour has to be unpaid because the 'labour-power' of husbands and sons needs to be reproduced without the economic cost becoming burdensome.

Therefore, only by going beyond capitalism can we achieve a society organized around a socialist principle of distribution, where each person is motivated to contribute ('from each according to their abilities') and no-one is left in need ('to each according to their needs') (Carens, 2003a). An 'historical materialist' analysis suggests that we will move from capitalism to socialism and eventually communism, once the capitalist system fails to resolve its basic contradiction: between the immense wealth it generates and the inequalities it needs to generate that wealth.

The base/superstructure model underwent many refinements over the years, with some insisting that the superstructure significantly affects the base, but it seems fair to state that for a theory to *be* Marxist a central place must be accorded to the economic relations and determinants of class. Two debates are especially relevant.[4]

Structures and agents (again)

One debate takes us back ultimately to the structure/agency distinction of Chapter 6.

Louis Althusser (1918–1990) rejects the humanist interpretation of individuals as 'prior' to the social conditions that form them. Instead, we are made by our environments, saturated with the contexts within which we find ourselves and 'interpellated' by institutions and social practices into the roles/positions that we occupy. Althusser (1969; Althusser & Balibar, 1971) regards the systems of the superstructure as possessing a relative autonomy that is determined 'in the last instance' by the economic base. Therefore, it is wrong to assume a mechanical, simplistic, one-way relationship between the base and the superstructure: ideology is not simply an inversion of the economic reality. Instead, the contradictions of capitalism are 'overdetermined' and multi-casual, so that only a scientific analysis can reveal the underlying oppression and exploitation of society.

Althusser also distinguishes between a 'repressive state apparatus' (RSA) – police, army and penal system – that helps to maintain capitalism through actual or threatened violence, and the 'ideological state apparatus' (ISA) – church, family and education system – that maintains capitalism by securing support for it by those (the poor, the exploited) who would have most to gain from its abolition. So, the welfare state qualifies largely as an element of the ISA, allowing capitalism to appear more humane than it really is.

However, Althusser is no simple structuralist. By dissolving the humanist, liberal, bourgeois view of the self, by presenting it as a construction of fragments that service capitalist imperatives, Althusser was influenced by and was a key influence upon post-structuralist ideas (e.g. Hindess & Hirst, 1977).

Herbert Marcuse (1898–1979) concentrates upon what he sees as the unity and homogeneity of capitalist society, arguing that its apparent diversity and plurality are mere surface features that camouflage an underlying sameness and uniformity. Modern societies constitute a 'totality' which cloaks its oppression within the vocabulary of freedom, merit and liberalism. Workers conspire in their own exploitation because rather than overthrow the system that exploits them, they buy into the capitalist dream – through advertising and commercialism – and waste their lives trying to own the goods and consumables that they themselves produced. Marcuse therefore highlights the one-dimensionality of society: the ways in which people fuel a totally administered and controlled society. On this reading, the welfare state is nothing more than an element of this total administration, a means by which injustice is made to seem just and servitude is made to resemble freedom.

The problem with Althusser and Marcuse is that, by offering neat 'theories of everything', they risk eliminating the human element from social and historical development. To disagree with Marcuse is to risk being labelled as a bourgeois apologist for the one-dimensional society. And Thompson (1978: 195) launched a famous attack on Althusserian Marxism as an 'intellectual freak'. Therefore, other Marxists have emphasized the movements and struggles of agents (including but not necessarily limited to workers).

For instance, in his famous argument with Poulantzas (1975), Ralph Miliband (1924–1994) acknowledged the centralization of social power around the capitalist state while also recognizing that opposing interests can mobilize themselves and occasionally change the organization and distribution of power, even within a capitalist context (Miliband, 1969). The working class, in particular, could take advantage of the relative autonomy of the state to seize some measure of control away from monopoly capital, and the welfare state could be interpreted as one such victory. So whilst it is facile to regard the welfare state as a prototype of a socialist society, it does represent a victory of sorts for the working class. Of course, the latter faces an uphill battle, and any victories short of a socialist transformation are likely to be modest and vulnerable to counter-attack. But if our politics omits reference to agency, free will and subjectivity, we become little more than detached observers, waiting for history to change according to some kind of inner, deterministic logic that we cannot affect.

Recall, then, the quote from Marx on p. 107: men make their history, but not under circumstances of their choosing. Thompson and Miliband stress the men-making-history part of the quote, while Althusser and Marcuse highlight the history-making-men element. As Chapter 6 noted, the either/or nature of this debate can appear old-fashioned.

This may explain the continued appeal of Antonio Gramsci (1891–1937) who argued that people are indeed subjugated by a system of power, both economically and ideologically (Gramsci, 1971). It is not enough for workers to *be* exploited, since if they recognize their exploitation for what it is then they might organize to change things. Therefore, they have to embrace and defend that exploitation as a result of their freely chosen actions. The work ethic is such a coping mechanism, allowing the exploited to feel virtuous, valued and productive. It is in this way that the interests of the ruling class become hegemonic, i.e. achieve moral and intellectual dominance.

But if ideology can repress, it can also liberate. The task for socialist parties is to engage in a war of ideas in order to win the hearts and minds of ordinary people, turning them away from their willing servitude. Ideology is part of the struggle for hegemony and dominance. For Gramsci, the war of ideas was as important as the wars taking place in workplaces and streets.

Systems

Attempts to accommodate agency and structure can also be found within the 'systems theory' school of thought. Habermas (1975) and Offe (1985, 1996) agree with the radical Right that there is a conflict between the need for capital accumulation and the welfare state's tendency to undermine it (cf. O'Connor, 1973). But whereas the radical Right insist this conflict can be resolved by scrapping the welfare state, or at least privatizing and commercializing it, Habermas and Offe argue that this can only *displace* capitalist crises, shifting them into a 'legitimation crisis'.

Capitalism, they observe, consists of three sub-systems: an economic system (capital), a political-administrative system (the state) and a socio-cultural system (values and norms). Capital provides the state with finance and, in return, the state ensures that the economic conditions of growth and accumulation are maintained. The state uses that finance to sustain social welfare provision, in return for which it receives mass loyalty back from its citizens. A welfare state, then, is integral to the functioning of 'organized capitalism'.

But welfare states always risk a 'crisis of accumulation' since they require high taxation and absorb wealth that would otherwise go into the private sector. This is why the Right constantly demands reduced welfare spending. But without state welfare, capitalism could not secure the popular legitimacy it requires. If the welfare state is slashed, social problems increase – leading to social disorder and alienation – and both middle- and working-class voters are likely to rebel. Thus,

> The contradiction is that while capitalism cannot coexist with the welfare state, neither can it exist without the welfare state. (Offe, 1984: 153)

Here, then, is an analysis that encompasses systems and structures without ignoring the human scale of conflict and culture.

A return to socialism?

Until recently, it would have been usual to explain Marxism through a series of conceptual contrasts: not only structure/agency, but also revolution versus reformism and socialism versus communism. The democratic socialism reviewed earlier was committed to democracy and incrementalist reform, often in contrast to what was seen as the Marxist predilection for a mass, revolutionary insurrection which was irresponsible and unrealistic. Today, if anything, the expulsion of democratic socialism from the social democratic lexicon has led to realignments on the Left where the old contrasts and disputes matter less.

Market socialism, for example, is the proposal to retain the efficiencies of markets while shifting the basis of the economy away from the private ownership of productive property to new, revitalized forms of social ownership (Roemer, 1994). The allocative efficiencies and price mechanisms of markets are retained but not the vast inequalities and injustices of capitalism. And while some object to markets on principle (Albert, 2003), market socialist ideas at least signal that philosophical and theoretical debates about the desirability of, feasibility of and prospects for socialism, and even communism, are still going strong.

Cohen (2009: 80–1) states that, 'The socialist aspiration is to extend community and justice to the whole of our economic life', while Wright

(2010), Žižek and Douzinas (2010) and Badiou (2010) have all argued that we are in more need of socialist alternatives and a revitalization of the utopian imagination than ever before. Thus, the question about whether and to what extent these philosophers are straight-down-the-line Marxists has become less important in a climate where boundaries, ideas, identities and labels are up for grabs and being rethought.

Criticisms

There are four major problems with Marxist theory.

Firstly, it has little to offer the practical reformer. Social policy is concerned with what is do-able in the here and now. Marxist analyses can be powerful but derive ultimately from a vision of an ideal society located decades – and possibly centuries – in the future. Some practical proposals do exist (Wright, 2010: chs. 6 and 7) but even here substantial conflicts remain. And even if Marxist reform is widely accepted as desirable the battle against entrenched, worldwide capitalist interests is always likely to be very long-term. So, rather than regard the welfare state as a Pyrrhic victory that falls short of socialist transformation, it may be the best we can hope for in an imperfect world.

Secondly, Marxism is vulnerable to the critiques we explore in the next chapter, where rather than treating social identity in simplified terms, e.g. worker vs. capitalist, identity is more an ambivalent, intersecting site of multiple subjectivities. By emphasizing class above all else, Marxism arguably ignores the significance of other social relations like gender and ethnicity. Of course, Marxists have been aware of this at least since Engels (2010) wrote about the family. But decades of tortuous attempts to show how, for example, domestic work contributes to surplus value do not eradicate the suspicion that Marxist theory starts from the wrong place.

Thirdly, and similarly, the supposition that economic power is the most important form of social power has been repeatedly questioned (e.g. pp. 97–8). Without wishing to go to the opposite extreme of *under*estimating the role economic power plays in human affairs, there are many who want to focus upon the other forms of power (in addition to the economic) that Marxists tend to lock away within the superstructure, e.g. political power, charismatic power, cultural power and military power (Mann, 1986).

Finally, just as they may overestimate the unity of 'class', so Marxists may underestimate the divisions and conflicts within the state. Even a definition of the state as relatively autonomous may overlook the extent to which it is an outcome of pluralistic struggle and political competition. If so, then Marxists may be accused of adopting functionalist accounts of the welfare state where everything is interpreted as serving the reproduction of capital. If we avoid such functionalism then we recognize the welfare state as progressive and as possessing a genuine, transformative potential.

Feminism

Feminism has frequently embraced questions of social identity (as we see in Chapter 8) while also possessing distinct ideological characteristics.

Feminism argues that above perspectives are all guilty of ignoring the specificities of gender inequalities and injustices (Daly, 2000; Kymlicka, 2002: ch. 9). Women may be exploited, but such exploitation involves more than just disputes over wages, working hours and workplace conditions. That said, and although some lean towards the Right, the vast majority of feminists are more comfortable with Centre-Left ideas. Feminists will typically voice support for social justice but insist that the concept incorporate the dimensions of gender (Nussbaum, 1999).

Take citizenship, for instance. Feminism argues that when we consider what it means to be a social participant, a bearer of rights and responsibilities, an implicit bias is woven into our languages, our cultures, our very psyches (McRobbie, 2009). Since men were the 'hunter-gatherers' of primitive times and since women are able to reproduce, the assumption is that the space outside the kinship unit is a masculine space while the domestic space (that of cooking and child-rearing) belongs to women. Doesn't it seem natural that men should hunt, kill, fight and run the tribe while women nurture, mother, cultivate and obey? Within what is now called the 'breadwinner model', masculinity dominates the public sphere of wage-earning and politics, with femininity inhabiting the private sphere of domesticity and male-dependency.

But feminists question this distinction between 'male citizen' and 'female homemaker' (Pateman, 1988, 1989; Lister, 2003). As we saw on p. 107, what appears to be natural can be a projection onto nature of social practices. Biology does not determine society. Women are not genetically predisposed to be tied to the home. Instead, their traditional confinement within the dutiful roles of wife and mother is itself a means by which the socioeconomic and cultural power possessed by men is used to *exert* control. This gender-specific relationship of oppression is known as 'patriarchy'.

Social justice is therefore important, but for feminists this means more than justice for the 'wage-earner'. Formal citizenship rights are accorded to all individuals and are, strictly speaking, gender neutral; but it is the inequalities (of opportunities and power) deriving from the basic 'sexual division of labour' which continue to ensure that women are more likely to be second-class citizens than men. Therefore, even as women have become more prominent and influential within politics and labour markets, the underlying inequality remains.

What is the answer to patriarchy, though? A rallying cry of 'second-wave feminism' in the 1960s was 'the personal is political', meant to draw attention to (1) the ways in which disadvantages in the private realm shape discriminations and inequalities in the public one, and (2) how a fairer allocation of public goods and opportunities will reconfigure the role, significance and composition of families and households. But what should this actually imply?

To a large extent this question goes to the heart of why there are many feminist critiques of, and proposed solutions towards, patriarchy (Okin, 1979). 'First-wave' feminists sought to promote gender-related issues within the context of the liberal principles of liberty and citizenship (Wollstonecraft, 1975; Friedan, 1983). Liberal institutions and existing democratic systems were held to be sufficiently flexible to allow women to gain equality with men. This brand of feminism is often regarded as simplistic and naive in that it underestimates the extent to which those institutions and systems are both dominated by men and embody masculine values.

By contrast, socialist and Marxist feminists (Hartmann, 1989) argued that a real equality between the sexes is ultimately dependent upon achieving a classless society. If capitalism requires a reserve army of labour, as well as the domestic reproduction of labour, then the subordination of women can be explained. Capitalism reduces women to the biological role of child-bearers, of mothers and homemakers, and so to a reserve army who can be drafted in and out of the periphery of the labour market depending upon the needs of the economy. Some critics allege that this analysis misreads the extent to which women have made, and are capable of making, real strides within capitalist society and renders gender equality dependent upon the utopian dream of a socialist revolution. Others have argued that this emphasis upon class neglects other social identities.

More recently, the following taxonomy from Fraser (1997: 44–62) has been influential.

Universal Breadwinner model

Perhaps women need to continue to force their way into the worlds of government and employment, competing with men as best they can as 'wage-earners'. Some will reject marriage and motherhood, while others will juggle public and private obligations. This is largely a liberal model.

Caregiver Parity model

Or, perhaps the above model requires women to become more like men: adopting the same behaviour, aspirations and values. Perhaps, instead, we ought to celebrate the private more, regarding it as the preserve of feminine values, but on a 'separate but equal' level to the public worlds of wage-earning and policymaking. This is more of a conservative model.

Universal Caregiver model

Yet, surely that would just preserve the fundamental bias: public = masculine, private = feminine. So perhaps the answer is for women to enter the public sphere, not as 'male surrogates' but as agents who will change it, making government and workplaces less hierarchical and adversarial. Men and women would share responsibilities in both the public and private worlds, with caring and parenting no longer viewed as inferior 'women's work'. This model owes much to socialist, egalitarian and radical politics.

Whichever feminist perspective is preferred, there are basic agreements about the significance of social policies in embodying and maintaining the economic, political and cultural power of a patriarchal society (Pascall, 1997; Charles, 2000; Bettio & Plantenga, 2004).

Most feminists express support for the *idea* of collectively organized state welfare services but this support translates into a broad criticism of existing provision and the socioeconomic context within which the welfare state is located (Lister, 2009; Orloff, 2009). Women are more likely to occupy part-time jobs and so experience lower pay, poorer conditions, worse entitlements and fewer opportunities for training and promotion than men. Women still tend to the occupationally segregated both 'horizontally', in that they are largely concentrated in clerical, secretarial, sales and service sector jobs, and 'vertically', in that they are more likely than men to be on the bottom rung of the career ladder. One consequence is that women have a greater incidence, a higher risk and longer durations of poverty compared with men (Pantazis & Ruspini, 2006).

So, a vicious circle is set in motion (Pascall, 1997: 30–72). Disadvantage in the labour market implies low pay and few entitlements so that many women are thrown back onto the least generous and most means-tested aspects of the welfare state which, in turn, fails to relieve their poverty and so contributes to the continuance of labour market disadvantage. In short, women's status as the dependent clients of welfare services is a construction, a consequence of their assumed dependency on the wage-earning status of men. Women have traditionally been defined as spouse and/or as mother whose job opportunities and welfare entitlements are effectively conditional upon assuming and performing these types of role.

Basically, the feminist critique of social policy, says that disadvantages in the welfare state, the family and the labour market feed into one another. Those assumptions were made explicit in Beveridge's Report and his infamous remark that married women have less need of the earned entitlements of social insurance because they have 'other duties'. In other words, a single (male) breadwinner is to act as a conduit between the household and market in order to ensure both the internal stability of the family and its external mobility within the economic.

What are the potential weaknesses of that critique? Many on the radical Right (Friedman, 1962) allege that a commitment to state welfare services implies an ignorance of the beneficial effects that the free market could have upon sexual equality: patriarchy has thrived because the state is a male-dominated institution resistant to change, whereas in an economy of free competition those employers who ignored the talents and abilities of female workers would be punished by those who did not. Sexual equality would therefore improve over the course of time and most feminists are consequently misguided in supporting the welfare state. Conservatives, by contrast, argue that a women's place really *is* in the home because men are essentially hunter-gatherers and women are essentially care-providers. Another possible criticism is that feminist prescriptions for welfare reform are either too utopian or too dependent upon the traditional ideologies we reviewed above. Feminists may make valuable *contributions* to social liberal or democratic socialist thought, but do not ultimately transcend the Left–Right political spectrum.

Ideological debates continue to be voiced even though, at periodical intervals, ideology is widely claimed to be dead or else the preserve of those political dinosaurs, over there, who refuse to realize their ideas have become extinct. Yet ideological analyses are more vibrant than their critics recognize. To abandon them would severely limit the scope of our political imaginations, reducing debates about welfare reform to technical and administrative questions. Welfare theorists must ask two questions: 'what is the best form of society?' and 'what kind of welfare systems facilitate that society?' By contrast, those who insist that we now live in a post-ideological society, attempt to close political debate down before it can really get started. Therefore, what is vital is not so much a commitment to any one ideology but a commitment to the breadth of ideas that any open, confident and healthy society must embody.

Questions for Further Discussion

- How consistent are right-wing theorists' conceptions of the economy with their conceptions of the family?
- Why do many Marxists and free market liberals agree about the failures of post-WW2 social policies?
- To what extent do feminist ideas and critiques represent an alternative to the left–right political spectrum?
- Does conservatism offer a distinct and coherent welfare ideology?

8
Identities

- Profiling Identity
- Identity Politics
- Reconstructing Welfare

- Recognition
- Social Divisions

Debates about identity have become vitally important. The previous chapters have suggested that identity is

- definitive of who we are and what we do;
- related to wellbeing, to the flourishing of long-term ambitions;
- something that unites humans, while also denoting differences and cultural diversities;
- both personal and social, a form of social agency which signifies membership within a particular way of life;
- multilayered, some layers being fundamental and others more ephemeral and contingent; and
- made through social practices, cultural representations and socioeconomic-political structures.

By the 1970s–1980s, 'identity politics' embodied the new emphasis upon individualization, demanding a turn away from materialism, structural analyses and ideology towards culture, discourse, new social movements and the postmodern. It represented a fracturing of old assumptions about solidarity and collectivism, but one which offered exciting possibilities for new 'decentred' alliances, political movements and theoretical critiques.

Identity is a slippery term but we can unpack its basic dimensions (cf. Appiah, 2005: Ch.1; Lawler, 2007; Parekh, 2008: Chs. 2–3) before going on to explore some recent ideas (pp. 151–9) and the implications of identity politics for social policy (pp.159–68).

Profiling Identity

Imagine you (person *A*) are alone in the universe and write a short auto-biography. In a universe of one, this autobiography might summarize your identity. Person *B* now appears. The account you previously gave of yourself *to yourself* is no longer adequate. What you are is to some extent a matter of how

148

and why you are perceived. When you were alone, you controlled how that presentation was received and interpreted. But when someone else arrives, you no longer have full control. Your identity is now partially dependent upon how *B* sees you. Their perception may correspond to yours or it may not but, either way, it is constitutive of your self. You might adjust your behaviour and appearance accordingly. But, of course, the identity of *B* is now partially dependent upon *your* perceptions and interpretations of *them*.

There are several correspondences going on, therefore:

1. *A*'s account of and to himself;
2. *B*'s account of *A*;
3. *B*'s account of and to herself;
4. *A*'s account of *B*.

1 will never correspond exactly to 2, nor 3 to 4. However, if 2 & 4 were completely dissimilar to 1 & 3, respectively, there might be no basis for social interaction. Therefore, meaningful social interaction depends upon a degree of convergence between how A & B see themselves *and* each other. *Identity is a projection of the self into a social space of mutual negotiations and reciprocities; and a projection onto the self of social roles, conventions and understandings.*

A & *B* now constitute a group which, over time, will form its own identity, history and cultural characteristics. You might become friends, enemies, or whatever. That group identity will shape your personal identity. A friendship will cause you to behave in ways you would not if you hated *B*. However, your personal identity will not correlate exactly to the group identity. Even if you perceive *B* as a friend there may be part of you standing back, monitoring the extent to which *B*'s friendship is genuine.

Now imagine that another group appears. Just as your identity became related to *B*, so the identity of *A* & *B* (group 1) is now related to that of group 2. In short, we have:

i.   Group 1's account of itself to itself;
ii.   Group 2's account of 1;
iii. Group 2's account of itself to itself;
iv.   Group 1's account of 2.

As before, a social space will involve mutual, back-and-forth projections of and onto each group. This will be a multilayered and constantly evolving space of identities and cultures: the meta-group (groups 1 + 2), the individual groups (1 or 2) and the sub-groups (each individual). See how quickly the concept of identity becomes complicated? Now imagine the addition of groups 3, 4 and so on, until billions of people are added.

Yet, it doesn't end there. We have assumed people and groups pop into existence. But this isn't how things happen. Your initial autobiography was only possible through the possession of language. In short, we already presupposed a social, cultural, political and communal context. Our self-images already accommodate communal membership and identifications. It would have made no sense to write 'I am a Caucasian, British female' without some understanding of what it means to be Caucasian, British and female, none of which you could invent *ex nihilo*.

So, representing yourself as Caucasian, British and female carries two implications. Firstly, these characteristics have a meaning which precedes your entrance into the world – even though you may interpret and reconfigure that meaning. Secondly, these characteristics denote differences. To be Caucasian, British and female means *not being* non-Caucasian, non-British and non-female. Furthermore, there are perhaps an infinite variety of ways in which someone can be non-Caucasian, non-British and non-female. Your identity is, then, both a presence (what you are) and an absence (the many characteristics you could possess but do not); it is one island in an archipelago of differences which may or may not connect together at some fundamental level.

In sum, we see that identity implies many overlapping textures:

- The self
- The self's relation to other selves in a group
- The group's relation to other groups
- The social, cultural and political contexts of groups
- The differences between contexts.

Debates about identity have gone in many directions but several questions are most relevant to the themes of this and previous chapters.

How social are our identities?

This relates back to the structure/agency debate. Individualists may regard a 'social identity' as, at best, an amalgamation of personal identities. An organic reading will find that nations, networks, groups, communities, etc. possess distinct, independent identities which shape and determine, but do not 'reduce' to, that of their members.

To what extent do we make our identities?

Liberals will insist that individuals possess a large degree of control over their identities. The self occupies any number of social roles (worker, father, husband, neighbour) without being absorbed completely into them. We can always withdraw from those roles and reconstitute our identities. Non-liberals propose that identities are discovered rather than made. To occupy a social role is to *be* it, e.g. a communitarian argues that personal identities are profoundly immersed in their social contexts.

How are identities made?

Some, like Marxists and socialists, insist that we should focus upon material processes and practices. Others propose that we look at discourse and culture – revisit the exploration of Foucault on pp.61–3, 97–8.

Is identity a form of unity or differentiation?

Post-structuralists argue that identity is always a highly transitory, fluid kaleidoscope of fragmentary 'subject-positions', none of which can dominate the others indefinitely (Laclau & Mouffe, 1985). Stabilities and solidarities are 'contingent'. However, it might be countered that without a fundamental substratum, e.g. a human nature, those fragments could never connect in the first place. The capacity to differentiate *x* from *y* must be shared, otherwise we would not be able to recognize differences *as* differences.

How do identities confer meaning?

For some, lives acquire meaning when inserted into a narrative which is bigger than the individual and which tells a story of our origins, destinations, purposes and projects. For others, such narratives are constructions which are always subject to re-narration. Life and social development are episodic and each chapter we add is not determined by what preceded, nor what will follow, it (Lawler, 2007: 16–29).

Identity Politics

Why is any of this important and why, if at all, should social policy take an interest?

In the 1950s and 1960s, Marxist debates revived with the discovery of the less scientistic, more humanist writings of Marx's youth. By the 1970s, that revival was waning, despite the efforts of the New Left to weave it into a counter-cultural politics. You could try to explain the oppressions of gender, ethnicity, etc. in terms of historical materialism (Hartmann, 1989; and C. L. R. James[1]) but many saw this as increasingly tenuous. Postmodernism, post-structuralism and interest in new social movements were post-Marxist attempts to understand and celebrate the specificities of diverse social identities without compacting them into a distorting 'grand narrative' (cf. Laden, 2009).

Identity politics, then, was the name given to a range of anti-oppressive theories and practices where the injustices of gender, ethnicity, sexuality, dis/ability, nationality, religion, etc. are explained in their own terms and not 'read off' from some all-encompassing critique. Spheres of injustice overlap, but not according to some inner logic or necessity. This explains the interest in culture and discourse. Where Marxism interpreted economic imperatives (the base) as the final determinants of the superstructures, the temptation now was to explain everything in terms of culture, context and discourse.

Culture is another slippery term we have frequently encountered. At its simplest it denotes the mores, values, histories, background understandings, customs, norms, symbols and representations of everything from clothing and architecture to entire civilizations. Within social policy, Clarke (2004: 31–51) has defined culture as something which is possessed (a property of social groupings), as a formation (a synthetic compound of different elements) and as a practice (that through which agents make and are made). Yet despite the ingenuity of these and other accounts (Van Oorschot et al., 2008; also Fitzpatrick, 2005: 181–98), the suspicion lingers that because the meaning of 'culture' is itself a cultural configuration, such debates have a self-justificatory, discomforting circularity.

Similar considerations apply to discourse. In one respect, few would doubt the importance of language. The use of 'he', 'his' and 'him' to stand for something or someone which is, strictly speaking, gender-neutral is perhaps indicative of an implicit gender-bias within our language. It may help to explain why the feminine is frequently pushed away as other and inferior, not only in our language but within our cognitive processes, social practices and wider cultural representations. With ideologies and ideological analysis beginning to feel tired and old-fashioned, the cultural turn toward discourse seemed innovative and exciting.

But this turn may lead into a cul-de-sac where *language becomes reality*, where everything is an interpretative context for everything else and anyone who declares that knowledge and being rest upon foundations is denounced as an 'essentialist'. For Baudrillard (1988) it is no longer possible to distinguish between reality and representation since everything is a sign which points to other signs. Reality has faded and we are left with endlessly proliferating 'hyperrealities' – that which is more real than the real; copies of copies of copies *ad infinitum*. The task of philosophers is no longer to understand the world, and certainly not to change it, but to immerse themselves within and shout into a continuously fragmenting maelstrom.

Some philosophers rebelled against the new fashions (Habermas, 1987b). Although postmodernists and post-structuralists saw themselves as tearing up all grand narratives and 'isms' they did so at a time when radical Right capitalism was in the ascendency. At best, dismantling the salience of concepts such as progress, emancipation and solidarity, when they were needed more than ever, was an unfortunate accident. If we 'need to eschew illusions of a top-down, objectivist science that can tell others what to do' (Schram, 2002: 133) then what is to stop me believing, apart from the fact that I don't, that poverty is caused by the laziness of the poor? At worst, those who triumphed over the death of humanist modernity were buying into a repressive politics.

Reconstructing Welfare

Despite such doubts, it is not difficult to see why questions of identity, culture and discourse should be of interest to social policy.

The U.K. welfare state was in many respects a project of national reconstruction. Whether it was (1) the Boer War turning policymakers' attention to questions of imperial strength and national efficiency, i.e. health, fitness and nutrition, (2) fears about the rise of socialism, or (3) genuine attempts to create a 'land fit for heroes', the nation-state was at the centre of it all.

But the nation is not just a series of borders, coastlines and lines on a map. The nation exists in the collective mind of those who identify with it for their sense of meaning and security. It is, in Anderson's (2005) famous phrase, an 'imagined community'. Thus, the nation is a cultural construction populated by a cross-generational series of self-images. The heroes for whom the land was to be made fit was the white man who was returning from war to reap the rewards, raise his family and maintain an empire. The archetypal citizen of the welfare state was the Christian, married, hard-working, patriarchal breadwinner (Williams, 1989; Clarke & Fink, 2008).

So what, though? Why does this matter? Because wherever you have the ideal, the centre and the dominant, you also have the non-ideal, the marginalized and the subordinated. If male full employment is the norm, then why worry about female domesticity and dependency? If whiteness is the norm, then race becomes a property of non-whites only. And if there are problems with social cohesion, then isn't it obvious that 'they' are failing to integrate into *our* society? If the welfare-citizen is a category of sameness then minorities and differences should either be assimilated into the mainstream or else remain concealed, silent and non-threatening.

For those concerned with justice and injustice, such tensions cannot be neglected indefinitely. If social policy is concerned with explaining and alleviating poverty, how can differential identities be ignored? If women are more vulnerable to poverty then men, and blacks more vulnerable than whites, then something other than inequalities of class is going on. Surely, there are forms of discrimination and subordination which are specific to those vulnerable groups. We can debate whether discrimination is due to overt bigotry, practices inscribed indirectly into social institutions, or fundamental discursive and cultural assumptions. But to imagine that the cause of, and solutions to, the poverty of the unemployed steelworker are exactly the same as those of the underpaid Caribbean nurse is not only to miss the point, it is to maintain the prejudicial beliefs which underpin social injustices. As such, practitioners, educators, policymakers and researchers within various policy sectors have, since the 1970s at least, sought to build 'anti-oppressive' practices into their respective fields.

But at this point we hit a possible objection. Let's agree that women, ethnic minorities and disabled people are discriminated against *as* women, ethnic minorities and disabled people. Discrimination involves locking people into stereotypical versions of their identities. If women are defined according to their reproductive capacity, then what could be more natural than the breadwinner model? But might anti-discriminatory practices involve similar risks? Even when valuing what was previously devalued, perhaps the anti-discrimination lobby are also guilty of locking people into their identities, of stressing differences rather than similarities and cultural representations rather than material relations.

Much of the sound and fury here concerns multiculturalism (Kymlicka, 2002: Ch.8; Fitzpatrick, 2005: 192–8; 2008a: 212–7; Appiah, 2005: 73–83; Parekh, 2006), i.e. support for ethnic and cultural diversity. One argument made by opponents of multiculturalism is that it defines individuals according to their group membership, symbolically trapping them within a kind of cultural ghetto to which everyone else is an 'outsider' who cannot understand the specifics of that cultural belonging. Since multiculturalism is just one aspect of the differential, identity politics which has been sketched above we can apply such critiques more generally. Three key arguments against identity politics and its influence on social policies stand out.

Firstly, liberal neutralists and/or universalists, like Barry (2001), attack multiculturalism and its politics of group rights. Properly theorized and instituted, he insists, a liberal egalitarianism can address social injustices without us having to favour this group rather than that. To think of interests and needs in terms of groups is not only anti-individualist, it potentially reifies the boundaries of groups, freezing and homogenising their membership. As such, the state should not try to become a cultural engineer. From a libertarian perspective, Kukathas (2003: 232–46) argues that favouring one group over another might breed resentment and make cultural conflict worse.

Or, secondly, we might prefer a communitarian politics of the common good (Goodhart, 2006). This is to agree that an emphasis on differences leads to a fracturing of what we hold in common, but the communitarian argues that what we hold in common is membership of a particular community rather than some abstract notion of universal humanity. An identity politics can be supported to the extent that it values specific social membership, but not in so far as it threatens to shatter the community into ever smaller sub-identities (Moore, 2009). In France, for instance, there is a strong politics of secular republicanism which is suspicious towards cultural-religious differences, manifesting itself in recent years as hostility towards certain Muslim practices

(Laborde, 2008). The state should engineer solidarity, bringing groups together rather than stressing their cultural differences.

Finally, perhaps differential identities distract us from an egalitarian and socialist politics of collective solidarity. Yes, there may be culturally-specific discriminations but these are overridden by the class-specific forms of injustice which characterize capitalist societies. The state should intervene mainly in the economy and its distributions of social wealth (Wolfe & Klausen, 1997).

Yet, against all this, the proponents of identity politics maintain that the job of the state and socio-political institutions more generally should be to rectify identity-related injustices. Since groups have been discriminated against *as* groups, Young (1990) recommends group-based forms of political representation and democratic participation.

Since at least the 1990s, wide-ranging debates concerning these issues have arisen, with questions of respect and recognition occupying centre stage.

Recognition

For a person who is disadvantaged because of their identity, *who they are* becomes an object of prejudice. The most fundamental part of themselves is used against them. Their status, their value, their very humanity is denied. One option is to suppress and conceal, e.g. a gay person may adopt hetero-sexual attitudes and habits. Another is to play to an inoffensive stereotype, to become 'different but harmless', e.g. the Uncle Tom figure, an inoffensive, obedient servant who accepts his place in the world. Another option is to resist, to assert the value of one's identity. This was a strategy of the new social movements.

A politics of recognition highlights the obligation of the wider society to change its assumptions and habits, so that groups are no longer measured in terms of higher/lower, or superior/inferior. Justice demands not that we be blind to differences, nor that we merely abide them. Instead, a cultural politics says that we ought to acknowledge and appreciate (or 'recognize') such differential identities and cultures, welcoming them not only as matters of fundamental rights but in terms of their contribution to social pluralism. We all benefit from social environments of diversity and mutual respect.

A recognition politics complicates simple notions of injustice (Anthias, 2001). Some identity-relations are mutually reinforcing. The economic power Alan possesses as an employer enables, and is enabled by, the cultural-symbolic power he possesses as a white man in a society of gender and racial inequalities. But other relations are contradictory, simultaneously dominating and subordinating. Gemma benefits from being middle-class and well educated but, as a woman, faces a glass ceiling at work and expectations that she will spend years out of employment to raise a child. Such contradictory relations and social positions make it harder to apply straightforward distinctions: affluent versus poor, exploiter versus worker.

Therefore, say the defenders of identity politics, the problem with the Left is that it has tried to be difference-blind. Although well-intentioned, its language of universalism has ignored the extent to which individuals are cultural beings, embedded in 'thick', dense contexts that cannot be discarded. Your identity is you and you cannot leave yourself to one side. In obsessing about capitalism, class and material resources, social democrats and Marxists ignore the extent to which harm and injustice is about more than distribution (Dean, 2008). Those committed to multiculturalism, identity politics, queer theory and cultural politics in general have argued that this 'distributive paradigm' should be replaced – in whole or in part, depending on who you read – by a 'recognition paradigm' (see Taylor, 1992, 1994; Honneth, 2007).

Yet, might this create more problems than it solves? It's not as if the distributive paradigm has become irrelevant (McNay, 2008: ch. 4; also Young, 2009). Inequalities of opportunity, wealth and property are widening; governments are still addicted to free markets, despite the repeated costs and damages this craving incurs. Class is not just another form of differential cultural identity. Diluting this paradigm might only surrender power to those who attack workers, trade unions, labour movements and the poor. Nor does it make much sense to celebrate identities which are the products of exploitation. You don't alleviate poverty by 'recognizing' the poor but by equalizing economic resources. Too much emphasis on identity and culture might only reify and homogenize (Appiah, 2005: 100–10; Parekh, 2008: 35–7). For example, a cultural politics might flatter those religious fundamentalists happy to agree that the self is involuntarily encumbered by faith and traditions. Liberals and universalists argue that such claims are themselves oppressive and that our cultural embeddedness is 'thinner' than the identity-obsessives like to believe (Kukathas, 2003: 246–54).

Recent debates concerning justice have centred around the question over whether and to what extent the distributive and recognition paradigms can be reconciled and, if so, what this implies (Lister 2001; Sayer, 2005: ch. 3; Olson, 2006: 4–6, 14–20; Parekh, 2008: 42–55). The contribution of Nancy Fraser has been central (Fraser & Honneth, 2003; Olson, 2008).

Fraser's position is that neither paradigm can be neglected because each supplies perspectives on the other which the other cannot supply for itself. Without the distributive paradigm we cannot explain why poverty and unemployment are indispensable to capitalism; but without the recognition paradigm we cannot explain why women, ethnic minorities, dis/abled people, etc. are typically more like to *be* poor and unemployed. The economic injustice accompanies an injustice whereby some individuals and groups are more likely to be marginalized, devalued and so 'misrecognized'. Injuries and insults feed off one another, but we cannot explain either simply as a manifestation *of* the other. Thus, Marxists would be wrong to conceptualize the black worker as no different to the white worker; and identity theorists would be wrong to imagine that poverty and unemployment are essentially matters of disrespect. Neither critique alone offers a path to a just society. A socialist society of distributive justice could conceivably still retain cultural prejudices; a capitalism of recognition and respect could still contain unjust inequalities of income and wealth.

As she refined this basic idea, Fraser clarified crucial aspects of her thinking. Firstly, she is not claiming that the social world is divided into two, with the cultural over there and the material over here. Obviously, we live within a complex reality in which the two are bound tightly together. A unit of money embodies and exchanges not just economic value but a symbolic value of worth. Popular opinion interprets the £20 Jeff earned as a sign of merit, while the £20 given to a benefit claimant is a sign of deficiency and failure. The economic and the symbolic are interwoven. Nevertheless, Fraser adopts a 'perspectival dualism' in which we retain 'the material' and 'the cultural' as ideal-types, reminding us not to collapse either into the other.

Secondly, Fraser argues that we have no obligation to respect the identity of the bigot or the fundamentalist. It is a condition of entry into the space of recognition that you are willing to recognize others. The bigot who agrees to respect everyone except black people, or the fundamentalist who devalues non-believers, are both guilty of contradiction. 'Participative parity' demands a recognition of cultural differences, but not a recognition of those who would themselves deny participative parity. We are allowed to be intolerant towards the intolerant (cf. Kukathas, 2003: 135–9). Fraser's larger point is that we ought to be concerned with institutions rather than identity *per se*. The idiot shouting racist chants at a football match is unpleasant, but what ultimately matters are social institutions. Those which allow subordination and hierarchies of status ought to be replaced by those which are egalitarian. The correct institutional context gives the racist less room to breathe. Ultimately, there are some identities which, over time, we ought to be eliminating.

Inevitably, Fraser's contribution has been subjected to important criticisms (see Olson, 2008).[2]

Firstly, there is a fundamental disagreement between those who draw from the Hegelian tradition and those, like Fraser, who are Kantian. For Taylor and Honneth identity presupposes an Hegelian philosophy because Hegel (1977: 111–9) viewed the identities of a master and his servant are interdependent. In acting as someone who has a right to be obeyed, the master constitutes the identity of his servant as someone whose role it is to obey. But, in obeying, the servant thereby constitutes the identity of his master. If the servant left his employ, then the identity of the master would undergo a drastic transformation. So, the master/servant relationship is paradoxical: it is hierarchical and yet also co-dependent.

Fraser (2001: 36–7) acknowledges an Hegelian influence but argues that Kant's stress upon what is universally right should predominate. We should not preserve identities in cultural amber. Instead, challenging misrecognition means being prepared to challenge those cultures which themselves misrecognize others. This implies 'measuring' cultures in terms of universal criteria which are sensitive to, but still independent of, any cultural context.

What we have here is a contrast between universalists and particularists. The former believe that we can identify principles and standards which apply to all places and all times; the latter agree with Hegel that a recognition politics should recognize the profound embeddedness of the self in its contexts. Both might agree that the distribution and recognition paradigms should be reconciled but disagree over what this implies.

Secondly, we might query Fraser's method. Does a perspectival dualism really advance our knowledge? Ideal-types and heuristic concepts are beloved of those who enjoy building theoretical models, but if our cultural identities are complex and radically embedded, then such models may not actually take us very far. Perhaps we are better off immersing ourselves into the social world's particularities.

Finally, some of those strongly attached to either the distributive or recognition paradigms deny that any concessions should be made to the other side. For Honneth (see Fraser & Honneth, 2003: 135–59), injustice is profoundly a question of disrespect. The unemployed person is a victim of an economic system, yes, but that system exists in the first place because civilization is founded on the human impulse to humiliate and disregard. A just economic system is one based upon esteem, respect and moral worth. Debates about modes of production and distribution are secondary to that fundamental *ethical* question.

Conversely, those attached to the distributive paradigm believe that concepts of culture and identity are a dead-end for the Left. We consider one possible argument presently.

In short, the question of whether and how to reconcile these paradigms is central to the radical theories and politics of the twenty-first century. At present, no consensus exists and it may be that, because of the very commitment to diversity, nothing which resembles the social democratic and Marxist consensus of old can ever re-emerge. Time, further discussion and experimentation will tell.

In terms of social policy, it seems likely that a fairly pragmatic, hybrid approach will prevail, albeit one complicated by the increased global scope of the subject (Fraser with Bedford, 2008: 229; also Touraine, 2000: ch. 2). The distributive paradigm is another description for social democracy as it has been traditionally understood. Social policy is rooted in the administrative, managerialist aspects of that tradition where social progress comes from producing the right kind of goods and distributing them fairly. Yet, social policy also possesses a well-established concern with discrimination, anti-oppressive practices and multiculturalism which speaks to the more cultural paradigm. In many respects, social policy already occupied the space that philosophers have started to theorize (Kymlicka & Banting, 2006).

Some of those grand philosophical disagreements will matter to social policy, but not all of them. Take decisions about the allocation of resources. There may be times when we want to address specific socioeconomic problems, e.g. issues of worker consultation, legal rights and pension contributions. At other times, forms of cultural intervention will prevail, e.g. combating prejudice against gay and lesbian pupils in school. Often, interventions will incorporate a spectrum of cultural *and* economic issues. But some decisions will be difficult. Should funding be provided to a religious group which experiences discrimination when such funding might conceivably support beliefs which violate the parity of participation? Philosophy can illuminate but will usually not specify which solution is best. Social policies are often matters of trial-and-error, of seeing what works and reflecting on philosophical guidelines in the light of experience.

Let's apply such considerations to some specific debates and issues.

Social Divisions

Social divisions are here defined as groupings of those who share similar identities and social positions (Payne, 2006a: 348). How might those divisions and identities be said to intersect?

Intersections

If you had to write that autobiography, detailing the components of your identity (nationality, gender, class, ethnicity, religion, age, dis/ability, sexuality), what would it look like? Would you give weight to one or more, or treat all of them equally? If your identity was a map, would there be hills and mountains or would the landscape be flatter? There are three basic ways of proceeding (see Bradley, 1996; Payne, 2006b; McCall, 2005; Yuval-Davis, 2006).

Firstly, we could be postmodernists or post-structuralists (Best, 2005). This means not only stressing diversity but also contingency. Identity is not a map at all because a map is something which endures. Instead, your identity resembles a labyrinthine, multidimensional jigsaw puzzle where the shapes of the pieces change incessantly and the picture the shapes reveal when they are slotted together is perpetually altering. Who we are and how we relate is not founded on solid ground. The social soil of our identity is always mutating. Someone is not a student *or* a female *or* a Christian; they are all of these things and more simultaneously. Identity is an ambivalent site of multiple intersections that cannot be resolved into the real you, somewhere, deep down.

Another possibility, secondly, returns us to the distributive paradigm. A socialist/Marxist might argue that identity is indeed multiple. However, it might also be the case that the constraints of capitalism 'underdetermine' our identities. If 'overdetermination' is like trying to pour many types of liquid into a vessel, then underdetermination is the opposite. One liquid only is used to fill the container. Your identity might imply multiple components but it is capitalism which defines you as a worker who spends most of your waking life trying to achieve economic security and fulfilment. By ignoring this, a cultural politics and identity politics represent a dead-end for the Left.

A third possibility corresponds to the hybrid politics that we explored in relation to Fraser. The problem with the distributive perspective is that it is unclear which system does the underdetermining. Capitalism might select and emphasize the wage-earner part of your identity but if, at the end of the day, you go home and are punched by your husband then which form of power is most important, the capitalist or the patriarchal? Instead, we ought to acknowledge that power flows along numerous axes where we position ourselves and are positioned in various locations, none of which can be conflated into the others. Your wife-ness has to be understood in its own terms and not as a manifestation of your worker-ness.

That said, relatively stable foundations *do* exist. We don't have to deconstruct everything. A social division is the name we here give to those who share similar locations within the social field, locations which are institutionally structured and which constitute the social symbolic places around which our lives circulate.

Let's revisit these perspectives by thinking about the body (see Turner, 1996). In one sense, the body is that thing currently standing, sitting or lying down while holding this book. Yet the body is more than its physical shape.

For a post-structuralist like Butler (1990) it is not a biological capacity for reproduction which does or does not make you a women, it is the performances by yourself and others which inscribe such categories into a body. What seems to be 'essential', 'biological' or 'natural' is no more than the sedimentation of performances and practices over time. We are called on to act as certain types of men or women who confirm the 'naturalness' of these constructs by willingly acceding to them. Gays, lesbians and transsexuals are ostracized and punished because their bodies project transgressive identities and appearances which are neither conventionally female nor male.

For a Marxist such critiques ignore the extent to which capitalism forces us to labour. Our bodies *might* be many things, but they become labouring bodies in the face of economic power, docile bodies in the face of political power and submissive bodies in the face of bureaucratic power. We are constrained by socioeconomic structures to either exploit or be exploited.

The hybrid, middle perspective says that the body circulates around a series of relational identities. In front of the computer screen, mine is a labouring body, but if my child interrupts me, it becomes a parental body. The body is many things all at once, though it *is* a physical, biological thing and not just a site of discursive inscription. Thus, some vectors and positionings are more important than others and we should not fixate on instability, fragmentation and contingency. We can understand how each part of an identity is constructed through every other part, without having to dissolve everything into a post-structuralist stream which sweeps away any hint of solidity and permanence.

Even within this perspective, though, we are still left with the questions posed on pp. 150–1 (see Lewis et al., 2000). Should we stress unity and narrative continuity or differentiation and fracture? Whether and to what extent we should emphasize *these* forms of inequality and subordination, rather than *those*, is a highly political question which may always elude a final answer.[3]

Gender

As we saw at the end of the last chapter, a gender-based critique offers a distinct and valuable contribution to ideological analyses (Abbott, 2006; McRobbie, 2009). But what does 'gender' imply?

We might refuse to identify gender as a fixed category (Butler, 1990). 'Gender' is not a reality out there beyond language and cognition, it is classification and a construction. Someone is not born a women, they become a women by performing the practices associated with femaleness. The feminine body implies certain (contingent) types of appearance and behaviour and the self-inscription of such practices into one's own body is what makes one a woman. But such inscriptions evolve. Think of how fashions for clothing, jewellery, cosmetics, etc. are more androgynous than they once were. Gender is not natural, therefore, since nature is itself a construct. To be identified as female is to be constantly located and re-located within a differential series of signs, symbols and cultural discourses.

The problem with this reading is that it threatens to dissolve the category of 'women' into a transitory signification of social power. If there is no nature beyond the discursive construction 'nature', then is there any need for feminism?

Or, we might interpret gender as *the* key social division (Daly, 1979). Perhaps humanity is characterized by a central distinction: a biological-psychological one between male and female and/or a cultural one between 'masculinity' and 'femininity'. Dominance is fundamentally patriarchal in nature, due to the male impulse to separate itself from its origins – the mother, the source of life – and control that which symbolizes lack and weakness, namely the feminine. Caring, nurturing impulses are thereby suppressed in systems of gender inequalities. Such hierarchies characterize all socio-political environments.

The problem with this perspective is that it immobilizes the interplay of social diversities. If it is simplistic to interpret everything in terms of class, then why would it be preferable to do so in terms of gender?

Thus, we come once again to the hybrid position, one which is both constructivist and realist. Gender should not be essentialized but neither is it just an interpretation of other interpretations, *ad infinitum*. When second-wave feminists promoted gender politics in the 1960s–1970s they often found themselves accused of treating white, Western, middle-class, heterosexual, able-bodied women as the archetype of what it was to *be* a woman (Lewis, 2000). What of non-western women, it was asked? What of lesbian women? And so forth. Therefore, the proliferation of identities was in many respects propelled by an advancing sensitivity to a vast spectrum of differences (Davis, 1982). And rather than feminism, what we really have are *feminisms*.

Yet if we follow this logic too far we might ignore the extent to which gender is a social division *encompassing* diversity. Thus while it is to some extent true that masculinity and femininity are lines of mutual intersection (in plainer language, each sex is characterized by elements of both), without some essentialist notion of what it is to be female it is unclear why resistance to patriarchy should be anything more than a language-game played within the confines of cultural politics.

This hybrid position arguably describes most of the feminist critiques within social policy (e.g. Dahl, 2004; cf. Smith, 2008). Discourse, culture and identity are vitally important, yet they do not fully justify the need for a fairer distribution of economic resources and a greater work-life balance. The broader devaluation of women's contribution to society and economy is a form of cultural power which was not created by, nor specific to, capitalism; but the vertical and occupational segregations to which most women are subjected *is* due to capitalism's socioeconomic need for cheap labour and unpaid domestic work. Thus, women are more likely to be poor than men (Hills et al., 2009: 348) due to a complex intermixture of materialist and culturalist elements. Economic redistribution of wealth and income must therefore accompany the symbolic redistribution of value through, for instance, the equitable sharing of carework. The proper resourcing of childcare, parental leave and equal pay has to accompany a shift away from social attitudes which conceive of women as natural carers who are dependent upon male earnings and protection. Degendered notions of citizenship, such as Fraser's universal caregiver model, spring from this kind of hybrid thinking.

Ethnicity and anti-racism

If the arguments of the previous section are persuasive then we cannot imagine 'race' to be *the* key social division either. Anti-racist politics is in large part dedicated to deconstructing and thus undermining the salience of the concept.

This easily offends popular opinion. Surely we can see different races around us all the time – white, black, Asian, oriental, etc. – differentiated by physical appearance, including skin colour. Yet, replies the anti-racist, why is skin colour any more important than other properties which differentiate us, e.g. eye colour, hair colour, height? 'Race' is thus not fundamental to humanity and we only believe otherwise because of historical, culturally constructed prejudices (Banton, 1987). Yes, there are genetic differences that could be categorized as racial differences, but they are largely insignificant; there is far greater genetic variation between individuals of the *same* 'race' than there is between individuals belonging to *different* races (Jones, 1996). This means that we assign such importance to race due to social reasons rather than biological ones: race is a social construction (Rex, 1970).

Does this mean we should interpret it via the distributive paradigm? Marxists argue that racism is a means by which the working-class is kept divided from itself, for if workers attribute their poverty and exploitation to 'the blacks' then they are distracted from the real causes of and solutions to their problems (see footnote 1). Yet, while capitalism might exploit racism, it did not create it. Other Leftist critiques are less conspiratorial but still concerned with the racial and class-based interactions of economic inequalities (Wilson, 2003).

Other critiques belong more to a cultural interpretation. Gilroy (1987) regards the struggles over racial identity as central to our notions of nationality and social belonging. In Britain, racism is bound up with its imperial past, e.g. Kipling's reference to the 'lesser breeds without the law' expresses an equation between 'the blacks' and 'the colonised'. With the passing of the empire Britons' collective identity experienced a sense of loss that could be blamed on 'the other', the invader. Moral panics about immigration, asylum seekers, etc. originate from this point (Hall et al., 1978): the attempt to exclude those who could not be assimilated and assimilate those who could not be excluded.

Again, therefore, we find a reconciliation of material/distributive and cultural/recognition politics seems appropriate. A key concept here has long been 'ethnicity' which draws attention away from biology towards language, customs and traditions, etc. (Donald & Rattansi, 1992).[4]

As we might expect, then, social policies play an important role (Mason, 2006: 112–27). Firstly, across English-speaking nations they were developed against the background of western colonialism and so may continue to embody notions of racial superiority and inferiority. Secondly, welfare systems and institutions may have discriminatory and prejudicial effects, whether directly or indirectly. Thirdly, appropriate welfare reforms *may* offer a means of rectifying the injustices of racial discrimination and oppression. Let us review each of these in turn.

The 'other duties' that Beveridge ascribed to women was the rearing of the children who would maintain the British Empire in a post-war world. The founding of the British welfare state, both before and after the Second World War, therefore occurred at a time prior to the emergence of the anti-racist movement, so the idea that poverty may bear a racial dimension was not initially taken into account. Rex (1986) notes how the importation of immigrant workers into the labour market was shaped by colonial relations, with far more attention being paid to black immigrants (the colonized) than to white ones, e.g. Australian immigrants in the 1950s and 1960s were more accepted than Caribbean ones. So, the black working-class was not only economically disadvantaged but also culturally excluded. This means that post-war social reforms took place in a context where black immigrants were perceived as an alien presence, as a threat that had to be neutralized and assimilated. Racial harmony implied that the 'blacks' should change to become British without the need to rethink the association of Britishness with whiteness. Within that association, to be ethnic is to be non-British.

Given this background, what effects have social policies had upon racial inequalities (Modood et al., 1997)? Indirect discrimination is now at least as important as direct discrimination in explaining the persistence of racial inequality. Indirect discrimination results not from the intentions of any one person, or group of people, but from a series of 'structural' interactions. Suppose that Gurch applies for a job that he fails to get. The employer is genuinely committed to racial equality, but Gurch's qualifications are simply too inadequate compared to those of the other (white) applicants. Why is this? After all, he attended a school that was also genuinely committed to racial equality, yet the school could do very little to compensate for the fact that Gurch grew up in a poor household. And why was his household poor? Because of the direct and indirect discrimination that his parents had experienced all their lives. In short, Gurch fails to get the job not because of any specific bigotry, but because of a vicious circle of circumstances. Direct and indirect discrimination are both present in what is referred to as 'institutional racism'.

Take the labour market. Unemployment figures consistently demonstrate that the economic inactivity of ethnic minority men and women is double that of white men and women, though variations between ethnic groups do occur (Phillips, 2009: 187–91). Black migrants were often channelled either into the public sector or into the low-waged, low-skilled parts of the private sector, and so have suffered disproportionately from economic restructuring. Those who find themselves in the 'secondary' labour market are often trapped there over the long-term and those who do penetrate the 'core' of well-paid, high-skilled, desirable and secure jobs still tend to occupy the lower rungs of the occupational ladder.

The same vicious circle that we noted on p. 146 is at work here, then. Disadvantage in the labour market leads to disadvantage in the benefit system and thus to poverty levels which are difficult to break free from given the persistence of institutional discrimination. Ethnic minority communities are three or four times more likely to be poor as a result. Further disparities exist in the housing sector, with ethnic communities more likely to be living in local authority housing, often in the poorest estates, and less likely to be owner-occupiers.

The record to date of social policies, therefore, appears to be less than admirable. However, anti-racist prescriptions rarely disregard the need for a welfare state (Solomos & Back, 1995, 1996). Indeed, defeating racial inequality would seem to require *more* welfare provision rather than less. It is obvious that reductions in overall social inequality would benefit ethnic minorities considerably, combined with continued attempts to eliminate discrimination in all its forms.

Dis/ability

The common image of a disabled person is of someone who is lacking or is incomplete: disability = personal handicap. The stereotypes here are of someone who is wheelchair bound or walking with a white stick and/or a guide dog. A rather patronizing sympathy for 'the disabled' then falls into place, perhaps accompanied with a feeling of 'Thank God that's not me' which can cause the able-bodied to experience discomfort in the presence of disabled people. Whilst they may not be able to put a name to it, these perceptions and attitudes derive from a 'medical model' of disability.

The medical model treats disability simply as a physical or mental impairment of the individual concerned. This model implicitly treats being able-bodied as the norm where disabled people therefore lack one or more characteristics of normality. So, if a person's mobility is reduced this is due to physiological or psychological conditions which mean that they cannot take full control of their lives and require outside, medicalized assistance from medical experts and social services. The medical model began to be challenged in the 1970s. For instance, the World Health Organization made a useful distinction between impairment (a physical or mental loss), a handicap (a limitation due to the impairment) and disability (the social restrictions that result).

The 'social model' goes still further and focuses not so much upon the individual as upon the inadequacies of the 'disablist' society within which he or she lives (Oliver, 2009): it is not that the individual *is* disabled but is *made* disabled by a society that does not accommodate varying levels of ability. If someone in a wheelchair cannot gain access to a building, this is due not to any inadequacy on her part but to the prejudicial assumptions of designers and administrators. The problem that disabled people have is not their disability but the perception which able-bodied people have of it. Accordingly, the disability movement emerged to challenge the perception of disabled people as 'charity cases', campaigning for their rights and resources.

Once more, then, we can see three perspectives at work here. An emphasis upon distribution alone potentially neglects the extent to which disabled people are subjected to cultural forms of devaluation and misrecognition. The capabilities perspective emphasizes that £1000 for an able-bodied person yields a level of wellbeing different to that for the disabled person (see pp. 30–1). And the social model draws attention to the often hidden assumptions and practices that reside within wider society.

But this does not mean we ought to be satisfied with a recognition paradigm either. Some deaf individuals have refused to accept implants that would improve their hearing on the grounds that it would subvert their identity as a deaf person and their membership of the deaf community. A strict politics of recognition might find this unproblematic. Yet, while such decisions can be respected, if we lived in a society which contained genuine respect for deaf people, it would be anachronistic to speak of identity and community in such separatist terms. Similarly, those like myself who refer to 'disabled people' are occasionally upbraided for defining individuals according to one facet of their identity. The correct description should be 'person of disability', we are told. Perhaps. But a point made above was that whereas we are discursive beings an obsession with the discursive to the exclusion of all else can also be a trap. You do not change the world merely by changing how it is spoken and represented. Language is something; it is not everything.

Thus, within a broad, hybrid politics some argue for a reconfiguration of the social model (Shakespeare, 1998). Although disability is undoubtedly a social construction perhaps the social model distracts too much attention away from the lived experience of impairment. Critics argue not for a return to the medical model but for a model that is more sensitive than its predecessors to the interaction of environmental factors with certain mental and physical conditions.

As before, social policies play several roles (Campbell & Oliver, 1996; Hyde, 2006). Firstly, they have responded only slowly and often reluctantly to the social model as this makes far greater demands upon economic and political resources than a medical model that concentrates upon the individual's impairments.

Secondly, social policies have not, generally, met the needs of disabled people, who are more likely to be in poverty than the rest of the population. Those disabled people who are in employment are twice as likely to be in the periphery of the labour market than their non-disabled counterparts, earning about three-quarters of the average weekly wage, and half as likely to be found in professional and managerial positions. Some of this is due to direct discrimination and some to the vicious cycles of indirect discrimination: poor social background, few qualifications, low skill-levels, infrequent work experience, etc.

The benefit system, though, hardly meets the additional costs of disability. These costs relate to nutrition and diet, heating and transport, special equipment and furniture, and home services. Disabled people have always been less entitled to claim social insurance benefits due to its contribution rules and so have been reliant upon means-tested benefits. Research suggests that disabled people spend approximately 25 per cent of their income meeting the costs that relate to their disability. The benefits available for disabled people constitute what is widely held to be the most complex and confusing element of the social security system. Nor do many people consider the benefits available for carers to be anywhere near sufficient.

Social policies, then, do not appear to have served disabled people particularly well. As before, however, this failure leads to demands for more welfare provision rather than less (Barnes et al., 1998). If future welfare reforms are to be effective, then they must be underpinned by strong and comprehensive legislation that emphasizes the social rights of disabled people. One implication is that disabled people must no longer be defined as the passive recipients of taxpayers' largesse, but as agents in control of their own welfare provision. Furthermore, the additional costs of disability must guide increases in income replacement benefits, in-work benefits and legislative reforms to the pay, entitlements and working conditions of disabled people.

Debates about identity have been crucial to social philosophy over the last few decades. By directing our focus onto the significance of culture and discourse they have, to some extent, challenged the ideological framework we explored in Chapter 7. However, it would be simplistic to imagine that earlier analyses have become irrelevant. Instead, it is now more usual to draw upon multiple perspectives and traditions: the material and the cultural, distribution and recognition, ideology and identity politics, universality and diversity. Sometimes these terms are in conflict with one another, but it is more usual than it was 10–20 years ago to find philosophers speaking of x *and* y rather than x *versus* y. Of course, this broad synthesis itself encompasses numerous possibilities. As ideas continue to evolve, we may or may not find things settling down into a new form of politics and socio-political philosophy whose implications for social policy will continue to strengthen.

Either way, it is also becoming clear that the themes of Chapters 7 and 8, and indeed of many others throughout this book, are occupying new arenas of debate. We go on to consider several vital developments in Chapters 9 and 10.

Questions for Further Discussion

- To what extent are the 'new' social divisions a product of the modern welfare state?
- Should social policy analysis welcome a 'politics of identity'?
- Are women more naturally caring than men?

9
Globalizations

- Economies of Knowledge
- Weightless Worlds
- Forever Bursting Bubbles
- Social Policy

Debates about social identity have increasingly had to consider new global contexts (e.g. Touraine, 2000; Parekh, 2008). This is also the case with the other themes of previous chapters.

Despite the international economic and political architectures of post-WW2 reform, *national* autonomy and policymaking persisted. By the 1970s, things were changing. Currencies and exchanges rates floated against one another; offshore trading exploded; information and communication technologies (ICTs) made it easier for financial centres and markets to integrate, eventually flowing together into a powerful torrent of capital and investment. By the 1990s, it was clear the ground was titling and welfare states would only remain upright by understanding and adapting to new circumstances.

What might this imply? Do the market flexibilities of global capitalism require welfare systems to be minimized, privatized and deregulated? Can welfare states more or less continue to perform the roles they have traditionally performed? Are we witnessing the birth of new priorities? What do equality, justice, citizenship, ideology, etc. mean in a global context? Or, is the entire debate about globalization a form of misdirection that obscures more than it reveals?

Chapters 9 and 10 are underpinned by two fundamental questions:

- What constraints and opportunities does globalisation present?
- In what kind of global society do we wish to live?

In response to the first question we first outline some historical developments (pp. 169–73), before exploring they key 'domains' of globalization debates (pp.173–80), investigating the recent financial crisis (pp.180–2) and finally reviewing the possible implications for social policy (pp.182–9).

Economies of Knowledge

Two debates in the 1970s–1980s anticipated much that followed. Both proposed that we were emerging into a new era, one where muscle-power (strength) was being replaced by brain-power (knowledge, problem-solving, data-processing) and voice-power (deliberative interaction, interpersonal skills). For centuries, prosperity and progress had depended upon the extraction and transformation of matter using machinery and tools. Now, it was alleged, societies were becoming 'knowledge societies' dependent upon the manipulation of screens, software, data, codes, signs, symbols and information. Through constant revolutions in microelectronics, the world was becoming lighter, smarter and smaller; no longer held down by the constraints of time and space, this new society was instantaneously present everywhere for everybody. Allied to a resurgence of free market ideas, discussions about globalization remain haunted by these earlier speculations.

Post-industrialism

The welfare state was a child of the industrial era. The growth of industrialism in the nineteenth century gave rise to social problems that demanded collective remedies and a labour movement that demanded substantial changes in industrial capitalism. Social and economic changes over the last 30 years have magnified to a point where few now describe western nations as industrial societies *per se*. In retrospect, we can see that the impetus for these changes was industrialism itself. As productivity increases and as machinery becomes more sophisticated and computerized, so the need for labour wanes. The post-war era of full employment came to an end and the economy began to 'de-materialize' as large smokestack industries disappeared or reorganized.

Bell (1973) alleged that just as agricultural society had given way to industrial society so, now, industrial society was giving way to a post-industrial one. The key feature of post-industrialism is employment in service sectors rather than manufacturing and production. This does not mean that manufacturing disappears (any more than agriculture vanished during the industrial era), but it does mean that physical commodities become less socially and economically important than the creation, exchange and processing of knowledge and information. Mining, shipbuilding and engineering have been outstripped by the growth of education, tourism, banking and financial services. And as information becomes central, those unskilled in using it can find themselves locked into the periphery of the labour market. Indeed, some announced the immanent demise of the industrial classes (see Chapter 6). The working-class would be replaced by new social movements dedicated to alternative forms of critique, organisation and change; while the industrial ruling class (tycoons like Carnegie and Morgan) would be replaced by the 'symbolic analysts' of the managerial middle-class (exemplified by Bill Gates).

For the welfare state, post-industrialism was thought to bring threats *and* opportunities (Esping-Andersen, 1999). It was a threat in so far as class structures looked set to be replaced by a more individualistic and market-dominated society; yet it was an opportunity, because welfare institutions already embodied the service ethic that post-industrialism seems to require.

The thesis of post-industrialism can be criticized (also Kumar, 1995: 31–5). Firstly, it perhaps over-estimates the degree of change that western societies have undergone. The post-industrial literature was often replete with an awful lot of starry-eyed futurism, wishful thinking, hyperbolic claims and non-verifiable hypotheses. Secondly, therefore, the service sector is perhaps too flimsy a peg upon which to hang a socioeconomic revolution. Services have long been an essential part of industrial capitalism, with employment in the manufacturing sector always being relatively modest. Thirdly, some post-industrialists were too quick to herald the death of the class system. The 'knowledge industries' have grown, yet it could be argued that this has *reinforced* class divisions. Finally, then, work practices for the poorest have not altered considerably: contemporary forms of scientific management (see below) are more than evident in call centres, recruitment agencies and fast-food restaurants (Ritzer, 2008). If such criticisms hold then the implications for the welfare state are not as significant as post-industrialists assume.

Post-Fordism

Fordism refers to mass production, large economies of scale and hierarchical workplace structures. The Chaplinesque assembly-line captures this notion of mass production, where the worker is a cog in a machine, an appendage of repetitive processes who is alienated from himself, his colleagues and his work, taking his orders from distant managers and overseen by aggressive supervisors. At the heart of Fordism is the scientific management of F. W. Taylor. Taylor took a typical job, such as the assembly of a car, identified its component parts and worked out how long it would take to complete each part at an efficient rate of production. The productivity of a plant could therefore be measured according to this rate and workplace practices suitably altered. However, this assembly-line process is inflexible and the commodities produced are identical to one another. Consequently, consumers must alter their tastes to suit the supply (as Henry Ford allegedly put it: 'you can have any colour car you want, so long as it's black'). Therefore, Fordism also implies mass consumption where demands are standardized, easily manipulated through the fashion and entertainment industries, and where sustaining the level of demand requires high social expenditure, full employment and a state-maintained compromise between employers and organized labour: corporatism.

According to some, Fordism began to break down in the 1970s (Amin, 1994). Fordist practices could no longer guarantee increases in productivity: as technology became more sophisticated, so the inflexible assembly-line became a counter-productive obstacle to workers' creativity and team-working. At the same time, consumers also became more sophisticated and were less willing to suppress their individual desires. Post-Fordism therefore refers to flexibility in production, or 'flexible specialisation' (Piore & Sabel, 1984), and diversification in consumption. Single-function machinery has been replaced by computerized systems that can be reprogrammed; vertical hierarchies have been replaced by horizontal networks as 'economies of scale' (centralized factories) become 'economies of scope' (decentralized sub-units to which work is contracted out); assembly-line practices have been replaced by team-working, with workers being treated less as supervisees to be ordered around and more as autonomous experts; a 9-to-5 culture has been replaced by flexi-time; mass marketing has been replaced by niche marketing, where supply is tailored to specialized demand; mass warehousing has been replaced by 'just-in-time' forms of storage and delivery. Furthermore, consumption becomes an even more vital part of society. Since people are less likely than before to follow single trends and fashions, shops and showrooms grow in number and diversity. Consumerism is less about 'keeping up with the Joneses' and more about being distinct from the Joneses. Following a crowd is less important than mixing styles according to one's own tastes and judgements.

However, many of the objections to the post-industrialist thesis apply here too (also Kumar, 1995: 54–65). Post-Fordism can be criticized as deterministic (concerned with technology and political economy) and too ready to exaggerate the changes that have occurred. Post-Fordists can also be accused of incorporating the ideology of managerialism into its theoretical accounts: e.g. 'flexicurity' (a combination of flexibility and security) may mask what continue to be hire-and-fire practices.

Some post-Fordist ideas are more critical, though. Jessop (2002) argues that the Keynesian welfare national state (KWNS) has gradually been replaced by a Schumpeterian workfare postnational regime (SWPR).

The KWNS prevailed for at least 30 years after the war and incorporated four dimensions. Firstly, it was Keynesian in so far as it secured the conditions for full employment through demand-side management of the economy. Secondly, it was concerned with welfare by generalizing the norms of mass consumption as well as the specific forms of collective consumption that perpetuated Fordist growth patterns. Economic and social policies were therefore closely attached to citizenship rights. Thirdly, the KWNS was predominantly national in that even local, regional and international states were subordinated to national economic and social priorities. Finally, the KWNS was statist in so far as the mixed economy was shaped and guided by state institutions. Jessop is at pains to acknowledge that the KWNS came in the diversity of shapes and sizes that comparative analysis (Esping-Andersen, 1990) has categorized as social democratic, conservative and liberal. Therefore, the transformation of the KWNS has taken a variety of paths towards a variety of destinations, all of which, though, share some basic features.

Therefore, the SWPR also incorporates four dimensions. Firstly, it is Schumpeterian rather than Keynesian. Schumpeter (1883–1946) famously described the capitalist economy as consisting of gales of 'creative destruction' (Schumpeter, 1992). In a Keynesian economy the aim is long-term macro-economic stability, whereas a Schumpeterian economy is characterized by a permanent revolution of innovation and flexibility in the name of competitiveness. Economic and labour market instability therefore becomes the organizing principle. Secondly, the SWPR is concerned with workfare rather than welfare, in that social policy is subordinated to the demands of competitive flexibility. The needs and rights of individuals take second place to the needs and interests of business. Social policies become less concerned with demand-side interventions and more with improving the supply of labour by equating 'citizens' with 'workers' and re-making the latter into dynamic, risk-taking entrepreneurs who embrace market insecurity. Those at the bottom of the income ladder can then be assisted with workfare policies, where claiming benefits becomes a highly conditional exercise (King, 1999). Thirdly, policies become postnational, as the nation-state is 'hollowed out' in three directions: upwards towards international agencies and inter-state forums, downwards towards regional and local levels and sideways towards cross-border forms of governance. Finally, the state enters into a variety of partnerships with the private and voluntary sectors in a 'mixed economy' of social welfare governance.

Weightless Worlds

As post-industrial and post-Fordist practices spread around the world, so they inspired and influenced debates about globalization.

We should be wary of the term, of course. Some cite the extent to which 'we have been here before' and warn against simplistic descriptions (Hirst and Thompson, 1999). Between the 1870s and World War One, we also experienced a series of economic, political and technological leaps. By over-emphasizing the extent to which we have broken with the past, globalisation debates potentially divert attention away from previous, successful attempts to tame global capital.

Interpretations

In any event, there are two strands to the debate: 'what is globalization?' and 'how should we respond to globalization?'

An entire book could be filled with the many definitions which have been offered but, at its basic, globalisation is both process (to globalize) and outcome (what the processes result in). Globalisation is here taken to refer to the increasing worldwide interdependency of individuals, localities, public and private organisations, economies, nations and socio-cultures. Held & McGrew (2007: 2–4) argue that globalisation involves the

- stretching of social relations as social, political and economic frontiers become porous, such that decisions, events and activities in one part of the world can have drastic and rapid effects elsewhere;
- magnification of interconnectedness as it becomes easier to trade, communicate and interrelate with those who are geographically distant;
- accelerating pace of transborder interactions and processes with ideas, news, goods, information, capital and technology moving around the world fluidly;
- deepening enmeshment of the local and the global, leading to a collective awareness of shared global spaces and problems.

Thus, while it was once the case that events happened and widespread knowledge of those events occurred subsequently (hours, days or even weeks later), the terrorist attacks on 9/11 were witnessed by hundreds of millions worldwide in 'real time'

So, terms like 'social' and 'national', 'centre' and 'periphery' become less relevant. In previous eras it was specific places (firms, cities, institutions, countries, etc.), or 'nodes', which defined the lines of relation between them. But with increased global interdependency, *the relations define the nodes.* Paradoxically, 'centres' take root anywhere and everywhere, becoming transitory points of relative stability where borders, planes and fields intersect. Space becomes detached from place.

Yet even venturing this far into definitions is problematic. There are those who argue that it is only reasonable to discuss globalization with specific reference to capitalism or the USA, neither of which appear in Held and McGrew's conceptualisation. What we have, then, is fundamental disagreement. To a large extent, this is due to the highly political nature of the debate. Rather than asking 'what is globalisation?' and then deciding whether it is desirable, people's opinions of what is desirable often shapes their views about the nature, causes and effects of globalization. Such considerations also affect the 'when?' (Robertson, 1992). Those who interpret globalisation positively are more likely to see it as a stage of post-imperialism, e.g. Giddens (1999: 9–19) identifies a rupture with the period before the advent of communication technology and infrastructures. But those who interpret globalisation as a new phase *of* imperialism tend to see it as being centuries old (Wallerstein, 1974).

At the risk of over-simplifying, we can identify three basic positions. The first is held by those who are in favour of globalisation: the *sponsors* (Wolf, 2005). Sponsors regard globalisation as the central truth of our time and they embrace it as both necessary and desirable. According to Tony Blair (2005):

> I hear people say we have to stop and debate globalisation. You might as well debate whether autumn should follow summer. They're not debating it in China and India. They are seizing its possibilities....In the era of rapid globalisation, there is no mystery about what works: an open, liberal economy, prepared constantly to change to remain competitive...Because the dam holding back the global economy burst years ago. The competition can't be shut out; it can only be beaten...

Friedman (2005) regards globalisation as a flattening of the world onto a single plane through the democratisation of markets and technology within an economic liberalism of decentralized political and economic power. Norberg (2003) worries that well-intentioned but wrong-headed obstructionism by the 'antiglobalisation movement' might wreck progress, while Bardhan (2006) argues that trade barriers need to be dismantled (especially in the developed world) for rates of global poverty to be reduced. Sponsors are typically those on the political right, who champion free markets, or those like Blair who believe that because 'there is no alternative' the Centre-Left must adapt itself to the realities of global capitalism.

The second position is held by those who are more sceptical and ambivalent about globalisation: the *reformists*. The reformists welcome some aspects of globalisation but not others. Bhagwati (2004) and Taleb (2008) are sponsors who make some concessions to the reformists. They both defend economic globalisation but are more attuned than Friedman and Norberg to its disadvantages and argue that better political management is needed to share the benefits more equitably.

As we move further into the reformists' camp we find those who identify globalisation as often exacerbating imbalances of power (Bauman, 1998: Ch.4). Affluent countries benefit more than poorer ones, capital more than labour, men more than women. Yet, for reformists, globalisation is ambivalent and Janus-faced. For Elliott and Lemert (2006: 12–15) social life is characterized by a 'new individualism', a strange admixture where the bad (anguish, anxiety) and the good (self-fulfilment, self-expression) morph into one another. For example, fears about global risks (epidemics, terrorism, etc.) can inspire new forms of collective action. Environmentalists highlight the destructive effects of consumption, international trade and deregulation but, in so far as Green ideas spread around the world, with people recognizing themselves as common inhabitants of a rather finite planet, they are also *pro*-globalisation. Reformists therefore tend to occupy any number of ideological positions but they stress the importance of *politics* and government intervention, whereas the sponsors are more likely to be economic determinists.

Finally, there are the *resisters* who argue that in recent decades capitalism has been deregulated while the non-market parts of society have become *re-regulated* in order to ensure the dominance of capital, producing a 'global apartheid' (Hardt & Negri, 2006: 160–79). Klein (2007: 14) argues that we are in the midst of an 'ideological crusade' where everything is being privatized, even wars and disaster-relief, and offered up to the God of profit-making. What we ought to be focusing upon is US-driven capitalism and militarism rather than some anonymous, agent-less force called globalisation. Resisters are therefore more likely than the reformists to highlight the negativities of contemporary capitalism. Bourdieu (1999) interprets globalisation as the intellectual colonisation of social consciousness, a hegemonic war waged by those who want to sweep away the few gains made by the poor and dispossessed in the middle decades of the twentieth century: it is the latest stage of a counter-reaction to the welfare state capitalism of the post-war era. Capital has become more dominant and mobile due to the power of Western governments (principally America) and multinationals who then invoke globalisation as a means of neutralizing criticism and resistance ('You might as well debate whether autumn should follow summer ...'). Therefore, 'globalisation' is a rhetorical sleight-of-hand, a means by which we interpret the consequences of our actions as processes over which we can have no control.

This account skips over many nuances and subtleties. For example, rather than labelling them as an *anti*-globalization movement (since most are in favour of global action to oppose economic liberalism), resisters typically belong to a series of 'global justice movements' incorporating a wide spectrum of interests and perspectives (Monbiot, 2003).[1] Such considerations bring us to the question of how and why we should respond to globalisation.

Economies

Economic globalisation encompasses six areas: finance, trade, multinationals, investment, labour and information.

Few doubt that flows of financial globalisation are truly global. By the mid-2000s $6 trillion, or about 12% of world GDP, was flowing through the foreign exchanges every day – about $4 billion every minute (Lechner, 2009: 93)! But this is not money as you and I understand it. This is 'virtual money'; figures on a screen that appear and disappear in a blur. Computers allow real-time transactions, the instantaneous flow of capital, and the proliferation of international bonds, portfolio investments and financial instruments. London, Tokyo and New York effectively merge into a single financial sector, dispersed across a number of geographical regions, which constitutes a global capital market, a frictionless economy.

Trade has also expanded rapidly. 1995 saw the creation of the World Trade Organisation (WTO), a powerful institution that can enforce the deregulation of protectionist measures. According to some, this created a global trading system, albeit one often centred on the most powerful blocs, with poorer countries frequently shut out of the world markets through any number of subtle measures. (Affluent countries preach the virtues of free trade more often than they practice it.) Resisters also point out that, as overseen by the WTO, globalized trade is undermining domestic legislation concerning social and environmental protection. By 2006, international trade had risen to $14 trillion per annum, and because it has been generally growing faster than GDP many countries are now dependent upon it (Lechner, 2009: 92).

Multinational corporations (MNCs) have bases in more than two countries, with some (especially Internet companies) being geographically rootless and mobile. MNCs have an internationalized management, an internationalized labour force, internationalized consumer markets and no specific national identification. MNCs account for 10% of the world's Gross National Product and a third of world exports (Ritzer, 2010: 199). So, they are often richer than many medium-sized countries and critics worry about their ability to play countries off against one another: 'lower your taxes and your wage costs or we'll invest somewhere else'. A great deal on international trade involves one part of a MNC trading with another part. Thus, many countries are dependent upon the investment and trade they bring.

Foreign direct investment (FDI) occurs when an investor owns and/or invests in an enterprise located in a country other than that of the investor (Held & McGrew, 2007: 89–93). FDI therefore represents the 'trans-nationalisation' of production and services. It has grown throughout the post-war period, reaching a peak ($1.4 trillion) at the turn of the century with the value of mergers and acquisitions subsequently growing to $3.9 trillion. Investment has traditionally clustered around the USA, Europe and Japan but has been gradually spreading out, encompassing more of the newly emerging economies.

Flows of labour, unsurprisingly, are fairly immobile compared to the above, but they have been increasing in recent years. By 2005, migrants totalled about 190 million or 3% of the global workforce (Held & McGrew, 2007: 95–6). With most migration occurring from South to North, 9% of the workforce of developed countries are now migrants, though they are concentrated in relatively few countries and cities. That said, it could be claimed that there is an international division of labour with companies able to relocate to low-wage countries with obvious implications for employment levels in developed nations. The latter then have to 'sell' the high-skilled, competitive flexibility of their workforces, through supply-side measures emphasizing education, training, multi-skilling and various wage/tax subsidies, in order to retain investment capital. Critics, though, insist that because firms are actually far less mobile than sometimes feared a competitive 'race to the bottom' of tax rates and labour regulations has not occurred.

Information Societies

Much of the world has experienced the informatization of economies and social relations (Fitzpatrick, 2005: ch. 5).

- The 'digital economy' helps to drive much of the 'real economy'. Online shopping and advertising are obvious examples. Even in the late 1990s many familiar high-street names had no web-presence. Today, this is no longer the case.
- There is also a sense in which the distinction between digital and real economies has faded with the emergence of new economic conditions and possibilities.
- It is also the case that the digital can *hide* the real. For all their online pizzazz, some big companies have a poor record when it comes to employee rights and trade union recognition.

Such changes have helped to reconfigure economy and society. Children are now exposed to more commercialisation than ever, possibly leading to emotional stresses and unrealistic expectations with damaging long-term effects. Social exchanges more generally are thus increasingly mediated through ICTs – social networking, new media, etc. – which can have immediate and drastic consequences in multiple locations across the social field. The Internet has revolutionized work, communication, social identities and associations, consumption and leisure to an extent that few can have anticipated even in the 1990s. New trends supersede one another at an ever-accelerating pace. It took years for email and blogging to become established and just months for texting and tweeting to proliferate. In the coming years, the distinction between computers, televisions and phones will fade, wireless applications will develop and 3-D technology – not limited to entertainment – will evolve via 'autostereoscopic' screens. For these and other reasons, some have long proffered the idea that ours have become 'information societies'.

According to Castells (2000, 2009a, 2009b), we now live in a network society. The Industrial Age was organized primarily around structures which produced and distributed energy, whereas the Information Age is organized primarily around flows of programmes, codes, binary digits and symbols. The former was hierarchical, bureaucratic and organized 'vertically', whereas the latter involves decentralized webs, networks and flexible, 'horizontal' forms of organisation. The 'new economy' is characterized by new forms of work and employment patterns. Part-time work, temporary work, self-employment, zero-hour contracts, informal or semi-formal labour arrangements, and relentless occupational mobility, are key features of the new labour market. The archetypal worker of the industrial age was 'organization man', a manual (male) labourer who expected to have a job for life and was resistant to change.

In the network society the archetype is a 'flexible woman', someone capable of multitasking, retraining and receptive to irregular patterns of work. The feminine qualities of flexibility, communication, emotional labour and people skills have replaced physical force and strength.

Polities

There are two key questions here. To what extent has the nation-state driven forward the processes of globalisation? Is the nation-state becoming obsolete?

The post-war decades were characterized by relative stability on the currency markets. The Bretton Woods System (BWS) fixed the exchange rates of all currencies to that of the dollar which, in turn, was fixed to the price of gold. Controls on capital ensured that financial flows were regulated and the IMF policed the system to avoid the uncontrolled and competitive devaluations of the interwar period. The BWS was the backbone of the post-war welfare state. By giving domestic objectives priority over global finance, it helped nations to maintain high levels of employment and growth. Why, then, did the BWS break down in the early 1970s (see Frieden, 2006: 339–60)?

Those such as Gowan (1999) draw attention to the deliberate actions of the USA. The Nixon administration felt that the BWS gave too much control to debtor nations, at the expense of America. Therefore, better to deregulate the international system, so that currencies would 'float' against one another, and allow American institutions to regain control both directly (through lending institutions) and indirectly (through the IMF). An alternative explanation suggests that it was the growth of eurocurrency markets (that could evade capital controls) in the 1960s that placed a fatal strain on the BWS. The US dollar came under pressure and Nixon had little choice but to end its convertibility into gold. The coffin lid of the BWS was then firmly nailed down by (1) the quadrupling of oil prices in the 1970s, thus giving international banks huge surpluses with which to fuel the money markets, and (2) the explosion in the financial markets in the 1980s.

So, to what extent has the nation-state driven forward the processes of globalisation? If globalisation is interpreted as possessing its own logic, e.g. technological innovations driving more technological innovations, then it may be that the nation-state has been overwhelmed by forces beyond its control (Ohmae, 1995). Reformists and resisters, however, insist that globalisation is, in large part, a consequence (partly intended and partly unintended) of the most powerful nation-states attempting to consolidate their power through liberalisation and deregulation (Harvey, 2006).

Such arguments also determine responses to the next question: is the nation-state becoming obsolete? Sponsors like Friedman (2005) insist that national borders are increasingly redundant in the face of the financial, trade and investment flows we examined above. With the growth of NGOs, for instance, political decision-making now has to be far more decentralized than in the past, so that the nation-state is becoming just another political actor on a borderless and increasingly crowded global stage. Hence the popularity of terms like 'governance'. By contrast, critics allege that political sovereignty may have *changed* but only because globalisation operates through and within *national* spaces (Sassen, 2007). Decision-making is now mediated horizontally across a range of interested parties as top-down, command-and-control models have faded. But, if anything, financial globalisation has *enhanced* the power of nation-states, e.g. the WTO was the product of several years of careful negotiation between governments eager to reap the benefits of the very globalisation they were encouraging.

Therefore, 'political globalisation' can imply different things to different commentators. For sponsors, it can mean nothing more than the regulation of global markets by the financial police of the IMF and the WTO. But for reformists and resisters, political globalisation has to imply governments regaining the control of markets which so many of them have ceded in recent decades.

Forever Bursting Bubbles

Much is at stake in these debates, given the implications recent events may have for the next few years. There is no space here to do more than summarize the 'Great Recession' of 2007–09 (Sorkin, 2009; Gamble, 2009).

Events began in the US housing boom. Following years of prices rising so high that many houses were overvalued – fooling owners into believing they were richer than they were – the real estate bubble began to deflate in 2006–07, throwing millions of middle-class families into negative equity. What this also exposed, was the vulnerability of the 'sub-prime' market where many low-income households found themselves unable to afford rising mortgage payments. Many households began to default, leading to foreclosures and, in a depressed market, to a large surplus of vacant homes that the banks could not now sell.

The subsequent losses triggered a crisis in the wider banking system. One problem was that American banks had sold mortgage 'bundles' to other banks and financial institutions throughout the world. As the housing crisis unfolded, it became clear that many of the debts thereby purchased were 'toxic', or valueless. Banks' assets tumbled and, with many American institutions owning large parts of non-American ones, and *vice versa*, the crisis went global. The result was the greatest run on the banks since the 1929 crash. The effects were especially pernicious in the 'shadow' banks, those institutions which act like banks but are not subject to the same regulations and guarantees (Krugman, 2008: 158–62). Lending to businesses, consumers and homeowners collapsed, as did stock markets. Having been the 'world's consumer', the USA could no longer purchase other nations' products and, if they could not sell their goods, they in turn could not earn the money to buy American ones. Causes and effects ricocheted back and forth and the first full-blown depression in 80 years loomed for many countries.

The initial response by governments was belated and inadequate. Conventional logic said that once interest rates had fallen, people would have incentives to borrow, invest and spend again. But this didn't happen. Confidence had plummeted so low that, following the age-old lesson that economic perceptions create economic realities, orthodox policies no longer worked. With economies facing meltdown, and in a world gone topsy-turvy, governments turned to some old foes. Keynesian demand management came back into fashion. 'Quantitative easing' was a fancy term for printing money and launching it into the economy in order to kick-start activity. And nationalisation reappeared. With banks freefalling, many were taken into public ownership and given huge injections of resources to steady nerves and underwrite reserves.

So had Keynes and Marx saved capitalism from itself? Not quite. This was crisis management. Depression (to date) has been avoided but any hopes that the a few *mea culpas* would presage a turn away from free market globalisation have so far been dashed. By 2010, European governments were insisting that unless high levels of public debt were reduced quickly, by slashing public spending, economic recovery would falter.

This is *what* happened but *why* did it happen? As always, it depends on who you consult (Gamble, 2009: 143–63).

For 'unrepentant sponsors', it was the state which failed (Gamble, 2009: 145–7). By being forced to lend to low-income households, banks had been exposed to the effects of a housing downturn that they could have avoided otherwise. Among the more 'repentant sponsors' some converts are more reluctant than others. Stelzer (2008: 22) recommends we adapt to a 'new capitalism' whose free markets would constitute an 'only slightly less invisible hand'. By contrast, Posner (2009) argues that the advocates of free market capitalism – like himself – got it wrong. Letting markets rip created a space for excessive risk-taking, selfishness and short-termism. A re-regulation of the financial system, akin to that performed in the earlier part of the twentieth century, is therefore warranted.

Reformists and those on the Centre-Left blame economic liberalism and advocate new regulations (Krugman, 2008: ch. 10; Stiglitz, 2010). This implies three basic elements. Firstly, a rejection of the free market, supply-side orthodoxy which got us into this mess by placing too much faith in (a) financial services, (b) rising levels of debt disguised as real wealth, (c) reckless, deregulated decision-making and (d) risky financial instruments. This requires a return to the Keynesian emphasis on demand-side management, public investment and firmer supervision of powerful institutions. Secondly, there needs to be significant banking reform. Bonuses should be rewards for genuine merit; banks 'too big to fail' should be broken up, with commercial banking separated from investment banking, for instance; and there needs to be a new system of insurance, to avoid future bailouts, along with a new ethos of social responsibility. Thirdly, a new global financial system is required, one which stimulates global demand, restricts reckless movements of financial capital, e.g. through a 'Tobin tax' on speculation, and ensures that there is a greater balance between debtor and creditor nations.

Further to the Left, resisters support re-regulation but go further than Keynesians (Harvey, 2010: ch. 8; Callinicos, 2010: 50–83). Booms and busts are endemic to capitalism; social democracy just spreads the pain around a bit more fairly. The system failed, they say, because insufficient economic demand is ultimately due to unfair and unequal distributions of social resources. Basically, as the post-war balance between labour to capital was undermined, with power shifting to the latter, most working people have too little to spend (due to relative cuts in benefits, wages and pensions) and so have sought cheap forms of credit that helped to fuel the debt boom. Furthermore, economic liberal deregulation liberated the corruption, fraud and mismanagement which is at the heart of capitalist exploitation.[2]

Resisters call for democratisation of the economy and a rebalancing of social distributions (Callinicos, 2010: 133–43). Like Harvey, Hardt and Negri (2006: 219–27, 290–306) identify a potential 'rippling effect' where those protest groups resisting one part of the capitalist system learn from others and, in turn, pass on their experiences to further groups. Waves of resistance which are both diverse *and* unifying thus begin to build and swell around the global social fabric. Many agree with Fraser (2008) that everyone should be able to participate in the systems and decision-making processes which govern their lives, requiring new forms of democratic representation, accountability and legitimacy. This might include a global constitution and parliamentary elections; what Held (1995) calls a 'cosmopolitan order'. Genuine democratic representation would therefore challenge the hegemony of the affluent and economic ideologies obsessed with profit.

Whatever the merits of the various arguments, what the 2007–09 crisis has done is left social policy in a less certain position that it has been in for decades.

Social Policy

The post-industrial and post-Fordist changes we reviewed above, provide many opportunities. Flexibility, for instance, can be defined in terms of a family-friendly, work-life balance rather than a corporate, hire-and-fire culture.

Still, much of the literature underscores the huge challenges presented on pp. 169–80 (Lister, 2010: 96–103):

- As labour markets fragment, it becomes harder for many to earn the entitlements of social insurance benefits.
- Women enter the labour force in greater numbers, with implications for equal pay, childcare, flexible hours, maternity leave, etc.
- Core/periphery divisions and insecurities make it harder to preserve universalist, redistributive services.
- Disciplinarian measures increase to curb social problems caused by 'peripheral citizens'.
- Welfare reforms are judged by their contributions to economic competitiveness and human capital, with 'activation' policies becoming central.
- Social policies must themselves become competitive so that international capital has incentives to invest.
- In an increasingly consumerist society, models of centralized, collectivist, standardized delivery are replaced by more personalised, marketized and customer-oriented forms of welfare organisation and delivery, including more financial and administrative input by the private sector.

The implications of living in an information society (pp. 178–9) are also much debated (Castells & Himanen, 2002). Families and networks, to take one example, have altered with the rise of social networking. Individuals, especially young people, are more connected than ever; but new risks have been introduced into the home through online forms of bullying, stalking and grooming. Interactive technologies enable new relationships to form between welfare producers and clients since physical presence matters less. Within education, distance-learning becomes easier. Within healthcare, diagnoses and even treatment can occur at a distance. But dangers lurk here too. Should you Google to find out what that pain might be? Should a doctor respond sympathetically to your self-diagnosis or condemn the increasing numbers of the 'worried well'?

Much commentary concerns the extent to which new forms of exclusion are emerging (Chen & Wellman, 2005). There are 'digital divides' *between* countries and *within* them. Those who are impoverished in terms of income, wealth, geography, etc. tend to have less access to new technologies and are more likely to experience the disadvantages of technological innovation (Patterson & Wilson, 2000: 85). It takes resources to keep up to date with the latest hardware and software, and those without ready access can miss important forms of information and opportunity. Thus, ICTs increasingly mediate the social relations within which they are embedded. They may exacerbate social problems or alleviate them, but rather than such effects inhering within the technology themselves, they are the result of political decisions and public management (Selwyn, 2004). Nations convinced that 'inequality is good for you', will go one way while egalitarian countries will go another.

Take the social security system (Henman & Marston, 2008). Technology makes it easier to apply for benefits, receive information and search for jobs. It is tempting to view this as a brave new world of user empowerment where bureaucracies subside into flat networks and administrative systems become frictionless, equitable encounters between clients and their advisors. But set against a background where benefit claimants have long been objects of public and political suspicion and hostility, the reality may be less favourable. Technology makes it easier for authorities to control and survey the habits and movements of claimants, distracting attention away from unjust social circumstances.

Before the crash

There are, therefore, many strands to the literature on globalisation and social policy (George & Wilding, 2002; George & Page, 2004; Deacon, 2007; Yeates, 2008):

- What effects are international organisations having on the principles, funding, organisation and delivery of welfare?
- How are social policies being influenced by globalisation 'from above' and 'from below'?
- What new forms of inter-state policy networks, agencies, coalitions and communities are forming?
- To what extent do nations possess autonomy over their welfare services?
- To what extent have transnational systems of welfare support, regulation and law begun to emerge?
- What are the prospects for social rights, poverty-alleviation and redistribution in a global context?

We addressed aspects of global citizenship in Chapter 4, and do so again in Chapter 10, but many of these questions relate to the issue of 'global governance'.

It was noted in pp. 92–3 that government now works 'at a distance', often in conjunction with other states and intergovernmental agencies, where policy processes and outcomes are mediated through a range of multiple sectors and dimensions. Much of this obviously involves global imperatives and actors. Studying social policies now means taking into account the multiple institutional levels into which national governments are integrated: supranational organisations (UN, WTO, IMF, OECD, World Bank), regional associations (EU, ASEAN, NAFTA) and sub-national agencies, plus NGOs, social movements and 'civil society' activists. A key question is: does global governance drive a convergence in national welfare systems? Two basic perspectives have been proposed.

Following the revival of free market politics in the 1980s, it was not uncommon for some to predict that, in a global context, welfare states would become characterized by selectivist, minimal safety-nets (Graham, 1994; World Bank, 1994). This is a kind of 'budget airlines' model where everyone receives minimal state provision, but if you want more-than-minimal services you have to pay for them yourself. In a globalizing economy, where are companies likely to invest? In you with your high taxes, restrictive regulations and generous benefits, or in your neighbour who offers tax breaks, light regulations and a de-unionized, disciplined workforce? Sponsors continue to argue that countries should slash social expenditure, privatize their welfare systems, reduce taxes, emphasize private sector investment, ensure wages are competitive and prevent welfare dependency (Norberg, 2003: 97). Does this mean that the social democratic welfare state is finished?

Not according to the evidence. In fact, despite a series of economic and political pressures, welfare states continue to embody a great deal of diversity and even expansion (Pierson, 2001; Navarro et al., 2004; Starke et al., 2008). One standard explanation for this goes by the name of 'path dependency' (Pierson 2004). This is the hypothesis that policies are historically and institutionally embedded. Global actors and firms are not able to swoop in and change everything because of the existing socio-political culture and because many interest-groups (including political parties and trade unions) will actively resist change. The fact that MakeProfits plc wants to buy and run your local school does not mean that the legislative framework, nor the actions of councillors, teachers, parents and other local stakeholders, will let them. Thus, policy regimes are set on 'sticky' evolutionary paths which are difficult to overturn. Social democratic systems may come under pressure but the evidence suggests that they have held up pretty well. The implication is that globalisation is not just 'one thing'. Instead, globalisation is adaptive, moulding itself whenever necessary to political systems, cultural ways of life and historical trajectories.

However, other commentators doubt that institutional contexts are so resistant to change (Dobrowolsky & Saint-Martin, 2005). The thesis of 'path departure' (or path-deviation) identifies various factors which drive welfare state change (Streeck & Thelen, 2005). The transfer of ideas from nation to nation might lead to a convergence in policymaking approaches. Furthermore, sustained ideological pressures from supranational organisations may erode resistance over time, overwhelming the ability of political and cultural contexts to resist. For instance, state welfare services may be threatened by the WTO's General Agreement on Trade in Services, which views state provision as a monopolistic restriction on private companies (Holden, 2008: 115–7). The ideology of free trade here demands the *de facto* privatisation of welfare systems. This is especially the case in post-communist nations where alternative welfare models are thin on the ground.

What then are the prospects for social democratic welfare in an era of global governance? Path-dependent and path-departure perspectives both argue against the economic determinism of the sponsors.[3] If welfare states are path-dependent, then social democracy does not risk extinction due to its own historical legacies, institutional stickiness and cultural particularities. However, this might also suggest that the prospects for a 'global social democracy' are fragile since other socio-political systems are unlikely to accommodate such developments. But if the path-departure argument is accurate then politics matters, not because of inherited legacies but because of ongoing battles and struggles. Social democracies are as strong and enduring as the willingness of their advocates to fight for what they believe.

After the crash

At which point we come back to the implications of recent events. At the risk of indulging in speculation, we can identify five possibilities.

Firstly, it may be that the sponsors will carry the day. The assumption here is that while some corrections to the financial system are needed a return to Keynesianism is unrealistic and the prospects for a global social democracy doubly so. No, the basic logic hasn't altered. Those countries which integrated themselves into the global economy have prospered the most, especially India and China. Despite occasional bouts of naive hyperbole, few have ever doubted that free market economies will hit occasional bumps in the road. 2007–09 was an admittedly large bump but this was an unprecedented, once-a-century confluence of economic accidents. Free markets bring prosperity for all while respecting the freedoms, choices and responsibilities of individuals and firms.

Therefore, the above prescriptions for social policy reform – privatization, deregulation and commodification – remain compelling. The European social model becomes weaker and weaker as power shifts towards the dynamic Asian economies. No wonder that European governments have recognized the need to slash social expenditure. According to sponsors, governments should facilitate the private welfare market and maintain means-tested safety-nets, but should divest themselves of the role of welfare providers.

Secondly, if reformists are correct it may be that some form of new, global regulatory framework *can* be constructed because it *has* to be. 2007–09 was not a unique, unpredictable event but the explosion of pressures that had been building up since the deregulatory mania of the 1980s. The Asian crisis of 1997–98 should have been a wake-up call, but continuing to sleep seemed easier. Western governments had allowed their economies to float on a sea of bubbles which were inflated by overvaluations and unsustainable levels of private borrowing. Because the illusion of good times was strong, vote-grabbing parties were unwilling to break the spell or challenge the ideological insistence that everyone can prosper through win-win free markets. But these self-deceptions could not continue indefinitely and the debts that had been masquerading as real wealth had to come down. Because we were unwilling to deflate the bubbles in a fair, managed way, the crisis which hit almost disabled western societies. Those on the Right complaining about high debt-to-GDP ratios conveniently obscure what might have happened if action had not been taken. Unless we reduce public debt in a sensible, equitable fashion we might be left with decimated public sectors, rising poverty and inequality, long-term stagnation and an inability to deal with the challenges – especially environmental ones – which lie ahead. And unless we re-regulate the systems and ethical cultures of financial management, then we may find ourselves heading for equally damaging recessions in the not-too-distant future. Rules which allow limited forms of protectionism and capital controls can be envisaged.

We need state welfare more than ever, therefore (Stiglitz, 2010: 196–205). Welfare expenditure:

- keeps levels of demand buoyant;
- facilitates economic stability;
- encourages savings and future security (through properly-funded retirement schemes);
- helps to educate and train the workforce;
- compensates for market failures, helping people back into work without experiencing the worst effects of unemployment;
- reduces inequalities (boosting consumption, because the poorest are more likely to spend money, and so creating jobs) and protects the most vulnerable.

The economic context of state welfare has changed, of course. The top-down, corporatist model cannot be recreated, but employee share ownership schemes, or some alternative, can give people a stake in their workplaces, so that individualisation and competition are counterbalanced by cooperation and participative belonging. Having re-experienced 1929, we now need to avoid a repeat of the 1930s by re-creating a global architecture that rejects the excesses of the last 30 years. We can do it because we have done it before.

Thirdly, resisters seek change on a number of fronts (Ritzer, 2010: Ch.16). The recent crisis was not a localized phenomenon, created by a few bad decisions. It was a result of a political-economic system which places profits before people. Resisters therefore advocate a shift from free trade to fair trade so that the laws governing systems of production, exchange, export and consumption are altered to serve social and ecological ends, demanding something resembling the care ethic mentioned in Chapters 2 and 7. For instance, at present prices often do not reflect a good's true costs and externalities. A way of ensuring that market prices reflect real costs must therefore be found. This means opening up the most powerful economic and political organisations to greater scrutiny and democracy. The 2007–09 crisis was allowed to happen because the most powerful institutions operated in a fog of secrecy. No-one should be allowed to operate unless they transparently meet basic standards. This requires not layers of state bureaucracy but communicative citizens active within a 'global civil society'. Democracy has to regain control of capitalism.

This means that we cannot continue to think of 'social policy' in old ways. If the political-economic system needs to turn away not only from free markets but also from a centrist social democracy then basic notions of social welfare need to change too. It is not desirable, for example, to create jobs which damage the environment. Any global social policy agenda is likely to carry us beyond a traditional concern with healthcare, income protection and education. A stated principle of the World Social Forum has been to encourage experiments in new forms of social provision and communal decision-making. We cannot pin down, therefore, what 'global social policies' might involve because these must be subject to continuous democratic negotiation and contestation.

Fourthly, it may be that we are faced with radical uncertainty and unpredictability. None of the above speculations matter because the future is unknowable. This is something alien to human experience. For most of human history, people could say with some certainty that the future would resemble some version of the present. But over recent decades the future has started rushing towards us with ever-increasing velocity. Any welfare systems we construct may themselves become sources of indeterminacy and insecurity.

Finally, it may be that some combination of the above is likely. For the time being at least, reformists and resisters have a common interest in arguing against those who propose a business-as-usual defence of the last 30 years of deregulatory capitalism. A less complacent, more ambitious response to recent events is capable of uniting a disparate set of ideas. Stiglitz (2010: 192) argues that long-term economic recovery has to involve raising global aggregate demand:

> A broader, longer-term vision – focusing on the plight of the poor and the challenge of global warming – will ensure that there is more than enough demand to absorb all of the world's production capacity.

This takes us into the themes of our tenth and final chapter.

We started with a series of questions. Is globalisation *this* or *that*? Does it do *x* or *y*? What should have become clear is that globalisation is multifaceted. Furthermore, what globalisation is and implies depends upon who you are talking to. Globalisation from the South, for example, is different to globalisation from the North. 'Globalisation' is thus not only a verb and a noun, it is a profoundly contested space, a signifier which expresses doubts and disagreement about where we are, how we got here and where we are going. However, if Stiglitz is even half-right, there are two remaining debates which we need to cover and which are crucial to many of the explorations pursued throughout this book.

Questions for Further Discussion

- To what extent is 'globalization' truly global?
- Does 'economic globalization' bring greater homogeneity or greater diversity?
- To what extent does the 'anti-globalization movement' possess a credible alternative to globalization?
- Who benefits the most from globalization?

10

Global Justice and Environmentalism

- Questions of Global Justice
- The Wellbeing of Nature
- Critiques
- Social Policy

Two questions were posed on p.169:

- What constraints and opportunities does globalization present?
- In what kind of global society do we wish to live?

Chapter 9 ended by quoting Stiglitz who argues that we are faced with two moral issues: the plight of the world's poor and the challenge of global warming. In this chapter, we therefore concentrate upon the second of the above questions.

Questions of Global Justice

Justice has traditionally been discussed in terms of national borders and belonging. What we have rights to, and what we owe to others, being framed by membership of specific social-national communities. This has been true even of those who appealed to universal categories.

For instance, Kant thought of individuals as citizens of a state, subject to the laws made possible by its constitution. The separation of nations could lead to war, yet separateness was better than nations fusing together into a 'universal monarchy'. But Kant did not imagine that national boundaries exhausted the scope of our moral duties. The task was to ensure that the relations between those separate nations was one of 'perpetual peace'. Just as a nation is a community of citizens, so the world is a community of interdependent nations where '...a violation of right on *one* place of the earth is felt in *all*...' (Kant, 1996: 330). A right for a state of nations (or a 'federative union'), governed according to universal laws, is what Kant (1996: 489–92) called a *cosmopolitan right*.

Widespread attention to global ethics and politics would not begin until the twentieth century. In the wake of the Second World War, Auschwitz and

Hiroshima, a range of topics emerged under the heading of 'international justice'. Such theories followed Kant in regarding nation-states as primary. Over the last few decades, though, debates about international justice have been subsumed within those concerning *global* justice (Weinstock, 2007; Pogge, 2008a). Here, the unit and object of study is *humanity as a whole*. Many continue to argue that the interests of humanity are best served through a political ethics which is nation-centred, but the significance of global justice debates is that we are now less confident about this than we once were.

How should we approach the subject?[1] Is global justice simply the global application of familiar notions of social and political justice? Can we take the latter and stretch such ideas across the planet? Or, does a global context fundamentally challenge our thinking? Are we required to revise our basic assumptions, concepts and methods?

This is largely a question about the role of states and nations: the extent to which they remain, and should remain, important. If we view the nation-state as indispensable and/or desirable then, by and large, we are likely to regard global justice as social and political justice 'writ large'. Alternatively, if we interpret the nation-state as an obstacle to justice, then the concept must flee the confines of domestic boundaries to accommodate a wider range of topics. Perhaps global justice even requires us to look beyond the human to the natural environment of which humanity is just one part.

Both options present considerable challenges. For example, because liberalism presumes the equal moral worth of all individuals isn't it obvious that liberals should support a universal ethics which refuses to discriminate on the basis of nationality? Yet, liberals also respect differences and the right to be different. National cultures matter because they matter to the very individuals whose freedoms liberalism wants to defend. Liberalism is therefore subject to a tension between the ideals of universalism and the particularities of national membership, cultural meanings and a sense of belonging, participation and value which is many respects local and tribal. Kant recognized this tension very early on and it remains central to contemporary debates (Habermas, 2008: ch. 10).

Although the picture is rather more complicated, let's preserve this contrast between humanity and the nation-state by examining two influential philosophers.

Singer versus Miller

Singer (1993: 229–46; 2009: 3–12) uses a famous example from applied ethics. Imagine you are walking passed a wood and are late for a job interview. Suddenly, you see a young child fall into a pool and start to drown. No other adult is nearby. If you don't help, the child will die. Doing so, however, will cause you to miss the interview and, because the pond is muddy, ruin your expensive suit. Should you save the child? Surely everyone would answer 'yes'. The cost to you is real but relatively minor compared to the cost to the child should you do nothing.

But now Singer observes that we do, in fact, 'walk by' every day. For the child drowning in the pond is equivalent to those dying in absolute poverty right now, as you read these words. Each of us can save a life at far less cost than a job and a suit. Therefore, just as we would have an obligation to save the drowning child, so we have an obligation to help those in absolute poverty. If we do not intervene – if we let them die – we are morally responsible. For Singer, letting someone die through inaction is as bad as killing them deliberately because the result in both cases is the same: a death you could have avoided had you acted differently.

Yet, how many of us who would save the drowning child fail to fulfil their obligations to the world's poor? There are all sorts of rationalizations we deploy.

- Perhaps our obligations spread outwards in concentric circles, like ripples in a pond becoming weaker and weaker. I should offer *some* help to the world's poor, but our principal obligations are local, owed to family, friends and fellow citizens in the first instance.
- Perhaps I own by money because I have earned it. I might donate some of it as a matter of humanitarianism or charity, but justice is an irrelevant consideration. It is farfetched to suppose that someone thousands of miles away has a *right* to my money. I didn't create world poverty, so why should I have a duty to relieve it?
- You can't help everyone. My assistance would be marginal, given the scale of the problem. Only governments can remedy such dire situations. If I help one person, there will be someone else in need. So am I unjust if I don't give away *all* my money?

But for Singer this is no more convincing than the equivalent justifications used by the person who ignores the drowning child:

- It's not my child, so why should I care? I have an obligation to myself first of all.
- Whether I do or do not help the child is not a question of justice. The child should be supervised by a parent. I don't acquire a duty just because other people have neglected their responsibilities.
- Am I supposed to help everyone who might be in distress? Even the Good Samaritan's help was only a drop in the ocean.

Singer's argument can be criticized. Many moral philosophers have doubted that 'letting die' is morally equivalent to 'killing'. The 'double-effect doctrine' makes a distinction between those consequences I intend and those I can foresee happening but which are *not* intentional

(Fitzpatrick, 2008a: 80–2). If I am racing to save five people from a flood and so do not have the time to stop and rescue you also, then I am permitted to ignore your plight in order to save the greater number. I do not intend your death, I merely foresee it. Your death in this instance is therefore not equivalent to me killing you. There are potentially millions of morally worthwhile actions I am not performing every second of my life. Surely I cannot be held responsible for these omissions in the same way that I can for the acts I actually perform.

Another objection concerns the depth of our obligations. If a life can be saved even by the last £1 I have in my pocket, am I obligated to donate it? Should I deprive myself to the point of starvation in order to help others (Fitzpatrick, 2008a: 221–3)? Singer is a realist who uses empirical research to establish how much it would cost each of us in the developed world to do what we can. His position has shifted over time. In the early 1990s, Singer (1993: 245–6) recommended that 10% of income in the affluent world should go to assisting the globally impoverished; by the early 2000s he mentions 1% (Singer, 2002: 191–5); and in a recent book this has gone back up to 5% (Singer, 2009: Ch.10). We might therefore be entitled to conclude that our obligations are fixed by more pragmatic considerations than suggested by the right-and-wrong absoluteness of a drowning child scenario.

Some have therefore questioned whether it is reasonable to extrapolate from such idealized examples. Miller (2007: 233–8) criticizes the analogy for placing all the emphasis on 'remedial responsibility' (the obligation to come to someone's aid) and none on 'outcome responsibility' (which identifies those responsible for creating the need for aid).

Miller (2007: 31–50) therefore rejects 'strong cosmopolitan' accounts of global justice, i.e. those which downplay the significance of national solidarities and memberships. Your country is not clothing that can be easily discarded; it is a substantive part of your identity. What we do or do not owe to others, as matters of justice, we owe *as* citizens *to* citizens. And because citizenship is a political category dependent upon political constitutions and means of enforcement, it makes no sense to speak of a generalized responsibility to everyone. National communities possess intrinsic value as sources of cultural meaning which enable us to distinguish between those we are close to (insiders) and those we are not (outsiders).

This does not mean we should ignore outsiders, acknowledges Miller (2007: 55–68). We do possess global responsibilities to show equal moral concern for all humans. But whereas 'strong cosmopolitanism' argues for equal treatment, a 'weak cosmopolitanism' proposes that we have an obligation to ensure that people everywhere have access to a minimum set of resources. Miller rejects a global egalitarianism on the grounds that there is no common set of cultural understandings which will tell us how to equalize resources or opportunities. Goods are meaningful and measurable only within specific cultural contexts.

For Miller (2007: 178–85), then, global justice implies setting a global minimum. Living a decent human life requires the realization of 'basic needs', e.g. for good health, and of 'societal needs' which vary from one society to the next (see p. 7). Everyone needs good health. But whether they need – and therefore have a right to – inoculations against malaria will depend. Only basic needs can ground human rights, insists Miller; furthermore, this applies only when such needs can feasibly and realistically be met (Brock, 2008). Ultimately, the claims of global justice become thinner and thinner, argues Miller (2007: 249–59), until what is left is largely a humanitarian duty rather than a duty of justice. It is better if I donate money to people in need, but I am not necessarily committing an injustice if I don't. Miller is defending a moral and political *contextualism*. There are universal needs and rights, he proposes, but these are highly dependent upon national contexts without which there is no meaningful obligation to address those needs and rights (O'Neill, 2009: 427–8).

The risk here is of becoming hostage to a cultural-national conservatism (also Caney, 2009: 400–3). By orienting itself so closely to the allegiances and identities that people currently demonstrate, Miller's approach perhaps neglects the prescriptive, allegiance- and identity-creating aspects of global justice debates (Sen, 2009: 383). Even if we grant his premise – we owe obligations to insiders and it is implausible to regard people as members of a world community – this is not itself a universal truth. Nation-states are constructs which grew as localities and kinship units mattered less and as societies became secularized with the separation of church and state. Strong cosmopolitans and universalists like Singer are trying to *prescribe* and not just *describe*.

So while Miller is correct to observe that a sense of global membership is the precondition for global egalitarianism – without the former the latter's institutions are unlikely to develop – it may also be true that a moral politics of global egalitarianism is one means by which that sense of global membership and world community can strengthen and proliferate (Ypi, 2010). This is surely the thesis of the green movement. Many environmentalists will acknowledge the human attachment to the familiarities of home while arguing that localities interpenetrate on a global scale so that we cannot preserve 'here' without also preserving what is 'over there'. An ethos of global concern can encompass local affiliations and memberships.

In short, while Singer can be accused of neglecting the demands placed on us by local relationships, Miller may ignore the extent to which local and global incorporate one other.

Seven perspectives

Singer and Miller represent opposite ends of the spectrum, but there are many other contributions to the debate, only a few of which can be sampled

Table 10.1 Seven varieties of global justice

	cosmopolitanism (strong)	contextualism (& nationalist)	Egalitarianism/ redistributive	human rights	humanitarianism	minimalism/ federative	universalism
Brian Barry			•				?
Charles Beitz			•	•			
Simon Caney			•	•			•
Joseph Carens				•	•		
Robert Goodin	?	•					?
David Miller		•	•	•		•	
Thomas Nagel				•			
Martha Nussbaum	•			•			•
Onora O'Neill	•			?	•		•
Thomas Pogge	•			•			
John Rawls		•				•	
Amartya Sen	?		•	•			?
Henry Shue				•			
Peter Singer	•			?			•
Hillel Steiner			•	•			?
Michael Walzer		•					

here. Table 10.1 lists some of the key contributors and cross-references them against various perspectives. (The appearance of question marks signals those points where is it unclear or I am just not sure.) Note that ideas and labels are still being worked out. For instance, Miller rejects strong cosmopolitanism but seems amenable to being described as a weak cosmopolitan. Others, though, might reject his definitions and deny that Miller can be described as a cosmopolitan at all.

Let's summarize the main perspectives on global justice (cf. Fabre, 2007).

Cosmopolitan

The view that 'all human beings have equal moral worth and that our responsibilities to others do not stop at borders' (Brock, 2005: 1; Caney, 2009: 388–90). There are, though, *degrees* of cosmopolitanism. Strong or radical cosmopolitans propose that there should be no bias in favour of compatriots; weak or moderate cosmopolitans argue that although we possess obligations to everyone, duties to those we know or with whom we share a similar cultural space (fellow citizens) will be more intense. The distinction is sometimes overdrawn. Singer (2009: 129–39) does not deny the importance of family, but argues that the needs of those in extreme poverty are stronger than your family's need for luxuries. Pogge (2008b: 356) is another leading cosmopolitan:

> The ultimate units of concern are *human beings*, or *persons* – rather than, say, family lines, tribes, or ethnic, cultural, or religious communities, nations, or states. The latter may be units of concern only indirectly....The status of ultimate unit of concern attaches to every living human being equally....This special status has global force. Persons are ultimate units of concern for everyone – not only for their compatriots, fellow religionists, or such like.

Contextualist

Miller represents the view that global justice requires institutions and citizens to be both just and global. Citizens can be just but they are not members of a world community; institutions can be global but offer a tenuous basic for justice, i.e. for the legitimizing solidarities of common membership. National communities are and are likely to remain the principal units of political association and any theory of global justice has to start from that realization. Miller's position is echoed by Nagel (2005: 146), who adds that, in a world dominated by the powerful, global injustice will and *must* precede any move towards global justice:

> Unjust and illegitimate regimes are the necessary precursors of the progress toward legitimacy and democracy, because they create the centralized power that can then be contested, and perhaps turned in other directions without being destroyed. For this reason, I believe the most likely path toward some version of global justice is through the creation of patently unjust and illegitimate global

structures of power that are tolerable to the interests of the most powerful current nation-states.

Egalitarian

The notion that global justice, like social justice, must imply substantive equalities. Barry (2008) argued that considerations of humanity require rich countries not just to give aid to poor ones but to transfer resources. Humanitarianism is not enough because it cannot define the level of sacrifice we are obliged to make. This position resembles an early contribution by Beitz (2008) when he proposed extending Rawls' difference principle to the entire world. If people in the original position were denied knowledge of their nationality, they would favour maximin distributions to the least well-off countries. Such distributions require that nation-states do not have exclusive property rights to those resources which happen to fall within their borders. If it is 'arbitrary from a moral point of view' for Jenny to have a face beautiful enough to make her a rich model, it is equally arbitrary for Lucksville to possess all the gold buried beneath some lines on a map. Such resources can therefore be subjected to a regime of global rights which strengthens claims for food aid, development assistance and monetary and trade reforms.

Human rights

If all individuals have equal moral worth, then it seems reasonable to regard everyone as possessing the same basic human rights. This is true, whether human rights are valued for their own intrinsic sake, or as instrumental factors generating desirable benefits and states of affairs. However, there are important divisions. Universalists see rights as ways of making legitimate claims against the restrictions and repressive injustices imposed by nations and cultures (Caney, 2005: ch. 3). For those like Miller, rights must be grounded in particular contexts, such as national-cultural institutions, since otherwise rights can have no corresponding, meaningful obligations. Capability theorists like Nussbaum and Sen may offer a third alternative. For Nussbaum (2006: 284–91), the capabilities approach is a species of the human rights approach, the latter justifying the freedoms that are necessary for the realization of human functionings.

Humanitarian

Those like Barry make a strict distinction between humanitarianism and justice. However, for those who are either sceptical towards the ideals of global justice, or at least doubtful that such ideals can be realized in the short-term, the picture is less clear-cut. Walzer (2003) argues that states have a right not to admit migrants, in order to preserve the cultural identities of their 'members'; but should, nonetheless, be Good Samaritans towards 'strangers'. Within moral philosophy there is a principle of supererogation: it can be morally commendable to do something even if it is not morally obligatory.

Therefore, the language of justice is not necessarily exhaustive of what we owe to others.

Minimalist

Rawls himself denied that the difference principle could be applied globally. Once people have a 'working liberal or decent government', Rawls (1999) proposed, no further redistribution is warranted. Justice as fairness implies a large degree of independence and self-determination. To impose strong egalitarian requirements on countries risks undermining that independence. The need for harmony amid global diversity demands that we recognize the many different ways in which people can choose to live together. This will often imply liberal and democratic constitutions but it is also possible to imagine people content to live in benign but hierarchical nations, e.g. theocracies. The best we can aim for is a 'law of peoples', the political autonomy of free and equal peoples. (This resembles Kant's federative union.) Liberalism demands the preservation of cultural differences, even in the case of non-liberal but tolerable governments. The minimalist and egalitarian perspectives begin to converge if by 'global equality' we mean 'global equality of opportunity' (Pogge, 2008b: 371–77).

Universalist

Universalism is the view that unless moral values apply to everyone, everywhere, they cannot be described *as* moral values. If all values are relative across time and space then 'what we do over here' is simply different to 'what they do over there'. Relativism offers no basic for evaluating here and there, and no means of subjecting both to evaluative criteria (Caney, 2005: ch. 2). Universalists can acknowledge the significance of local cultures and ways of life, but argue that contextualists go too far in allowing universal foundations to erode. Global justice has to be *universal* justice. In the drowning child example, if it would not be morally permissible for a white passerby to save a white child, but not a black one, why should national membership and cultural proximity be a legitimate criterion?

Social policy

Debates about global justice and social policy are both concerned with citizenship, communal membership, cultural belonging and identity, the reorganization of social institutions and the fair distribution of resources and other welfare-enhancing goods (Bertram, 2008; Straehle, 2010). The essential questions are as follows:

- What are the implications for existing social policies (especially in the developed welfare states) of global justice?
- Do we have to fundamentally rethink the social policy agenda?

There are numerous ways of coming at these questions.

If we accept the drowning child analogy, then arguably every penny dedicated to welfare expenditure is money which cannot now be spent on the world's poor. Singer's example is a powerful argument against regarding those from whom we are geographically distant as being morally distant too. There is a case for diverting at least some expenditure away from domestic social policies towards foreign aid or some other form of global redistributive fund.

Yet it is difficult to ignore Miller's point. Nations may be lines on a map, yet they matter because these are lines to which most people attach emotional, symbolic and political significance. There is a coherent case for regarding our obligations to fellow citizens as stronger than those towards non-compatriots. From this perspective, social policies as they are currently justified, funded and organized should *not* undergo some revolutionary change.

There is a way of getting ourselves off the philosophical hook. Recall that Singer is not arguing that the developed world should impoverish itself. This is because the amount of money required to alleviate the extremes of world poverty is much less than many imagine – a transfer of 1% of global GDP from North to South according to Pogge (2008c: 304). Nor did Miller deny that we have an obligation to ensure that people everywhere have access to a minimum set of resources so that their basic needs can be met. If, therefore, we agree that our record on global poverty is currently pretty dire, then the differences between Singer's and Miller's philosophies matter a bit less. Either approach would be an improvement on the current state of affairs. Perhaps we do not have to think of domestic and global social policies, of domestic justice and global justice, in either/or terms.

But this pragmatic solution only gets us so far. As social policy students, what we want to know is *how* to get from here to there. Take one important debate (see Fitzpatrick, 2008a: ch. 11).

Some have argued that national borders should be open, allowing the free migration of people from country to country (Carens, 2003b). If your French nationality is an accident of birth, then why should you have more access to France's resources than non-French citizens? Yet if migration was entirely open, then welfare states in developed countries might be subjected to greater financial pressures (as new-arrivals become entitled to full benefits and services) and cultural pressures (since existing populations may feel resentful at the granting of those entitlements). This is partly why others have called for migration *restrictions* (Miller, 2005).

One argument for open migration is that it redistributes money from guest countries back to home countries. If the former is wealthier than the latter then this constitutes a global redistribution from rich to poor. A guest country might then claim that it is fulfilling responsibilities it does not have to repeat elsewhere, e.g. in foreign aid donations. By contrast, if a wealthy nation prefers restrictions on migrations, for whatever reason, this might increase its global justice obligations:

> If the rich countries do not want to let foreigners in, then the very least they must do is send much more money to compensate them for their being kept out. (Goodin, 2002: 565)

So, if we set a goal to which both Singer and Miller can assent, one which quantifies the obligations of developed nations and their citizens, then countries can either (1) prefer open migration to other forms of redistribution, (2) restrict migration and prefer other forms of redistribution as compensation, or (3) effect some other trade-off between redistributive mechanisms. Thus, we can imagine establishing a Global Resources Fund, as proposed by Pogge (2008c), through which resources are transferred to the developing world. But there is potentially a diversity of in-cash and in-kind contributions that developed nations could make to this fund in order to fulfil their obligations, depending upon the wishes of their populations and the needs of their economies.

In short, even if we set a baseline obligation, the actual policies which it demands are subject to a host of political determinations which cannot be anticipated in advance through theoretical debate alone. But what this also suggests is that we do not have to redesign our welfare systems from scratch. The demands of saving a life are considerable (and may cost you the equivalent of a job or a suit) but they are not debilitating. If anything, this makes the developed world's ongoing failure to deal adequately with global poverty even less excusable.

Efforts to address global poverty will ultimately be redundant unless these are ecologically as well as socioeconomically sustainable. I do not attempt a grand synthesis of global justice and environmentalist debates since the literature is still in its early stages. Instead, as with the above debate, we take a step back to appreciate the fundamentals of what is at stake.

The Wellbeing of Nature[2]

Don't imagine that environmentalism depends entirely upon establishing that global warming is increasing as a result of human activity. Although environmentalists have powerful evidence to this effect, their case is not dependent upon it. Even if by some miracle global temperatures reverted to their pre-industrial level tomorrow, greens would still be in possession of some challenging ideas. This is because the roots of environmentalism precede the 1960s, when awareness of the dangers of pollution, unrestricted population growth and the depletion of key resources began to increase.

Back in the nineteenth century, the earliest pioneers of green thinking were warning about certain modern tendencies. Individualists like Thoreau (1995) worried that industrialization and urbanization were distancing humans from nature and from a sense of the wilderness. Thoreau did not reject the benefits of civilization but argued against a divergence of the social from the natural. From more of a left-wing stance, Morris (1986) believed that people were being increasingly asked to serve an industrial machine whose real purpose should be to serve *us*! Freedom, creativity, feeling and the cooperative spirit were being stifled, he alleged, by capitalist competition, greed and ugliness. In short, environmentalism's roots stretch back to the romanticism and pastoralism of previous centuries, drawing upon important thinkers like Rousseau. It is interested in improving the quality of life (of personal and social wellbeing), as well as saving the planet.

That said, it is certainly true that contemporary environmentalism sets out to establish the causes of, and propose solutions to, climatic changes associated with global warming (Monbiot, 2007). The challenge can be summarized as follows:

When nature is converted into products that can be bought, sold and consumed we emit the greenhouse gases which have been 'stored' within nature, especially when we burn fossil fuels. As those gases build up in the atmosphere, less of the sun's energy can radiate back out into space. Some warming is fine – without it the world would be much colder – but the vast majority of scientists now worry that we are reaching a point that will have dramatic effects upon our planet, its species and ourselves.

So, the extinction of species is accelerating, sea levels are rising, ice-shelves melting, extreme weather events are increasing in rate and severity, large areas of rainforest and arable land are threatened, as is biodiversity. The health of millions of people, especially in developing countries, is likely to be affected through increases in malnutrition and a variety of diseases. As levels of potable water and crop yields decline, we are likely to see more 'ecological migration' as people flee those parts of the world which are increasingly uninhabitable.

So, what *should* we do about this? And what *can* we do? Since we are already committed to an increase in average global temperature of at least 2°C (above pre-industrial levels) we are going to have to adapt. 'Adaptation' implies making improvements in flood defences, water, agriculture and the use of land, medical care and the built environment. But if we are to slow down, halt and eventually reverse global warming then we also need policies of 'mitigation'. This is where political and ethical disagreements really begin to bite.

'Sustainability' is a key principle associated with green movements, parties and activists. We ought to take urgent steps to make our societies and economies sustainable again. At its most basic, this means not taking out of nature more than we can put back in. If you cut a tree down, you had better plant enough new trees so that the same rate of carbon dioxide as before can be absorbed. But even this basic definition raises numerous questions. Crucially, does sustainability imply drastic reductions in wealth and affluence? Must we now abandon economic growth and development? In the late 1980s, the Brundtland Commission (1987: 43) famously defined sustainable development as 'development that meets the needs of the present without compromising the ability of future generations to meet their own needs'. This seems to suggest that we can have growth *and* sustainability, a view which has allowed green ideas some influence on governments' thinking in the form of 'ecological modernization' (see below). Many greens, though, worry that rather than converting the political mainstream to environmentalism, environmentalism risks being converted to the business-as-usual assumptions of the mainstream (Christoff, 1996).

Environmentalisms

In short, there are numerous strands and schools of thought within environmentalism. The following lists are far from exhaustive.

Politics & Ideology

1. Libertarians & Free Markets
Libertarians and free market advocates are not identical – as we saw in Chapter 3 – but both argue that the state ought to be much smaller. Ecological problems have been caused by the state intruding into the sphere of private property and not giving markets enough space to develop sustainable technologies and products (Anderson & Leal, 2001). The solution is to divide the environmental 'commons' into private holdings that, for reasons of self-interest, agents will work to preserve and develop. At best, only light-touch regulation is needed in order to encourage markets – through incentives, prices and profits – in the right direction. However, leftist libertarians and anarchists disagree with this, arguing that we ought to detach ourselves from both states *and* markets by forming self-organizing, radically democratic communities (Bookchin, 2005).

2. Conservatives
Green conservatives are more willing to see free markets as problematic, imposing costs on the planet for the purpose of profit (Goldsmith, 2009). Capitalism needs a new ethic of stewardship, so that we nurture the roots of prosperity rather than exploiting and ultimately destroying them. The statism and utopianism of the Left has been as reckless in regarding nature as a resource to be utilized and discarded. Conservatism respects nature, as the source of our sense of local belonging, because it respects tradition. We benefit future generations by preserving the legacy bequeathed to us from the past.

3. Centrists/Liberals
Green liberalism states that a green society should and must be a free society (Wissenburg, 1998). Rather than *forcing* people to act and think green, we should recognize that people have green preferences (because they care about nature and the welfare of their children) and organize society accordingly. The state should steer society, but not try to reengineer it. A centrist politics

of 'ecological modernization' brings states and markets together productively (Stern, 2007). This implies that with the right technologies and institutions, growth can be decoupled from damaging, high-carbon activities and the latter eventually abolished.

4. Social Democrats

Agree that ecological modernization is the way forward, but offer strong arguments against free markets and in favour of social justice (Giddens, 2009). Ecological crises have been exacerbated by the selfish materialism promoted by the Right, in contrast to the Centre-Left stress on needs and cooperation. Principles of social justice, equality and fairness need revising so that they are consistent with notions of environmental sustainability and justice. Equally, the latter must ensure that the least advantaged are protected and assisted by the development of a green society and economy.

5. Socialist/Marxists

Capitalism is held to be *the* cause of ecological problems (Pepper, 1993). O'Connor (1998) identifies a 'second contradiction' of capitalism: that between its propensity for endless economic expansion and the capacity of the environment to (a) supply the necessary resources, and (b) absorb the resulting pollution. Unless it is stopped, capital tries to expand everywhere into everything, conflicting with the limits and scarcities of the natural world. Capitalist markets are viral, infecting and transforming anything it can into a source of exchange-value. Because the costs of pollution fall on everyone, but the profits which the polluter created are acquired by him alone, capitalism ignores the 'externalities' it creates, undermining its own foundations by ignoring the fact that wealth originates in nature. Sustainability therefore requires a new system of social ownership, social economy and community property.

6. Feminists

For eco-feminists, ecological problems are patriarchal. The impulse to control, dominate and waste is a masculine one and manifests itself in the subordination of women, the exploitation of animals and the degradation of nature more generally. Nature is seen as a resource to be harvested, just as women are defined as child-bearers, servants and chattels. The solution is a deep-seated revision of how we think about ourselves, each other and the natural world (Salleh, 2009). Rather than seeing everything in terms of hierarchies we should develop new forms of 'cultural ecology' and identity.

Ethics

Additional debates and divisions can be found within moral philosophy. Most notably, there are long-standing disagreements between anthropocentrists and biocentrists.[3]

1. Anthropocentrism

Describes those ideas which are 'human-centred'. When we think about the ecosystem and the environmental problems we face, it is impossible to do so without making our own needs and interests central. We are ourselves part of nature and so to treat nature as if humans don't exist, don't matter or (even worse) as if they infect the purity of the natural world is both objectionable and counter-productive. It is of course possible for humans to demonstrate a kind of 'selfish speciesism'. But a green ethic requires us to explore our interconnectedness with living things. By ignoring this, biocentrists actually *replicate* the error made by a destructive anthropocentrism, of separating the human from the natural.

2. Biocentrism

Biocentrists can of course acknowledge that humans are rooted in nature, while denying the doctrine of human-*centredness*. The problem with anthropocentrism is that it represents nature in human terms. It is biased in favour of sentience and so neglects the value of non-sentient life-forms and the fact that there are many different forms of consciousness (including the very ecosystem itself). We ought, instead, to appreciate the 'intrinsic value' of nature, where nature and all living things are valued for their own sake. Anthropocentrists are more likely to view nature as possessing 'instrumental value', as something which is valuable only in so far as it serves human objectives. A green ethic should correspond to what some have called 'deep ecology'. Humans must live for the good of nature by abandoning their humanist chauvinism and radically altering our perceptions of what we are in the scheme of things.

3. Ecocentrism

Becoming dismayed by the standoff between anthropocentrists and biocentrists, some philosophers have tried to develop insights which draw upon both. Ecocentrists believe that everything within nature belongs to the moral community, but that since morality is a human construct, we cannot ignore the special role humans play. If we have the power to destroy or preserve the rest of nature, then humans have obligations to other species that other species do not have towards us. Therefore, the fact that nature possesses intrinsic value does not rule out moral deliberations which are instrumentalist, where some parts of nature are used to achieve goals that benefit nature as a whole. Rather than deep ecology, ecocentrism is probably more consistent with a philosophy of *social* ecology where a sustainable society is that based around a politics of egalitarian justice and personal freedom.

What these 'isms' give rise to, are numerous perspectives on a vast series of debates (Dobson, 2003). Anthropocentrists and ecocentrists are more likely to develop concepts of environmental citizenship, responsibilities and rights, categories that biocentrists may regard with suspicion.

For instance, while all agree that environmental justice should imply an ethic of care, biocentrists argue that care cannot be limited to humans, for if we view humans as having dominion over non-human animals then what we call 'care' is really just another form of 'speciesism'. For anthropocentrists, care implies a social context; we care from within a set of social identities and reciprocities. Ecocentrists might agree that care is socially bounded but propose that we can expand the boundaries of social and moral obligations, nevertheless.

These and many other debates influence how philosophers approach some key questions (see Carter, 2011).

Future generations:

What legacy should we leave for future generations? Should we risk global warming in order to make them materially wealthier? To what extent can we even be said to harm future generations? Should we preserve nature on the basis that it possesses intrinsic value? How far into the future do our obligations extend?

Developing world:

Environmental debates intersect with those concerning global justice, though the literatures largely remain only partly integrated. The intersection occurs because of 'distance'. Sitting in Britain in 2010 I am geographically-distant from people currently residing in Zambia; temporally-distant from British citizens of the year 2110; and both geographically- and temporally-distant from Zambians living a century from now (Fitzpatrick, 2003: Ch.7).

Can those distances be bridged and, if so, how? How similar are our duties to those who are geographically- and/or temporally-distant? It is possible that there are synergies between environmental and global justice; that each is just another way of looking at the other. However, it is also possible that there are trade-offs to be managed. A rising world population places unsustainable demands on the environment. Since those in a lifeboat cannot save everyone in the water they cannot offer justice *to* everyone. Is it better to sacrifice a million (through famine, war, disease) than risk the lives of a billion? Or, if the real problems include global poverty and insufficient redistribution from North to South then, so long as growth and development are ecologically sustainable, environmental and global justice *are* presumably compatible.

Since he is a long-standing advocate of environmental and global justice, should we adopt Singer's approach and minimize the harm we do to others, wherever and whenever they are found? Or, is Miller correct to propose that, whatever our obligations may be to others, they start from within our geographical and temporal *localities*?

Animals:

This notion of distance extends to non-humans, too. I am ontologically- and cognitively-distant from other species. As Nagel (1979: 165–80) once asked, how can I really know what it's like to be a bat? So, how should I relate to animals? Do they have rights or is the notion of 'animal rights' too anthropocentric? Are activities like meat-eating and animal experimentation morally wrong? Is speciesism equivalent to sexism and racism? To what extent should our concern for animals who possess a recognisable consciousness and intelligence extent to non-sentient life-forms? Do plants and rocks have an intrinsic value?

We are therefore presented with a bewildering array of questions and perspectives, of which the above is just a sample. But despite this diversity, there are some ideas that characterize environmentalism.

Critiques

Let me summarize the main points under two headings (see Hannigan, 2011)

Limits to growth

Environmentalists argue that planetary resources are finite, in contrast to the insatiable, apparently endless demands made by the ethos and practices of economic growth (Jackson, 2009). The planet can neither supply all of the resources that are ultimately required, nor absorb all the pollution created by rampant production, travel and consumerism. Greens have devised and popularized terms such as the 'ecological footprint' to highlight the unsustainable demands that we make.

Critics argue that announcements of the death of growth are premature (Nordhaus, 2008). We could, for instance, decarbonize the economy, assisted by new products, technologies and markets. Green pragmatists are likely to agree that a knee-jerk anti-growth politics is little better than a pro-growth one, while insisting that the emphasis should nevertheless be upon sustainability. Other environmentalists, though, may feel that we should no longer confuse growth with 'quality of life'. What we need is a social-ethical revolution and not just a few changes to the methods of economic accounting. At best, sustainable growth has to imply 'zero growth' where economic activity remains within the physical limits of the Earth's capacity (Daly, 1996: Ch.1).

Treadmills of production and consumption

The desire for growth has characterized many socioeconomic systems. Greens, though, draw particular attention to the toxic combination of capitalist competition and neglect by the state in creating ecological deterioration.

Capitalism does not just satisfy needs and desires; it creates them. It has an interest in keeping people in a state of permanent angst – as if fulfilment always requires the purchase of just a few more goods – in order to sell products, make a profit and keep the cycle of desire-consumption-anxiety-desire going.

Consumers don't create capitalism; capitalism creates consumers. This occurs through the advertising industry and the constant, hyperactive bombardment by brands, icons, images of celebrity and signifiers which impel and feed off emotional-psychological distress and yearning. The most profitable consumers are those fighting an impoverished status and self-image. This isn't necessarily to paint consumers as dupes, it is to portray agents as having to continually struggle within a system which dominates and exploits them.

The state both colludes in and drives the processes of production, consumption and ecological crisis (Catney & Doyle, 2011). The identification of 'wellbeing' with 'wealth' and ever-rising expectations of material affluence has been encouraged by politicians fishing for votes and by a bureaucratic machine that is deeply entwined with the economy. Consequently, many greens have been traditionally hostile to the state, with environmentalism continuing to possess a reputation for anarchism, localism, radicalism and utopianism. Bookchin (2005) is one of many advocating that decision-making processes be decentralized and democratized into a cooperative, communal system.

More recently, though, many green theorists have sought to reconcile environmentalism to the principles of representative democracy, both because they regard communalism as naïve and as a response to the accommodations of ecological modernization. Thus, Eckersley (2004) and Meadowcroft (2005) both advocate a green state system where sustainability becomes the priority overarching all other governmental functions. This may be a forlorn hope, of course. If the state is a capitalist state and therefore essentially destructive of the natural environment, then any green paint applied to the state will be wafer thin and soon flake off. If, instead, what is being advocated is a reconstruction of the state-market apparatus around sustainable growth, then this seems more desirable. However, whether this implies the greening of capitalism or the realization of a post-capitalist society, such a goal also seems more difficult to achieve. Either way, a global regime of coordination is required so that some, ecologically destructive states are not allowed to free ride on green ones.

Furthermore, it also requires a revision of what it means to be a responsible human being. People value lots of things in their lives, yet is it their identities as workers and spenders which are made to predominate. Greens are often accused of being killjoys. But what they really want to kill is waste, not enjoyment; indeed, the expectation is that lives not dedicated to the endless accumulation of 'stuff', which give the other faces of our identities room to breathe, will be *more* satisfying.

Social Policy

How, then, does all of this pertain to social policy and welfare reform (Cahill, 2001; Cahill & Fitzpatrick, 2002; Fitzpatrick & Cahill, 2002; Adebowale, 2008; Fitzpatrick, 2011c)? There are four basic critiques we might make of social policies from an environmentalist perspective.

Firstly, Greens identify and criticize the extent to which social policies are dependent upon levels and forms of growth which are unsustainable. This growth-dependency – or 'productivism' – underpins all welfare systems. A related charge is that social policies *contribute* to unsustainability. By perpetuating the ideologies of productivism, welfare systems help to fuel more unsustainable growth. One implication is that welfare reforms tend only to address what environmentalists regard as the surface symptoms of social problems and miss the fact that the roots of many problems lie in people being asked to spend most of their lives serving a socioeconomic system that benefits the most powerful corporations, interests, individuals and elites. People are impelled to run ever faster on an economic wheel, wasting the most precious currency we all possess (our time), from fear of the poverty and loss of status that would result should they fall off. Environmentalists have long articulated the idea which has recently become popular (see Chapter 1), where wellbeing is only partially related to the accumulation of income, wealth, property and other 'things'. The satisfaction we gain from ownership is outweighed by the time and energy the acquisition takes.

For Greens, we need a more reasonable equilibrium in our personal and communal lives between time and material prosperity (the so-called 'work-life balance') and in our economies between 'standard of living' and 'quality of life', between competitive aspiration and cooperative interaction. Sustainable growth won't be about adding quantity to our possessions but about adding quality to our lives and communities. A 'caring society' is that where people use resources only in so far as they replenish them, nurture rather than discard, recognize their natural and social interdependencies and form convivial systems of association, organization and social progress.

Secondly, this 'politics of time' implies that social policy has to think globally and across the long-term (Dryzek, 2008). Environmental problems are unprecedented, affect a global arena, occupy a longer timescale and are subject to collective unpredictability. It is no surprise that people find it difficult to make links between London and Zambia, or between their own behaviour and mass flooding, or between 2010 and 2110. A new social policy agenda has to help them make the connections, recognize their own roles and responsibilities and reorganize social institutions accordingly.

Thirdly, this might imply taking the emphasis away from wage-earning as a source of economic security, moral value, social identity and communal participation. The 'classic' welfare states of the mid-late twentieth century were based upon male, full-time, full employment; for only if employment was high could social expenditure be maintained at generous levels. To the extent that 'green-collar' jobs and practices assist the goal of sustainable growth, they are welcome. Where jobs and labour markets do not, we urgently need to revise our assumptions and objectives. So, in questioning the prevailing 'employment ethic', many environmentalists are arguing not for the abolition of employment but for a recognition that security, value, identity and membership derive from far wider sources and activities. So rather than 'work' being equated with 'employment' we should recognize a broader spectrum of participative and socially valuable contributions. Greens are among those calling for the expansion of mutualist, social economy enterprises, civic associations and informal economies.

And if our notions about employment should change, what of related ideas? Social insurance is based upon the notion that the collectivization of risks can and should derive from labour market participation. When it comes to climate change, however, *collective unpredictability* becomes central (Gough, 2008). If so, then job- and wage-based forms of insurance alone may no longer offer the secure bridge, linking the past, present and future, that their architects anticipated.

Finally, Greens challenge the general lack of political and economic democracy which continues to characterize our societies. The allegation is that existing forms of social organization and welfare provision underestimate the extent to which citizens can be self-organizing. The state, political party and electoral systems are too distant and elitist. Representative democracy needs to be reconfigured around deliberative, participative, reflexive institutions and networks. This means addressing the 'clientalization' of welfare, where wellbeing is all too often delivered by outside experts and bureaucrats (whether public or private). Greens envisage new processes and outcomes where the state provides a universalistic framework which makes greater room for civic associations and policy communities that would control funds and so reduce the distance between the users and producers of services (Offe, 1996). In short, Green social policies seem to require a greater degree of decentralization and the emergence of a newly empowered 'welfare citizen'.

All of which adds more questions to those already accumulated in the section on global justice. In particular, would a Green welfare state resemble existing systems or would it be something that we have not yet envisaged? Though the above ideas are slowly entering the mainstream their eventual impact is far from certain and dependent upon a vast array of circumstances and debates.

It should now be clear why relating global justice to environmental debates is a daunting challenge. It is tempting to claim that environmental ethics and politics should be cosmopolitan, since surely our responsibilities to the natural world do not end at the nation's edge. Yet this assumption may be premature. Because ours is still largely a world of nation-states – and because we may care for the environment through a love of the local – it is not obvious that a contextualist perspective is irrelevant. Besides, to a biocentric, even many of the assumptions which dominate cosmopolitan debates may also appear too anthropocentric.

To fit these debates together we need a three-dimensional map. Draw a line horizontally. Cosmopolitanism can be found at one end of the line and contextualism at the other (pp.196–8). Starting at one end of this first line, now draw a second line at right-angles so that we have standard vertical and horizontal axes. The vertical line represents the contrast between anthropocentrism and biocentrism (pp.203–4). Now, where the vertical and horizontal axes touch, draw another line at right-angles to the others, up out of the page. Our three lines form the corner of a cube so that we have three spatial dimensions. This third line describes the ideological components of green thinking (pp.202–3).

So we have three axes and a bewildering array of positions we could occupy within this three-dimensional space. And it may of course be that the axes do not embody fixed categories. Ideas are fluid and so theorists may not occupy a single point but multiple points that flow across our cubed map. Charting and exploring this map could practically take a lifetime, as would a proper justification of where – and why – each of us would want to locate ourselves when we think about the future of justice. The above chapter gives barely a hint of a vast, still unexplored universe.

Questions for Further Discussion

- To what extent is it possible to be both a cosmopolitan *and* a contextualist?
- Is it credible to imagine that domestic welfare states can help to create global justice?
- How relevant is environmentalism to the future of state welfare?

Concluding Remarks

If nothing else, this book has provided evidence for the following three claims.

First, it is often necessary to take social policy themes and issues into account when discussing social and political theory. Social policy students do not simply debate how to translate principles into practical reality. Instead, they ask distinctive questions that enhance the method and assumptions of social philosophy. To explore social and political thought without substantial reference to the battles fought over social policies is to miss a key feature in the development of modern societies. Welfare theory (the philosophy of social policy) is not quite the same as social theory (the philosophy of sociology and social science) and political theory (the philosophy of politics and government).

Second, social policy researchers, scholars and students should not neglect the theoretical foundations of the subject. Although it is highly reliant upon generating and disseminating empirical research and data to a variety of audiences, including non-academic ones (policymakers, practitioners, charities and voluntary organizations, etc.), there are few occasions when this practical focus cannot be enriched by philosophical debates. The theoretical and the empirical inform one another.

Finally, therefore, welfare theory has roots that extend far into history. We need to be aware of the extent to which present debates evolved out of those which occupied our predecessors. Yet welfare theory is by no means limited to the history of ideas, for as the last chapter has demonstrated the subject is forever renewing itself, adding imaginative and innovative issues to its panorama of concerns. The roots of history carry us far into the future. Any account of welfare theory which veers too closely towards the ideological will reduce itself to little more than a political party manifesto, yet any account that ignores the ideological will miss the most exciting question which social policy asks: how can we improve our social environments?

For that remains the task ahead of us.

In the early 1990s, Fukuyama (1992) announced the 'end of history'. With the fall of the Berlin Wall, he believed, future social developments would occupy the terrain marked out by liberal, capitalist democracies with their respect for freedom and the rule of law. This pronouncement was spectacularly overblown. Not only has democratic capitalism received challenges from without (e.g. religious fundamentalism) but it has also created rods for its own back, as well as the backs of others (e.g. the Great Recession and global warming). Today, the association of 'capitalism' with 'liberal democracy' is less automatic than it was in the 1990s. Furthermore, for freedom to be real it must imply the capacity to rethink the practices and institutions which make freedom a meaningful, lived experience for all individuals *as* individuals and as members of groups and networks. In this book, we have investigated – among other topics – renewed interest in community, the return of class and the rise of new social identities, all of which present challenges *to* and *for* liberal democracy *originating from within* liberal democratic contexts.

Yet nor was Fukuyama entirely wrong. For such challenges to be met, they need to be addressed in a spirit of openness, rationality, mutuality, tolerance, self-reflection and consensual agreement. If these are not the enduring principles of liberal democracy then it is the latter which has come to an end. Yet there is no guarantee that the institutions and procedures of liberal democracy will not turn against such principles. Thus, liberal democracy needs to combine the thankless business of organization and administration with a socioeconomic and political system which is self-renewing and fortified against the dangers of ossification.

As theorists of social policy, then, our task is daunting. We need to open ourselves to, and influence, new possibilities and new developments in the laboratories of philosophical debate – activities which can feel like academic, clouds-in-the-sky luxuries. We also need to ensure that we can translate those debates into realities which will improve the lives of real people in real societies. Welfare theory is poised in that space between the ideal and the real. It does not indulge in philosophy-for-philosophy's-sake. Nor is it rooted in discussions of today's legislation, politicians' speeches, party manifestoes, opinion polls or media fashions.

This book comes at that space from a number of different angles, identifying where they intersect and where they do not. But beware. The best we can do is to step forwards with ambition, responsibility and rational, critical awareness. There is no single future waiting for us to insert ourselves into it. Theory is not a distraction from the real business of improving social institutions. The more we debate the alternatives the more we become capable of making a future in which we would all wish to live, even though mortality is patient, waiting to play his biggest joke on you.

What Fukuyama pronounced was the end of history. What he represented was closure – the start of an unwillingness to imagine different social possibilities. Our task is to re-imagine ourselves, our freedoms and our capacity to shape society together. To get our jokes in first.

Since the first edition of this book we have received more and more evidence that those who announced the closure of society or the end of history, who tried to convince the rest of us that 'there is no alternative' and who decorated freedom in the iron clothing of necessity were playing a dangerous game. Not just because they were wrong instead of right, but because they eroded our ability to tell the difference. The more people they could delude, the more their delusions became the new reality. Only not quite. Their dreamworlds have been defaced again and again. History keeps breaking open.

Yet in my more pessimistic moments I am unsure whether we are any more willing and able than we were then to take back our social environments, to reintroduce markets to society and morality again. Like some endless, inescapable, historical re-enactment, mainstream politics continues to fight the battles of the 1980s and 1990s. In too many countries political parties, separated by barely a few feet of centre-ground, launch missiles against one another from their trenches. Too many of the newspapers we read and the politicians we hear are still, mentally, perched on top of that bloody wall, heralding the death of communism and parading before the cheering crowds inside their heads. They have been joined by the bloggers, tweeters and texters in a cacophony of infinite voices. The more of us there are, the harder it is to be heard and the louder we become. Our societies deafen themselves. Yet as public debate softens and flows along countless millions of tributaries, each individual stream is weak, connections are ephemeral and the *status quo* itself flows contentedly on.

Democracy now faces a challenge greater than that ever posed by the church, the aristocracy, capitalist plutocrats, totalitarian dictatorships or the newest apostles of anti-modern irrationality. Democracy's best friend is also its most deadliest enemy: democracy itself. The challenge we face is deeply paradoxical, therefore. How can we be more participative without allowing reason and tolerance to become just another sound in the crowd? How can we organize and collectively control our fate without succumbing to new demagogues and elitists? Democratic conversation is the best weapon we have, but the price to be paid if we get the conversation wrong is the highest we have ever faced.

A century ago or more, the social policies of reformist liberals and socialist administrators promised an historic victory over the cold doctrines of Victorian self-satisfaction. The world that was built after World War Two was both imperfect and heroic and utterly worth defending against those who would reinvent the darker centuries which preceded it. Yet that world became complacent too, imagining that the war was over. But wars are never over, and our enemies realized this sooner than we did. The task for today's progressives – the heirs to those early pioneers – is to be both defensive and aggressive, to find and nurture the micro-utopias, those ideas and experiments capable of making a difference.

As I suggested in the first edition, perhaps what we need is utopia without the utopians. We need the ideals, the heavens; but we also need to be sceptical about the preachers and prophets who would lead us there. What we lack is, first, a convincing macro-utopian account of social progress and, second, the willingness to translate the micro-utopias we do possess into practical schemes of reform. The notion of real utopias has become fashionable recently. Fine. But never forget that to be real a utopia must be self-limiting, attuned to its own fallibilities. If we get things right we may surprise ourselves by building something far beyond the dull, regimented paradises envisaged by the bureaucratic radicals of old.

This is where welfare theory has a role to play. For the job of welfare theory is not only to provide the theoretical resources by which critiques of the immediate can be carried out but also to stoke the flame of the utopianism that can light the way towards that imaginary horizon, if and when we decide we want to make the journey. It is not possible for any single text to perform this task alone, but a book such as this can help to keep the tradition of welfare theory alive. Indeed, my influence is far less considerable than yours: since welfare theory is ultimately something that has to be *done*, rather than merely written about, it can only be done collectively by those, yourselves, who decide to step out of the path of the onrushing storm.

All of which returns us to the caveat noted at the beginning of the book: it is as dangerous to arrive at utopia as it is to avoid its call. Utopianism is a journey without a destination, a target that we must aim to miss, and progressive social policies are most effective when this contradiction is admitted. If we fail to dream of utopia then we may sleepwalk forever through the infinitely replicated aisles of global capitalism, but if we forget that these are just dreams then we might never wake up from the nightmares that utopianism can also conjure. Wars never end. The utopian needs the pragmatist as much as the pragmatist needs the utopian. Wars may never end but some wars are more just than others, some horizons are wider than others, and the battles that are fought within them are more capable of improving social welfare than those we seem to be engaged in at the moment.

Notes

Chapter 1

1 Note that we will not be looking at the social choice literature, which deals with the highly technical question of how individual preferences and choices can be aggregated into social ones (Nitzan, 2010).
2 The question of whether someone is better or worse-off is based upon the value judgements and preferences of the individual concerned.

Chapter 2

1 Consider the similarities between this argument and that of capabilities on pp.30–1.
2 The American Declaration of Independence states that individuals have a right not to happiness but the *pursuit* of happiness.
3 Note that ambition-sensitivity is not the same as equality of opportunity for welfare. Resource egalitarians are either unconcerned with wellbeing or content to leave its determination to individuals.
4 It can be objected that Rawls is justifying *inequalities* rather than social equality (Temkin, 1993). If it could be shown that massive inequalities were to the benefit of the least well-off (something approximating to Blue society) then, according to Rawlsian justice, so be it. In one sense this is true. Yet given that natural talents and inheritances tend to generate vast inequalities and given that these talents and inheritances are undeserved according to Rawls, the translation of Rawlsian principles into real-world settings would seem to require a politics of equalization. So his liberalism does imply a distinct egalitarian dimension. Not everyone accepts this argument, however; see Chapter 3.
5 This definition of equal outcomes refers to the effects that a particular service has for its users and is therefore slightly different to the definition discussed above which referred to the overall consequences that social policies could be said to have for society.
6 Or we might prefer a kind of 'affirmative action' whereby preferential treatment is given that falls short of a 'quota system'.

Chapter 3

1 A distinction is sometimes made between liberty and freedom, but we shall here treat the two as synonymous for reasons of simplicity. 'Autonomy' is a more philosophical term still, denoting self-government and self-will.
2 Don't make the mistake of imagining that defenders of free markets must be libertarian.
3 This is a version of the 'Wilt Chamberlain argument' (Nozick, 1974: 160–4).
4 It should be noted that Nozick himself later repudiated key aspects of *Anarchy, State and Utopia*.

5 Therefore, income is categorically distinct from body-parts and talents. My arm is definitive of my personhood to an extent that my income is not. And while my talents constitute an internal resource, this does not mean I am entitled to each and every external resource that they could generate. My talent for public speaking doesn't mean that I should be allowed to make money by preaching hatred. Therefore, the redistribution of income *is* distinct from that of body-parts and talents.

6 This might describe the view of communist anarchists, for instance. Such anarchists will agree with their right-wing counterparts that state coercion is an unwarranted intrusion on the rights of individuals to govern themselves. However, left-wing anarchists typically extend such ideas to markets – indeed, any kind of capitalistic practice which undermines the capacity of individuals to live together in cooperative solidarity and conditions of 'direct democracy'. Yet the problem for Left anarchists is to explain how private property can be abolished, and social equality maintained, without the countervailing force of the state. Market capitalism might expire if the vast majority of the world's population simultaneously decided to form themselves into self-sufficient, communist associations; but anything falling short of this is unlikely to be effective. Pure anarchism therefore tends be more imaginable on a small-scale than on a large one.

7 For a Foucauldian account of welfare services in terms of the modern city, interpreted as a social body, see Joyce (2003: 65–75).

Chapter 4

1 Civil society denotes a social space which includes markets and workplaces, households, neighbourhoods and voluntary associations, but is not necessarily reducible to any of them. It is both a real space of individual interaction and an imagined space which defines the distance between individuals and government. It is shaped *by* the state yet constitutes that which *separates* states and citizens.

2 My use of the term 'non-liberal' is not meant to suggest that someone is *anti-liberal* or illiberal, but denotes those who are attracted to one or more the perspectives reviewed on pp.75–81.

3 Properly funded workfare schemes tend to *increase* social expenditure.

Chapter 5

1 The other forms of authority are traditional, or historical authority, and charismatic authority.

2 For a discussion of social psychological theories dealing with power, see Fitzpatrick (2005: 137–41).

3 It should also be noted that whereas pluralists invariably welcome the idea of a pluralist state, elitists are split between those who dislike the idea of elitist power and those who regard it as natural and inevitable.

4 Those who read the first edition of this book and have turned to the endnote again have now been duped twice. Idiots.

5 Personal correspondence.

Chapter 6

1 Recall the Prisoners' Dilemma from Chapter 1.
2 There is an additional, stronger theory of social *constructivism* but since this leads us more firmly into philosophies of science, I am going to ignore it.

Chapter 7

1 More common terms are 'New Right' and 'Neoliberalism'. I avoid the former because the New Right stopped being new a long time ago, and the latter because there are significant conservative (and illiberal) aspects to radical Right thinking. When 'economic liberalism' is used in this book it is with specific reference to free market ideas only.
2 For an account of neoconservatism, see Fitzpatrick (2005: 7–11).
3 Some refer to this broad alliance as a 'reluctant collectivism' but this is too negative and party political, e.g. there was nothing reluctant about the social liberalism of Leonard Hobhouse (1864–1929) when arguing that liberalism and socialism were often in agreement (Hobhouse, 1994).
4 For a discussion of eco-socialism see Chapter 10.

Chapter 8

1 See the James archive at http://www.marxists.org/archive/james-clr/index.htm.
2 A fourth is presented in Chapter 9.
3 Obviously, what follows is not comprehensive but designed to illustrate the important debates. For accounts of age and sexuality see the first edition of this book as well as Estes *et al* (2003), Gilleard & Higgs (2009), Hines (2009) and Richardson (2000).
4 However, use of the term 'black' is still widespread in the academy as an umbrella term for the diversity of non-white ethnic groups.

Chapter 9

1 Some prefer the term 'alter-globalization'.
2 The Great Recession affected those countries with currency and banking controls the least.
3 It is of course possible that neither thesis is true. Genschel (2004) argues that we should avoid simplified models.

Chapter 10

1 I will not discuss those who deny outright there can be any such concept as 'global justice' (e.g. Kukathas, 2006).
2 Much of what follows is discussed in more depth in Fitzpatrick (2011b/c).
3 Be aware that terminology can vary, see Eckersley (1992).

References

Abbott, P. (2006) 'Gender', in Payne, G. (ed.) *Social Divisions*, Basingstoke: Palgrave.

Ackerman, B. & Alstott, A. (1999) *The Stakeholder Society*, Yale: Yale University Press.

Ackerman, B. & Fishkin, J. (2005) *Deliberation Day*, New Haven: Yale University Press.

Adebowale, M. (2008) 'Understanding Environmental Justice', in Craig, G., Burchardt, T. & Gordon, D. (eds) *Social Justice and Public Policy*, Bristol: Policy Press.

Albert, M. (2003) *Parecon*, London: Verso.

Alcock, P. (2006) *Understanding Poverty*, 3ʳᵈ ed., Basingstoke: Palgrave.

Alesina, A. & Glaeser, E. (2005) *Fighting Poverty in the US and Europe*, Oxford: Oxford University Press.

Althusser, L. (1969) *For Marx*, London: Allen Lane.

Althusser, L. & Balibar, E. (1971) *Reading Capital*, London: New Left Books.

Amin, A. (ed.) (1994) *Post-Fordism*, Oxford: Blackwell.

Anderson, B. (2005) *Imagined Communities*, new edition, London: Verso.

Anderson, E. (1999) 'What is the Point of Equality?', *Ethics*, 109(2): 287–337.

Anderson, J. & Honneth, A. (2005) 'Autonomy, Vulnerability, Recognition, and Justice', in Hirstman, J. & Anderson, J. (eds) *Autonomy and the Challenges to Liberalism*, Cambridge: Cambridge University Press.

Anderson, T. & Leal, D. (2001) *Free Market Environmentalism*, 2ⁿᵈ ed., Boulder: Westview Press.

Annetts, J., Law, A., McNeish, W. & Mooney, G. (2009) *Understanding Social Welfare Movements*, Bristol: Policy Press.

Anthias, F. (2001) 'The Concept of "Social Divisions" and Theorising Social Stratification', *Sociology*, 35(4): 835–54.

Appiah, K. A. (2005) *The Ethics of Identity*, Princeton: Princeton University Press.

Archer, M. (1995) *Realist Social Theory*, Cambridge: Cambridge University Press.

Archer, M. (2007) *Making our Way through the World*, Cambridge: Cambridge University Press.

Arendt, H. (1958) *The Human Condition*, Chicago: University of Chicago Press.

Aristotle (1955) *Nichomachean Ethics*, Middlesex: Penguin.

Aristotle (1988) *Politics*, Cambridge: Cambridge University Press.

Arneson, R. (1989) 'Equality and Equal Opportunity for Welfare', *Philosophical Studies*, 56: 77–93.

Arneson, R. (1997) 'Egalitarianism and the Undeserving Poor', *Journal of Political Philosophy*, 5(4): 327–50.

Arneson, R. (2002) 'Why Justice Requires Transfers to Offset Income and Wealth Inequalities', in Paul, E. F., Miller, F. D. & Paul, J. (eds) *Should Differences in Income and Wealth Matter?*, Cambridge: Cambridge University Press.

Arneson, R. (2004) 'Luck Egalitarianism: An Interpretation and Defense', *Philosophical Topics* 32 (1&2): 1–20.

Aron, R. (1970) *Main Currents in Sociological Thought: Volume 2*, Middlesex: Penguin.

Aronowitz, S. (1992) *The Politics of Identity*, London: Routledge.

Badiou, A. (2010) *The Communist Hypothesis*, London: Verso.

Baker, J. (1987) *Arguing for Equality*, London: Verso.

Ball, T. & Dagger, R. (1991) *Political Ideologies and the Democratic Ideal*, New York: HarperCollins.

Banting, K and Kymlicka, W. (eds) (2006) *Multiculturalism and the Welfare State*, Oxford: Oxford University Press.

Banton, M. (1987) *Racial Theories*, Cambridge: Cambridge University Press.

Barbalet, J. (1988) *Citizenship*, Milton Keynes: Open University Press.

Barber, B. (1995) *Jihad vs. McWorld*, London: Ballantine Books.

Bardhan, P. (2006) 'Globalisation and the Limits to Poverty Alleviation', in Bardhan, P., Bowles, S. & Wallerstein, M. (eds) *Globalisation and Egalitarian Redistribution*, New Jersey: Princeton University Press.

Barnett, C. (1986) *The Audit of War*, London: Macmillan.

Barry, B. (1995) *Justice as Impartiality*, Oxford: Oxford University Press.

Barry, B. (2001) *Culture and Equality*, Cambridge: Polity.

Barry, B. (2005) *Why Social Justice Matters*, Cambridge: Polity.

Barry, B. (2008) 'Humanity and Justice in Global Perspective', Pogge, T. (ed.) (2008a) *Global Justice: Seminal Essays*, St. Paul: Paragon.

Barry, N. (1987) *The New Right*, London: Croom Helm.

Barry, N. (1997) 'Conservative Thought and the Welfare State', *Political Studies*, 45(2): 331–45.

Barry, N. (1999) *Welfare*, 2nd edition, Milton Keynes: Open University Press.

Baudrillard, J. (1988) *Selected Writings*, edited by M. Poster, Cambridge: Polity.

Bauman, Z. (1993) *Postmodern Ethics*, Oxford: Blackwell.

Bauman, Z. (1998) *Globalization*, Cambridge: Polity.

Bauman, Z. (2005) *Liquid Life*, Cambridge: Polity.

Bauman, Z. (2007) *Liquid Times*, Cambridge: Polity.

Beck, U. (1992) *Risk Society*, London: Sage.

Beck, U. (2007) 'Beyond Class and Nation: reframing social inequalities in a globalizing world', *British Journal of Sociology*, 58(4): 679–705.

Beck, U. & Beck-Gernsheim, E. (2002) *Individualization*, London: Sage.

Beck, U., Giddens, T. & Lash, S. (1994) *Reflexive Modernisation*, Cambridge: Polity.

Beitz, C. (2008) 'Justice and International Relations', Pogge, T. (ed.) (2008a) *Global Justice: Seminal Essays*, St. Paul: Paragon.

Bell, D. (1973) *The Coming of Post-Industrial Society*, New York: Basic Books.

Bennett, T. Savage, M. Silva, E. & Warde, A. (2009) *Culture, Class, Distinction*, London: Routledge.

Bentham, J. (1984) *Chrestomateia: The Collected Works of Jeremy Bentham*, Oxford: Clarendon.

Benton, T. (ed.) (1996) *The Greening of Marxism*, New York: Guilford Press.

Berger, P. & Luckmann, T. (1966) *The Social Construction of Reality*, London: Allen Lane.

Berlin, I. (1984) 'Two Concepts of Freedom', in Sandel, M. (ed.) *Liberalism and Its Critics*, New York: New York University Press.

Bertram, C. (2008) 'Globalisation, Social Justice and the Politics of Aid', in Craig, G., Burchardt, T. & Gordon, D. (eds) (2008) *Social Justice and Public Policy*, Bristol: Policy Press.

Best, S. (2005) *Understanding Social Divisions*, London: Sage.

Bettio, F. & Plantenga, J. (2004) 'Comparing Care Regimes in Europe', *Feminist Economics*, 10(1): 85–113.

Bevir, M. (2010) *Democratic Governance*, Princeton: Princeton University Press.

Bhagwati, J. (2004) *In Defence of Globalization*, Oxford: Oxford University Press.

Blair, T. (2005) speech reported in *The Globalist*, October 5th.

Block, W. (1994) 'Libertarianism and Libertinism', *The Journal of Libertarian Studies*, 11(1): 117–128.

Bonoli, G. (2005) 'The Politics of the New Social Policies', *Policy and Politics*, 33(3): 431–49.

Bookchin, M. (1980) *Towards an Ecological Society*, Montreal: Black Rose Books.

Bookchin, M. (2005) *The Ecology of Freedom*. Edinburgh: AK Press.

Bottero, W. (2005) *Stratification*, London: Routledge.

Bourdieu, P. (1984) *Distinction*, London: Routledge.

Bourdieu, P. (1999) *Acts of Resistance*, Cambridge: Polity.

Bourdieu, P. & Passeron, J. (1977) *Reproduction in Education, Society and Culture*, London: Sage.

Bowles, S. (2006) 'Egalitarian Redistribution in Globally Integrated Economies', in Bardhan, P., Bowles, S. & Wallerstein, M. (eds) *Globalisation and Egalitarian Redistribution*, New Jersey: Princeton University Press.

Bradley, H. (1996) *Fractured Identities*, Cambridge: Polity.

Brock, G. (2005) 'Egalitarianism, Ideals, and Cosmopolitan Justice', *Philosophical Forum*, 36(1): 1–30.

Brock, G. (2008) 'Taxation and Global Justice: Closing the Gap between Theory and Practice', *Journal of Social Philosophy*, 39(2): 161–84.

Brown, W. (2006) 'Power After Foucault', in Dryzek, J., Honig, B. & Phillips, A. (eds) *The Oxford Handbook of Political Theory*, Oxford: Oxford University Press.

Brundtland Commission (1987) *Our Common Future*, Oxford: Oxford University Press.

Bulmer, M. & Rees, A. (eds) (1996) *Citizenship Today*, London: UCL Press.

Burchardt, T. (2008) 'Monitoring Inequality: Putting the Capability Approach to Work', in Craig, G., Burchardt, T. & Gordon, D. (eds) (2008) *Social Justice and Public Policy*, Bristol: Policy Press.

Burke, E. (1968) *Reflections on the Revolution in France*, Middlesex: Penguin.

Butler, J. (1990) *Gender Trouble*, London: Routledge.

Byrne, D. (2005) *Social Exclusion*, 2nd ed., Buckinghamshire: Open University Press.

Cahill, M. (2001) *Social Policy and the Environment*, London: Routledge.

Cahill, M. & Fitzpatrick, T. (eds) (2002) *Environmental Issues and Social Policy*, Oxford: Blackwell.

Callinicos, A. (2000) *Equality*, Cambridge: Polity.

Callinicos, A. (2010) *Bonfire of Illusions*, Cambridge: Polity.

Campbell, J. & Oliver, M. (1996) *Disability Politics*, London: Routledge.

Caney, S. (2005) *Justice Beyond Borders*, Oxford: Oxford University Press.

Caney, S. (2009) 'Cosmopolitanism and Justice', in Christiano, T. & Christman, J. (eds) *Contemporary Debates in Political Philosophy*, London: Wiley-Blackwell.

Cannadine, D. (2000) *Class in Britain*, 2nd ed., Middlesex: Penguin.

Carens, J. (2003a) 'An Interpretation and Defence of the Socialist Principle of Distribution', in Paul, E. F., Miller, F. D. & Paul, J. (eds) *After Socialism*, Cambridge: Cambridge University Press.

Carens, J. (2003b) 'Who Should Get in? The Ethics of Immigration Admissions', *Ethics and International Affairs*, 17(1): 95–110.

Carlyle, T. (1971) *Selected Writings*, Middlesex: Penguin.

Castells, M. (2000) *End of Millennium*, 2nd ed., Oxford: Blackwell.

Castells, M. (2009a) *The Power of Identity*, 2nd ed., Oxford: Blackwell.

Castells, M. (2009b) *The Rise of the Network Society*, 2nd ed., Oxford: Blackwell.

Castells, M. & Himanen, P. (2002) *The Information Society and the Welfare State*, Oxford: Oxford University Press.

Chambers, S. & Kopstein, J. (2006) 'Civil Society and the State', in Dryzek, J., Honig, B. & Phillips, A. (eds) *The Oxford Handbook of Political Theory*, Oxford: Oxford University Press.

Charles, N. (2000) *Feminism, the State and Social Policy*, Basingstoke: Palgrave.

Chen, W. & Wellman, B. (2005) 'Minding the Cyber-Gap', in Romero, M. & Margolis, E. (eds) *Blackwell Companion to Social Inequalities*, Oxford: Blackwell.

Christiano, T. (2007) 'A Foundation for Egalitarianism', in Holtung, N. & Lippert-Rasmussen, K. (eds) *Egalitarianism*, Oxford: Clarendon Press.

Christoff, P. (1996) 'Ecological Modernisation, Ecological Modernities', *Environmental Politics*, 5(3): 476–500.

Clark, T. & Lipset, S. (2000) *The Breakdown of Class Politics*, Woodrow Wilson Centre Press.

Clarke, J. (2004) *Changing Welfare, Changing States*, London: Sage.

Clarke, J. & Fink, J. (2008) 'Unsettled attachments: national identity, citizenship and welfare', in W. van Oorschot, M. Opielka, and B. Pfau-Effinger (eds) *Culture and Welfare State*, Cheltenham: Edward Elgar.

Clarke, J., Newman, J., Smith, N. & Vidler, E. (2007) *Creating Citizen-Consumers*, London: Sage.

Cochrane, A. (2004) 'Modernisation, Managerialism and the Culture Wars', *Local Government Studies*, 30(4): 481–96.

Cohen, G. A. (2008) *Rescuing Justice and Equality*, Cambridge: Harvard University Press.

Cohen, G. A. (2009) *Why Not Socialism?*, Princeton: Princeton University Press.

Cohen, J. (2009) 'Reflections on Deliberative Democracy', in Christiano, T. & Christman, J. (eds) *Contemporary Debates in Political Philosophy*, London: Wiley-Blackwell.

Cole, G. D. H. (1920) *Guild Socialism Re-stated*, London: Leonard Parsons.

Coleman, J. & Fararo, T. (1993) *Rational Choice Theory*, London: Sage.

Cox, O. C. (1970) *Caste, Class and Race*, New York: Monthly Review.

Craig, G., Burchardt, T. & Gordon, D. (eds) (2008) *Social Justice and Public Policy*, Bristol: Policy Press.

Crompton, R. (2008) *Class and Stratification*, 3rd ed., Cambridge: Polity.

Crosland, T. (1956) *The Future of Socialism*, London: Jonathan Cape.

Dagger, R. (1997) *Civic Virtues*, Oxford: Oxford University Press.

Dagger, (2009) 'Individualism and the Claims of Community', in Christiano, T. & Christman, J. (eds) *Contemporary Debates in Political Philosophy*, London: Wiley-Blackwell.

Dahl, H. (2004) 'A View from the Inside: Recognition and Redistribution in the Nordic Welfare State from a Gender Perspective', *Acta Sociologica*, 47(4): 325–337.

Dahl, R. (1961) *Who Governs?*, New Haven: Yale University Press.

Dahl, R. (1985) *Polyarchy*, New Haven: Yale University Press.

Daly, M. (1979) *Gyn/Ecology*, London: The Women's Press.

Daly, M. (2000) *The Gender Division of Welfare*, Cambridge: Cambridge University Press.

Daniels, N. & Sabin, J. (2002) *Setting Limits Fairly*, Oxford: Oxford University Press.

Darwell, S. (2002) *Welfare and Rational Care*, Princeton: Princeton University Press.

Darwin, C. (2004) *The Descent of Man*, Middlesex: Penguin.

Davis, A. (1982) *Women, Race and Class*, London: The Women's Press.

de Jasay, A. (1989) *Social Contract, Free Ride*, Oxford: Clarendon.

de Jasay, A. (2004) 'Pious Lies: the justification of states and welfare states', *Economic Affairs*, 24(2): 62–4.

de Tocqueville, A. (1990) *Democracy in America*, New York: Vintage Books.

Deacon, A. (2002) *Perspectives on Welfare*, Buckinghamshire: Open University Press.

Deacon, A. & Mann, K. (1998) 'Agency, Modernity and Social Policy', *Journal of Social Policy*, 28(3): 413–35.

Deacon, B. (2007) *Global Social Policy and Governance*, London: Sage.

Dean, H. (2006) *Social Policy*, Cambridge: Polity.

Dean, H. (2010) *Understanding Human Needs*, Bristol: Policy Press.

Dean, H. & Taylor-Gooby, P. (1992) *Dependency Culture*, Hemel Hempstead: Harvester Wheatsheaf.

Dean, J. (2008) 'Enjoying Neoliberalism', *Cultural Politics*, 4(1): 47–72.

Dean, M (1999) *Governmentality*, London: Sage.

Dean, M. (2007) *Governing Societies*, Maidenhead: Open University Press.

Della Porta, D. & Diani, M. (2006) *Social Movements*, 2nd ed., Oxford: Blackwell.

Devine, F. (2004) *Class Practices*, Cambridge: Cambridge University Press.

Devine, F. & Savage, M. (2005) 'The Cultural Turn: sociology and class analysis', in Devine, F., Crompton, R., Savage, M. & Scott, J. (eds) *Rethinking Class*, Basingstoke: Palgrave.

Diener, E., Lucas, R., Schimmack, U. & Helliwell, J. (2009) *Well-Being for Public Policy*, Oxford: Oxford University Press.

Dobrowolsky, A. & Saint-Martin, D. (2005) 'Agency, Actors and Change in a Child-Focused Future: "path dependency" problematised', *Commonwealth & Comparative Politics*, 43(1): 1–33.

Dobson, A. (2003) *Citizenship and the environment*, Oxford: Oxford University Press.

Donzelot, J. (1979) *The Policing of Families*, Baltimore, Maryland: John Hopkins University Press.

Dorling, D. (2010) *Injustice*, Bristol: Policy Press.

Doyal, L. & Gough, I. (1991) *A Theory of Human Needs*, London: Macmillan.

Driver, S. & Martell, L. (2006) *New Labour*, 2nd ed., Cambridge: Polity.

Dryzek, J. (2000) *Deliberative Democracy and Beyond*, Oxford University Press.

Dryzek, J. (2005) *The Politics of the Earth*, 2nd ed., Oxford: Oxford University Press.

Dryzek, J. (2008) 'The Ecological Crisis of the Welfare State', *Journal of European Social Policy*, 18(4): 334–7.

Dworkin, R. (1977) *Taking Rights Seriously*, London: Duckworth.

Dworkin, R. (2000) *Sovereign Virtue*, Harvard: Harvard University Press.

Easterlin, R. (2005) 'Building a Better Theory of Well-Being', in Bruni, L. & Porta, P. (eds) *Economics and Happiness*, Oxford: Oxford University Press.

Eckersley, R. (1992) *Environmentalism and Political Theory*, London: UCL Press.

Eckersley, R. (2004) *The Green State*, Cambridge: MIT Press.

Elliott, A. and Lemert, C. (2006) *The New Individualism*, London: Routledge.

Elster, J. (1985) *Making Sense of Marx*, Cambridge: Cambridge University Press.

Elster, J. (2007) *Explaining Social Behaviour*, Cambridge: Cambridge University Press.

Engels, F. (2010) *The Origin of the Family, Private Property and the State*, Middlesex: Penguin.

Esping-Andersen, G. (1990) *The Three Worlds of Welfare Capitalism*, London: Sage.

Esping-Andersen. G. (ed.) (1993) *Changing Classes*, London: Sage.

Esping-Andersen, G. (1999) *Social Foundations of Post-Industrial Economies*, Cambridge: Cambridge University Press.

Estes, C. Biggs, S. & Phillipson, C. (2003) *Social Theory, Social Policy and Ageing*, Buckinghamshire: Open University Press.

Etzioni, A. (1994) *The Politics of Community*, London: Fontana.

Etzioni, A. (2004) *The Common Good*, Cambridge: Polity.

Fabre, C. (2007) *Justice in a Changing World*, Cambridge: Polity.

Finlayson, A. (2003) *Making Sense of New Labour*, London: Lawrence & Wishart.

Fishkin, J. & Laslett, P. (eds) (2003) *Debating Deliberative Democracy*, Blackwell.

Fitzpatrick, T. (1998) 'The Implications of Ecological Thought for Social Welfare', *Critical Social Policy*, 18(1): 5–26.

Fitzpatrick, T. (1999a) *Freedom and Security*, London: Macmillan.

Fitzpatrick, T. (1999b) 'Social Policy for Cyborgs', *Body & Society*, 5(1): 93–116.

Fitzpatrick, T. (2000) 'Critical Cyber Policy: Network Technologies, Massless Citizens, Virtual Rights', *Critical Social Policy*, 20(3): 375–407.

Fitzpatrick, T. (2001) 'New Agendas for Social Policy and Criminology', *Social Policy & Administration*, 35(2): 212–29.

Fitzpatrick, T. (2002) 'The Two Paradoxes of Welfare Democracy', *International Journal of Social Welfare*, 11(2): 159–69.

Fitzpatrick, T. (2003) *After the New Social Democracy*, Manchester: Manchester University Press.

Fitzpatrick, T. (2005) *New Theories of Welfare*, Basingstoke: Palgrave.

Fitzpatrick, T. (2008a) *Applied Ethics and Social Problems*, Bristol: Policy Press.

Fitzpatrick, T. (2008b) 'From Contracts to Capabilities and Back Again', *Res Publica*, 14(2): 83–100.

Fitzpatrick, T. (2009) 'Deliberative Democracy, Critical Rationality and Social Memory', *Studies in Philosophy and Education*, 28(4): 313–27.

Fitzpatrick, T. (2011a) 'Social Paternalism and Basic Income', *Policy & Politics*, 39(1): 81–98.

Fitzpatrick, T. (2011b) 'The Potential Contradictions of a Phronetic Social Policy: Social Science as Phronesis?', *Journal of Social Policy*, 40(1): 31–9.

Fitzpatrick, T. (ed.) (2011c) *Understanding the Environment and Social Policy*, Bristol: Policy Press.

Fitzpatrick, T. & Cahill, M. (eds) (2002) *Environment and Welfare*, Basingstoke: Palgrave.

Flaherty, J., Veit-Wilson, J. & Dornan, P. (2004) *Poverty: the Facts*, 5th ed., London: CPAG.

Fleurbaey, M. (2008) *Fairness, Responsibility, and Welfare*, Oxford: Oxford University Press.

Foucault, M. (1967) *Madness and Civilisation*, New York: Pantheon.

Foucault, M. (1980) *Power/Knowledge*, New York: Pantheon.

Foucault, M. (1984) *The Foucault Reader*, edited by Paul Rabinow, Middlesex: Penguin.

Fraser, N. (1989) *Unruly Practices*, Cambridge: Polity.

Fraser, N. (1997) *Justice Interruptus*, London: Routledge.

Fraser, N. (2001) 'Recognition Without Ethics?', *Theory, Culture and Society*, 18(2–3): 21–42.

Fraser, N. (2008) *Scales of Justice*, Cambridge: Polity.

Fraser, N. with Bedford, K. (2008) 'Social Rights and Gender Justice in the Neoliberal Movement', *Feminist Theory*, 9(2): 225–45.

Fraser, N. & Honneth, A. (2003) *Redistribution or Recognition?*, London: Verso.

Freeden, M. (1996) *Ideologies and Political Theory*, Oxford: Oxford University Press.

Freeman, S. (2007) *Rawls*, London: Routledge.

Friedan, B. (1983) *The Feminine Mystique*, Middlesex: Penguin.

Frieden, J. (2006) *Global Capitalism*, New York: W. W. Norton & Co.

Friedman, D. (1989) *The Machinery of Freedom*, New York: Harper and Row.

Friedman, M. (1962) *Capitalism and Freedom*, Chicago: Chicago University Press.

Friedman, T. (2005) *The World is Flat*, New York: Farrar, Strauss, Giroux.

Fudge, S. & Williams, S. (2006) 'Beyond Left and Right: Can the Third Way Deliver a Reinvigorated *Social* Democracy?', *Critical Sociology*, 32(4): 583–602.

Fukuyama, F. (1992) *The End of History and the Last Man*, New York: Free Press.

Gamble, A. (2009) *The Spectre at the Feast*, Basingstoke; Palgrave Macmillan.

Gaus, G. (2003) 'Backwards into the Future: Neorepublicanism as a Postsocialist Critique of Market Society', in Paul, E. F., Miller, F. D. & Paul, J. (eds) *After Socialism*, Cambridge: Cambridge University Press.

Genschel, P. (2004) 'Globalization and the Welfare State: a retrospective', *Journal of European Public Policy*, 11(4): 613–36.

George, V. & Page, R. (eds) (1995) *Modern Thinkers on Welfare*, Hemel Hempstead: Harvester Wheatsheaf.

George, V. & Page, R. (eds) (2004) *Global Social Problems*, Cambridge: Polity.

George, V. & Wilding, P. (1994) *Welfare and Ideology*, Hemel Hempstead: Harvester Wheatsheaf.

George, V. & Wilding, P. (2002) *Globalization and Human Welfare*, Basingstoke: Palgrave.

Geras, N. (1989) *Discourses of Extremity*, London: Verso.

Giddens, T. (1984) *The Constitution of Society*, Cambridge: Polity.

Giddens, T. (1994) *Beyond Left and Right*, Cambridge: Polity.

Giddens, T. (1998) *The Third Way*, Cambridge: Polity.

Giddens, T. (1999) *Runaway World*, London: Profile Books.

Giddens, T. (2009) *The Politics of Climate Change*, Cambridge: Polity.

Gilleard, C. & Higgs, P. (2009) 'The Power of Silver: Age and Identity Politics in the 21st Century', *Journal of Aging & Social Policy*, 21(3): 277–295.

Gilligan, C. (1982) *In A Different Voice*, Cambridge, MA: Harvard University Press.

Gilroy, P. (1987) *There Ain't No Black in the Union Jack*, London: Hutchison.

Ginsburg, N. (1979) *Class, Capital and Social Policy*, London: Macmillan.

Goldsmith, Z. (2009) *The Constant Economy*, London: Atlantic Books.

Goldthorpe, J. & Jackson, M. (2007) 'Intergenerational Class Mobility in Britain: evidence from national surveys, 1972–2005', *British Journal of Sociology*, 58(4): 525–46.

Goleman, D. (2007) *Social Intelligence*, London: Arrow Books.

Goodhart, D. (2006) *Progressive Nationalism*, London: Demos.

Goodin, R. (1988) *Reasons for Welfare*, Princeton, NJ: Princeton University Press.

Goodin, R. (2002) 'Free Movement: if people were money', in LaFollette, H. (ed.) *Ethics in Practice*, Oxford: Blackwell.

Goodin, R. (2003) *Reflective Democracy*, Oxford: Oxford University Press.

Goodin, R. & Le Grand, J. (eds) (1987) *Not Only the Poor*, London: Allen & Unwin.

Gordon, D. (2006) 'The Concept and Measurement of Poverty', in Pantazis, C., Gordon, D. & Levitas, R. (eds) *Poverty and Social Exclusion in Britain*, Bristol: Policy Press.

Gornick, J. & Meyers, M. (2009) *Gender Equality*, London: Verso.

Gough, I. (1979) *The Political Economy of the Welfare State*, London: Macmillan.

Gowan, P. (1999) *The Global Gamble*, London: Verso.

Graham, C. (1994) *Safety Nets, Politics and the Poor*, Washington DC: Brookings.

Graham, C. (2009) *Happiness around the World*, Oxford: Oxford University Press.

Gramsci, A. (1971) *Selections from Prison Notebooks*, London: Lawrence & Wishart.

Gray, J. (1993) *Beyond the New Right*, London: Routledge.

Green, T. H. (1986) *Lectures on the Principles of Political Obligation*, Cambridge: Cambridge University Press.

Gutmann, A. & Thompson, D. (2004) *Why Deliberative Democracy?*, Princeton University Press.

Habermas, J. (1975) *Legitimation Crisis*, London: Hutchison.

Habermas, J. (1984) *Reason and the Rationalisation of Society*, Boston: Beacon Press.

Habermas, J. (1987a) *The Theory of Communicative Action*, 2 volumes, Cambridge: Polity.

Habermas, J. (1987b) *The Philosophical Discourse of Modernity*, Cambridge: Polity.

Habermas, J. (1990) *Moral Consciousness and Communicative Action*, Cambridge: MIT Press.

Habermas, J. (1994) 'Citizenship and National Identity', in van Steenbergen, B. (ed.) *The Condition of Citizenship*, London: Sage.

Habermas, J. (2008) *Between Naturalism and Religion*, Cambridge: Polity.

Hacking, I. (1999) *The Social Construction of What?*, Cambridge: Harvard University Press.

Halsey, A. H., Lawder, H., Brown, P. & Wells, A. (eds) (1997) *Education*, Oxford: Oxford University Press.

Hardin, G. (1977) 'The Tragedy of the Commons', in Hardin, G. & Baden, J. (eds) *Managing the Commons*, San Francisco: W. H. Freeman & Co.

Hardt, M. & Negri, A. (2006) *Multitude*, London: Penguin.

Hartmann, H. (1989) 'The Unhappy Marriage of Marxism and Feminism', in Gottlieb, R. (ed.) *An Anthology of Western Marxism*, Oxford: Oxford University Press.

Harvey, D. (2005) *A Short History of Neoliberalism*, Oxford: Oxford University Press.

Harvey, D. (2006) *Spaces of Global Capitalism*, London: Verso.

Harvey, D. (2010) *The Enigma of Capital and the Crises of Capitalism*, London: Profile.

Haugaard, M. (ed.) (2002) *Power: a Reader*, Manchester: Manchester University Press.

Haybron, D. (2008) *The Pursuit of Unhappiness*, Oxford: Oxford University Press.

Hayek, F. (1944) *The Road to Serfdom*, London: Routledge & Kegan Paul.

Hayek, F. (1960) *The Constitution of Liberty*, London: Routledge & Kegan Paul.

Hayek, F. (1976) *Law, Legislation and Liberty: Volume 2*, London: Routledge.

Hayek, F. (1979) *Law, Legislation and Liberty: Volume 3*, London: Routledge.

Heath, A. & Payne, C. (2000) 'Social Mobility', in A. H. Halsey with J. Webb (eds) *Twentieth-Century British Social Trends*, London: Macmillan.

Hegel, G. (1967) *Philosophy of Right*, Oxford: Oxford University Press.

Hegel, G. (1977) *Phenomenology of Spirit*, Oxford: Oxford University Press.

Held, D. (1995) *Democracy and the Global Order*, Cambridge: Polity.

Held, D. (2010) *Cosmopolitanism*, Cambridge: Polity.

Held, D. & McGrew, A. (2007a) *Globalization/Anti-Globalization*, 2nd ed., Cambridge: Polity.

Henman, P. & Marston, G. (2008) 'The Social Division of Welfare Surveillance', *Journal of Social Policy*, 37(2): 187–205.

Herrnstein, R. & Murray, C. (1994) *The Bell Curve*, New York: Free Press.

Hills, J. (2009) 'Future Pressures, Intergenerational Links, Wealth, Demography and Sustainability', in Hills, J., Sefton, T. & Stewart, K. (eds) *Towards a More Equal Society?*, Bristol: Policy Press.

Hills, J., Sefton, T. & Stewart, K. (2009) 'Conclusions: Climbing every Mountain or Retreating from the Foothills?', in Hills, J., Sefton, T. & Stewart, K. (eds) *Towards a More Equal Society?*, Bristol: Policy Press.

Hindess, B. (1996) *Concepts of Power*, Oxford: Blackwell.

Hindess, B. & Hirst, P. (1977) *Mode of Production and Social Formation*, Basingstoke: Macmillan.

Hines, S. (2009) 'A Pathway to Diversity? Human rights, citizenship and the politics of transgender', *Contemporary Politics*, 15(1): 87–102.

Hirsch, F. (1977) *The Social Limits to Growth*, London: Routledge.

Hirst, P. & Thompson, G. (1999) *Globalisation in Question*, 2nd ed., Cambridge: Polity.

Hobbes, T. (1973) *Leviathan*, London: J. M. Dent & Sons.

Hobhouse, L. (1994) *Liberalism and Other Writings*, Cambridge: Cambridge University Press.

Holden, C. (2008) 'International Trade and Welfare', in Yeates, N. (ed.) *Understanding Global Social Policy*, Bristol: Policy Press.

Holtung, N. (2007) 'Prioritarianism', in Holtung, N. & Lippert-Rasmussen, K. (eds) *Egalitarianism*, Oxford: Clarendon Press.

Holtung, N. & Lippert-Rasmussen, K. (2007) 'An Introduction to Contemporary Egalitarianism', in Holtung, N. & Lippert-Rasmussen, K. (eds) *Egalitarianism*, Oxford: Clarendon Press.

Holzman, R. (2006) 'Risk', in Fitzpatrick, T., Manning, N., Pascall, G., Kwon, H-J. & Midgley, J. (eds) *International Encyclopaedia of Social Policy*, London: Routledge.

Honderich, T. (2005) *Conservatism*, 2nd edition, Boulder: Westview Press.

Honneth, A. (2007) *Disrespect*, Cambridge: Polity.

Hume, D. (1969) *A Treatise on Human Nature*, Middlesex: Penguin.

Huntington, S. (1997) *The Clash of Civilisations and the Remaking of World Order*, London: Simon & Schuster.

Hurley, S. (2003) *Justice, Luck and Knowledge*, Harvard: Harvard University Press.

Hyde, M. (2006) 'Disability', in Payne, G. (ed.) *Social Divisions*, Basingstoke: Palgrave.

Inglehart, R. (1990) *Culture Shift in Advanced Society*, Princeton, NJ: Princeton University Press.

Jackson, B. (2010) 'At the Origins of Neo-Liberalism: The Free Economy and the Strong State, 1930–1947', *Historical Journal*, 53(1): 129–51.

Jackson, T. (2002) 'Quality of Life, Sustainability and Economic Growth', in Fitzpatrick, T. & Cahill, M. (eds) *Environment and Welfare*, London: Palgrave.

Jackson, T. (2009) *Prosperity Without Growth*, Sustainable Development Commission.

Jacobs, L. (2004) *Pursuing Equal Opportunities*, Cambridge: Cambridge University Press.

Jessop, B. (2002) *The Future of the Capitalist State*, Cambridge: Polity.

Jessop, B. (2008) *State Power*, Cambridge: Polity.

Jones, C. & Novak, T. (1999) *Poverty, Welfare and the Disciplinary State*, London: Routledge.

Jordan, B. (2008) *Welfare and Wellbeing*, Bristol: Policy Press.

Jordan, B. (2010) *Why the Third Way Failed*, Bristol: Policy Press.

Joyce, P. (2003) *The Rule of Freedom*, London: Verso.

Kahneman, D., Diener, D. & Schwarz, N. (1999) *Well-Being*, New York: Russell Sage.

Kant, I. (1996) *Practical Philosophy*, Cambridge: Cambridge University Press.

Kekes, J. (1998) *A Case for Conservatism*, New York: Cornell University Press.

Kenworthy, L. (2004) *Egalitarian Capitalism*, New York: Russell Sage.

Keynes, J. M. (1954) *The General Theory of Employment, Interest and Money*, London: Macmillan.

Kierkegaard, S. (1992) *Either/Or*, Middlesex: Penguin.

King, D. (1999) *In the Name of Liberalism*, Oxford: Oxford University Press.

Kirk, R. (1985) *The Conservative Mind*, 7th edition, Washington: Regnery Publishing Inc.

Klein, N. (2007) *The Shock Doctrine*, London: Allen Lane.

Knight, C. (2009) *Luck Egalitarianism*, Edinburgh: Edinburgh University Press.

Korpi, W. (1983) *The Democratic Class Struggle*, London: Routledge & Kegan Paul.

Kraut, R. (2007) *What is Good and Why*, Cambridge: Harvard University Press.

Kropotkin, P. (2009) *Mutual Aid*, Mineola, NY: Dover Books.

Krugman, P. (2008) *The Return of Depression Economics and the Crisis of 2008*, London: Penguin.

Kuhn, T. (1970) *The Structure of Scientific Revolutions*, 2nd ed., Chicago: University of Chicago Press.

Kukathas, C. (2003) *The Liberal Archipelago*, Oxford: Oxford University Press.

Kukathas, C. (2006) 'The Mirage of Social Justice', Social Philosophy & *Policy*, 23: 1–28.

Kumar, K. (1995) *From Post-Industrial to Post-Modern Society*, Oxford: Blackwell.

Kymlicka, W. (1995a) *The Rights of Minority Cultures*, Oxford: Clarendon.

Kymlicka, W. (1995b) *Multicultural Citizenship*, Oxford: Oxford University Press.

Kymlicka, W. (2002) *Contemporary Political Philosophy*, 2nd ed., Oxford: Oxford University Press.

Laborde, C. (2008) *Critical Republicanism*, Oxford: Oxford University Press.

Lacey, A. (2001) *Robert Nozick*, Chesham: Acumen.

Laclau, E. & Mouffe, C. (1985) *Hegemony and Socialist Strategy*, London: Verso.

Laden, A. (2009) 'Relational Liberalism and Demands for Equality, Recognition, and Group Rights', in Christiano, T. & Christman, J. (eds) *Contemporary Debates in Political Philosophy*, London: Wiley-Blackwell.

Laing, R. D. (1970) *The Divided Self*, London: Pelican.

Lash, S. & Urry, J. (1987) *The End of Organised Capitalism*, Cambridge: Polity.

Laski, H. (1935) *The State in Theory and Practice*, London: George Allen & Unwin.

Lavalette, M. & Mooney, G. (eds) (2000) *Class Struggle and Social Welfare*, London: Routledge.

Lawler, S. (2007) *Identity*, Cambridge: Polity.

Layard, R. (2005) *Happiness*, London: Allen Lane.

Lazzarato, M. (2009) 'Neoliberalism in Action: Inequality, insecurity and the reconstitution of the social', *Theory Culture & Society*, 26(6): 109–33.

Le Grand, J. (1982) *The Strategy of Equality*, London: Allen & Unwin.

Le Grand, J. (2003) *From Knight to Knave and From Pawn to Queen*, Oxford: Oxford University Press.

Le Grand, J. (2007) *The Other Invisible Hand*, Princeton: Princeton University Press.

Lechner, F. (2009) *Globalization*, Oxford: Wiley-Blackwell.

Levitas, R. (2005) *An Exclusive Society?*, 2nd ed., Basingstoke: Palgrave.

Lewis, G. (2000) *'Race', Gender, Social Welfare*, Cambridge: Polity.

Lewis, G., Gewirtz, S. & Clarke, J. (eds) (2000) *Rethinking Social Policy*, London: Sage.

Lister (2004) *Poverty*, Cambridge: Polity.

Lister, R. (2001) 'Towards a Citizens' Welfare State: the 3+2 "R's" of Welfare Reform', *Theory, Culture and Society*, 18(2–3): 91–111.

Lister, R. (2003) *Citizenship: Feminist Perspectives*, 2nd ed., London: Macmillan.

Lister, R. (2009) 'A Nordic Nirvana? Gender, citizenship, and social justice in the Nordic welfare states', *Social Politics*, 16(2): 242–278.

Lister, R. (2010) *Understanding Theories and Concepts in Social Policy*, Bristol: Policy Press.

Locke, J. (1960) *Second Treatise on Government*, Cambridge: Cambridge University Press.

Lopez, J. & Potter, G. (eds) (2005) *After Postmodernism*, London: Continuum.

Lukes, S. (ed.) (1986) *Power: readings in social and political theory*, Oxford: Blackwell.

Lukes, S. (2005) *Power: A radical agenda*, 2nd ed., Basingstoke: Palgrave.

Macintyre, A. (1981) *After Virtue*, London: Duckworth.

Macintyre, A. (1987) *Whose Justice? Which Rationality?*, London: Duckworth.

Mack, E. (2009) 'Individualism and Libertarian Rights', in Christiano, T. & Christman, J. (eds) *Contemporary Debates in Political Philosophy*, London: Wiley-Blackwell.

Mack, E. & Gaus, G. (2004) 'Classical Liberalism and Libertarianism', in Gaus, G. & Kukathas, C. (eds) *Handbook of Political Theory*, London: Sage.

Macmillan, H. (1938) *The Middle Way*, London: Macmillan.

Mandeville, B. (1988) *The Fable of the Bees*, Indianapolis, IL: Liberty Press.

Mann, M. (1986) *The Sources of Social Power: Volume 1*, Cambridge: Cambridge University Press.

Marcuse, H. (1964) *One-Dimensional Man*, London: Routledge & Kegan Paul.

Marmot Review (2010) *Fair Society, Healthy Lives*, available at: www.ucl.ac.uk/marmotreview.

Marquand, D. (2004) *Decline of the Public*, Cambridge: Polity.

Marshall, T. H. & Bottomore, T. (1992) *Citizenship & Social Class*, London: Pluto.

Marx, K. (1977) *Selected Writings*, edited by D. McLellan, Oxford: Oxford University Press.

Maslow, A. (1954) *Motivation and Personality*, 2nd edition, New York: Harper & Row.

Mason, D. (2006) 'Ethnicity', in Payne, G. (ed.) *Social Divisions*, Basingstoke: Palgrave.

Masson, J. M. (1992) *The Assault on Truth*, London: Flamingo.

Matravers, M. (2007) *Responsibility and Justice*, Cambridge: Polity.

McCall, L. (2005) 'The Complexity of Intersectionality', *Signs*, 30(3): 1771–1800.

McGee, R. (2002) 'Ending Welfare as We Know It', *Economic Affairs*, 22(1): 12–16.

McKay, S. (2011) 'Response 1: Scientific Method in Social Policy Research Is Not a Lost Cause', *Journal of Social Policy*, 40(1).

McLaughlin, E. & Baker, J. (2007) 'Equality, Social Justice and Social Welfare', *Social Policy & Society*, 6: 53–68.

McNay, L. (2008) *Against Recognition*, Cambridge: Polity.

McRobbie, A. (2009) *The Aftermath of Feminism*, London: Sage.

Mead, L. (1986) *Beyond Entitlement*, New York: Free Press.

Mead, L. (2005) 'Welfare Reform and Citizenship', in Mead, L. & Beem, C. (eds) *Welfare Reform and Political Theory*, New York: Russell Sage.

Meadowcroft, J. (2005) 'From Welfare State to Ecostate', in Barry, J. & Eckersley, R. (eds) *The State and the Global Ecological Crisis*, Cambridge: MIT Press.

Meadows, D., Randers, J. & Behrens, W. (1972) *The Limits to Growth*, New York: Universe Books.

Meiksins-Wood, E. (1985) *The Retreat from Class*, London: Verso.

Melucci, A. (1989) *Nomads of the Present*, London: Radius.

Miliband, R. (1969) *The State in Capitalist Society*, London: Weidenfeld & Nicolson.

Mill, J. S. (1962) *Utilitarianism*, London: Fontana.

Miller, D. (1999) *Principles of Social Justice*, Cambridge, Mass: Harvard University Press.

Miller, D. (2003) 'What's Left of the Welfare State?', in Paul, E. F., Miller, F. D. & Paul, J. (eds) *After Socialism*, Cambridge: Cambridge University Press.

Miller, D. (2005) 'Immigration: the case for limits', in Wellman, C. & Cohen, A. (eds) *Contemporary Debates in Applied Ethics*, Oxford: Blackwell.

Miller, D. (2007) *National Responsibility and Global Justice*, Oxford: Oxford University Press.

Miller, D. & Walzer, M. (eds) (1995) *Pluralism, Justice and Equality*, Oxford: Oxford University Press.

Mills, C. W. (1956) *The Power Elite*, Oxford: Oxford University Press.

Monbiot, G. (2003) *The Age of Consent*, London: Flamingo.

Monbiot, G. (2007) *Heat*, London: Penguin.

Montesquieu, C-L. (1989) *The Spirit of the Laws*, Cambridge: Cambridge University Press.

Moore, M. (2009) 'Liberalism, Communitarianism, and the Politics of Identity', in Christiano, T. & Christman, J. (eds) *Contemporary Debates in Political Philosophy*, London: Wiley-Blackwell.

More, T. (1989) *Utopia*, Cambridge: Cambridge University Press.

Morris, W. (1986) *News from Nowhere and Selected Writings and Designs*, Middlesex: Penguin.

Morriss, P. (2002) *Power*, 2nd ed., Manchester: Manchester University Press.

Murphy, L. & Nagel, T. (2002) *The Myth of Ownership*, Oxford: Oxford University Press.

Murray, C. (1984) *Losing Ground*, New York: Basic Books.

Murray, C. (2000) 'Genetics of the Right', *Prospect*, April: 28–31.

Murray, C. (2006) *In Our Hands*, Washington: The American Enterprise Institute.

Nagel, T. (1979) *Mortal Questions*, Cambridge: Cambridge University Press.

Nagel, T. (2005) 'The Problem of Global Justice', *Philosophy & Public Affairs*, 33–114–37.

Narveson, J. (2001) *The Libertarian Idea*, Peterborough, Canada: Broadview Press.

National Equality Panel (2010) *An Anatomy of Economic Inequality in the UK*, LSE: CASE.

Navarro, V., Schmitt, J. & Javier, A. (2004) 'Is Globalisation Undermining the Welfare State?', *Cambridge Journal of Economics*, 28: 133–52.

Nisbet, R. (2001) *Conservatism*, Milton Keynes: Open University Press.

Nitzan, S. (2010) *Collective Preference and Choice*, Cambridge: Cambridge University Press.

Norberg, J. (2003) *In Defence of Global Capitalism*, Washington: Cato Institute.

Nordhaus, W. (2008) *A Question of Balance*, New Haven: Yale University Press.

Nozick, R. (1974) *Anarchy, State and Utopia*, Oxford: Blackwell.

Nussbaum, M. (1999) *Sex and Social Justice*, Oxford: Oxford University Press.

Nussbaum, M. (2001) *Upheavals of Thought*, Cambridge: Cambridge University Press.

Nussbaum, M. (2006) *Frontiers of Justice*, Harvard: Balknap Press.

O'Connor, J. (1973) *The Fiscal Crisis of the State*, New York: St. Martin's Press.

O'Connor, J. (1998) *Natural Causes*, New York: Guilford Press.

O'Connor, J. (1998) *Natural Causes*, New York: Guilford Press.

O'Neill, O. (2009) 'The Dark Side of Human Rights', in Christiano, T. & Christman, J. (eds) *Contemporary Debates in Political Philosophy*, London: Wiley-Blackwell.

Oakeshott, M. (1962) *Rationalism in Politics and Other Essays*, London & New York: Methuen & Co.

Offe, C. (1984) *Contradictions of the Welfare State*, London: Hutchison.

Offe, C. (1985) *Disorganised Capitalism*, Cambridge: Polity.

Offe, C. (1987) 'Challenging the Boundaries of Institutional Politics: Social Movements Since the 1960s', in Maier, C. S. (ed.) *Changing Boundaries of the Political*, Cambridge: Cambridge University Press.

Offe, C. (1996) *Modernity and the State*, Cambridge: Polity.

Offer, A. (2006) *The Challenge of Affluence*, Oxford: Oxford University Press.

Offer, J. (2006) *An Intellectual History of British Social Policy*, Bristol: Policy Press.

Ohmae, K. (1995) *The End of the Nation-State*, London: HarperCollins.

Okin, S. M. (1979) *Women in Western Political Thought*, Princeton, NJ: Princeton University Press.

Oldfield, A. (1990) *Citizenship and Community*, Routledge.

Oliver, M. (2009) *Understanding Disability*, 2nd ed., Basingstoke: Palgrave.

Olson, K. (2006) *Reflexive Democracy*, Cambridge: MIT Press.

Olson, K. (ed.) (2008) *Adding Insult to Injury*, London: Verso.

Olson, M. (1965) *The Logic of Collective Action*, Cambridge: Harvard University Press.

Ophuls, W. (1977) *Ecology and the Politics of Scarcity*, San Francisco: W. H. Freeman.

Orloff, A. (2009) 'Gendering the Comparative Analysis of Welfare States: an unfinished agenda', *Sociological Theory*, 27(3): 317–343.

Ostrom, E. (1990) *Governing the Commons*, Cambridge: Cambridge University Press.

Page, R. (1996) *Altruism and the British Welfare State*, Aldershot: Avebury.

Page, R. (2007) 'Without a Song in their Heart: New Labour, the welfare state and the retreat from democratic socialism', *Journal of Social Policy*, 36(1): 19–37.

Pantazis, C. & Ruspini, E. (2006) 'Gender, Poverty and Social Exclusion', in Pantazis, C., Gordon, D. & Levitas, R. (eds) (2006) *Poverty and Social Exclusion in Britain*, Bristol: Policy Press.

Parekh, B. (2006) *Rethinking Multiculturalism*, 2nd ed., Basingstoke: Palgrave.

Parekh, B. (2008) *A New Politics of Identity*, Basingstoke: Palgrave.

Parfit, D. (2001) 'Equality or Priority?', in Harris, J. (ed.) *Bioethics*, Oxford: Oxford University Press.

Parsons, T. (1961) 'The School Class as a Social System: Some of its Functions in American Society', in Halsey, A. H., Floud, J. & Anderson, C. A. (eds) *Education, Economy and Society*, New York: Free Press.

Pascall, G. (1997) *Social Policy: A New Feminist Analysis*, London: Routledge.

Pateman, C. (1988) *The Sexual Contract*, Stanford: Stanford University Press.

Pateman, C. (1989) *The Disorder of Women*, Stanford University Press.

Pateman, C. & Mills, C. (2007) *Contract and Domination*, Cambridge: Polity.

Patterson, R. and Wilson, E.(2000) 'New IT and Social Inequality: Resetting the Research and Policy Agenda', *The Information Society*, 16(1): 77–86.

Payne, G. (2006a) 'Social Divisions as a Sociological Perspective', in Payne, G. (ed.) *Social Divisions*, Basingstoke: Palgrave

Payne, G. (ed.) (2006b) *Social Divisions*, Basingstoke: Palgrave

Pepper, D. (1993) *Eco-Socialism*, London: Routledge.

Pettit, P. (1997) *Republicanism*, Oxford University Press.

Phillips, A. (1999) *Which Equalities Matter?*, Cambridge: Polity.

Phillips, C. (2009) 'Ethnic Inequalities' in Hills, J., Sefton, T. & Stewart, K. (eds) *Towards a More Equal Society?*, Bristol: Policy Press.

Pierson, C. (2006) *Beyond the Welfare State?*, 3rd edition, Cambridge: Polity.

Pierson, P. (ed.) (2001) *The New Politics of the Welfare State*, Oxford: Oxford University Press.

Pierson, P. (2004) *Politics in Time*, Princeton: Princeton University Press.

Pigou, A. C. (1965) *Essays in Applied Economics*, London: Frank Cass.

Piore, M. & Sabel, C. (1984) *The Second Industrial Divide*, New York: Basic Books.

Plant, R. (1993) *Social Justice, Labour and the New Right*, London: Fabian Society.

Plant, R. (2009) *The Neo-Liberal State*, Oxford: Oxford University Press.

Plato (1955) *Republic*, Middlesex: Penguin.

Pogge, T. (ed.) (2008a) *Global Justice: Seminal Essays*, St. Paul: Paragon.

Pogge, T. (2008b) 'Cosmopolitanism and Sovereignty', in Pogge, T. (ed.) *Global Justice: Seminal Essays*, St. Paul: Paragon.

Pogge, T. (2008c) *World Poverty & Human Rights*, 2nd ed., Cambridge: Polity.

Polanyi, K. (1944) *The Great Transformation*, Boston: Beacon Press.

Posner, R. (2009) *A Failure of Capitalism*, Cambridge: Harvard University Press.

Poulantzas, N. (1975) *Classes in Contemporary Capitalism*, London: New Left Books.

Przeworski, A. (1985) *Capitalism and Social Democracy*, Cambridge: Cambridge University Press.

Putnam, R. (2000) *Bowling Alone*, New York: Simon & Schuster.

Rawls, J. (1972) *A Theory of Justice*, Oxford: Oxford University Press.

Rawls, J. (1993) *Political Liberalism*, New York: Columbia University Press.

Rawls, J. (1999) *The Law of Peoples*, Harvard: Harvard University Press.

Rawls, J. (2001) *Justice as Fairness*, Cambridge: Harvard University Press.

Reisman, D. (2005) *Democracy and Exchange*, Aldershot: Edward Elgar.

Rex, J. (1970) *Race Relations in Sociological Theory*, London: Wiedenfeld & Nicolson.

Rex, J. (1986) *Race and Ethnicity*, Milton Keynes: Open University Press.

Richardson, D. (2000) 'Constructing Sexual Citizenship: Theorising Sexual Rights', *Critical Social Policy*, 20(1): 105–35.

Richardson, H. (2002) *Democratic Autonomy*, Oxford: Oxford University Press.

Ritzer, G. (2008) *The McDonaldization of Society*, 5th ed., Thousand Oaks, CA: Pine Forge Press.

Ritzer, G. (2010) *Globalization*, Oxford: Wiley-Blackwell.

Robertson, R. (1992) *Globalisation*, London: Sage.

Roemer, J. (1993) 'A Pragmatic Theory of Responsibility for the Egalitarian Planner', *Philosophy & Public Affairs*, 22: 146–66.

Roemer, J. (1994) *A Future for Socialism?*, London: Verso.

Rose, N. (1999a) *Powers of Freedom*, Cambridge: Cambridge University Press.

Rose, N. (1999b) *Governing the Soul*, London: Freedom Association Books.

Rose, N. (2007) *The Politics of Life Itself*, Princeton: Princeton University Press.

Rothstein, B. (1998) *Just Institutions Matter*, Cambridge: Cambridge University Press.

Rousseau, J-J. (1973) *The Social Contract and Discourses*, London: J. M. Dent & Sons.

Saad-Filho, A. & Johnston, D. (eds) (2004) *Neoliberalism*, London: Pluto Press.

Salleh, A. (2009) *Eco-sufficiency and Global Justice*, London: Pluto.

Sandel, M. (1982) *Liberalism and the Limits of Justice*, Cambridge: Cambridge University Press.

Sandel, M. (1996) *Democracy's Discontent*, Cambridge: Harvard University Press.

Sandel, M. (2009) *Justice*, London: Allen Lane.

Sartre, J-P. (1958) *Being and Nothingness*, London: Methuen & Co.

Sassen, S. (2007) 'The Places and Spaces of the Global', in Held, D. & McGrew, A. (eds) *Globalization Theory*, Cambridge: Polity.

Sassoon, D. (2010) *One Hundred Years of Socialism*, 2nd ed., London: I. B. Taurus.

Satz, D. (2007) 'Liberalism, Economic Freedom, and the Limits of Markets', in Paul, E. F., Miller, F. D. & Paul, J. (eds) *Liberalism: old and new*, Cambridge: Cambridge University Press.

Saunders, P. (1996) *Unequal but Fair?*, London: IEA.

Savage, M. (2000) *Class Analysis and Social Transformation*, Buckingham: Open University Press.

Sayer, A. (2005) *The Moral Significance of Class*, Cambridge: Cambridge University Press.

Schaefer, D. (2007) 'Procedural versus Substantive Justice: Rawls and Nozick', in Paul, E. F., Miller, F. D. & Paul, J. (eds) *Liberalism: old and new*, Cambridge: Cambridge University Press.

Scheffler, S. (2003) 'What is Egalitarianism?', *Philosophy and Public Affairs*, 31(1): 5–39.

Schmidtz, D. (ed.) (2002) *Robert Nozick*, Cambridge: Cambridge University Press.

Schmidtz, D. (2006) *Elements of Justice*, Cambridge: Cambridge University Press.

Schmidtz, D. & Brennan, J. (2010) *A Brief History of Liberty*, London: Wiley-Blackwell.

Schram, S. (2002) *Praxis for the Poor*, New York: New York University Press.

Schram, S. (2006) *Welfare Discipline*, Philadelphia: Temple University Press.

Schram, S. & Caterino, B. (eds) (2006) *Making Political Science Matter*, New York & London: New York University Press.

Schumacher, E. F. (1973) *Small is Beautiful*, New York: Harper & Row.

Schumaker, P. (2008) *From Ideologies to Public Philosophies*, Oxford: Blackwell.

Schumpeter, J. (1992) *Capitalism, Socialism and Democracy*, London: Routledge.

Schwartz, B. (2004) *The Paradox of Choice*, New York: HarperCollins.

Scott, J. (2001) *Power*, Cambridge: Polity.

Scruggs, L. & Allan, J. (2006) 'The Material Consequences of Welfare States Benefit Generosity and Absolute Poverty in 16 OECD Countries', *Comparative Political Studies*, 39(7): 880–904.

Scruton, R. (2006) *A Political Philosophy*, London: Continuum.

Searle, B. (2008) *Well-Being*, Bristol: Policy Press.

Segall, S. (2010) *Health, Luck, and Justice*, Princeton: Princeton University Press.

Selwyn, N. (2004) 'Reconsidering Political and Popular Understandings of the Digital Divide', *New Media & Society*, 6(3): 341–62.

Sen, A. (2009) *The Idea of Justice*, London: Allen Lane.

Sennett, R. (2003) *Respect*, London: Penguin.

Shakespeare, T. (ed.) (1998) *The Disability Reader*, London: Cassell.

Shapiro, D. (2007) *Is the Welfare State Justified?*, Cambridge: Cambridge University Press.

Singer, P. (1993) *Practical Ethics*, 2nd edition, Cambridge: Cambridge University Press.

Singer, P. (2002) *One World*, New Haven & London: Yale University Press.

Singer, P. (2009) *The Life You Can Save*, London: Picador.

Skeggs, B. (2004) *Class, Self, Culture*, London: Routledge.

Skidelsky, R. (2003) *John Maynard Keynes, 1883–1946*, Basingstoke: Macmillan.

Skinner, Q. (1998) *Liberty Before Liberalism*, Cambridge University Press.

Skinner, Q. (2008) *Hobbes and Republican Liberty*, Cambridge: Cambridge University Press.

Smith, A. (1970) *The Wealth of Nations*, Middlesex: Penguin.

Smith, A. (2008) 'Neoliberalism, Welfare Policy, and Feminist Theories of Social Justice', *Feminist theory*, 9(2): 131–144.

Solomos, J. & Back, L. (1995) *Race, Politics and Social Change*, London: Routledge.

Solomos, J. & Back, L. (1996) *Racism and Society*, London: Macmillan.

Sorkin, A. (2009) *Too Big to Fail*, London: Allen Lane.

Spencer, H. (1969) *The Man Versus the State*, Middlesex: Penguin.

Spicker, P. (2011) 'Generalisation and Phronesis: rethinking the methodology of social policy', *Journal of Social Policy*, 40(1).

Starke, P., Obinger, H. & Castles, F. (2008) 'Convergence Towards Where: in what ways, if any, are welfare states becoming more similar?', *Journal of European Public Policy*, 15(7): 975–1000.

Stedman Jones, G. (2004) *An End to Poverty?*, London: Profile.

Steiner, G. (2002) *Grammars of Creation*, London: Faber & Faber.

Steiner, H. (1994) *An Essay on Rights*, Oxford: Blackwell.

Steiner, H. (2002) 'How Equality Matters', in Paul, E. F., Miller, F. D. & Paul, J. (eds) *Should Differences in Income and Wealth Matter?*, Cambridge: Cambridge University Press.

Stelzer, I. (2008) *The New Capitalism*, Washington: Hudson Institute.

Stern, N. (2007) *The Economics of Climate Change*, Cambridge: Cambridge University Press.

Stevenson, N. (2003) *Cultural Citizenship*, Buckinghamshire, Open University Press.

Stiglitz, J. (2010) *Freefall*, London: Allen Lane.

Straehle, C. (2010) 'National and Cosmopolitan Solidarity', *Contemporary Political Theory*, 9(1): 110–20.

Streeck, W. & Thelen, K. (2005) 'Institutional Change in Advanced Political Economies', in Streeck, W. & Thelen, K. (eds) *Beyond Continuity*, Oxford: Oxford University Press.

Sumner, L. W. (1996) *Welfare, Happiness and Ethics*, Oxford: Oxford University Press.

Taleb, N. (2008) *The Black Swan*, Middlesex: Penguin.

Tawney, R. H. (1964) *Equality*, 4th ed., New Jersey: Barnes & Noble.

Taylor, C. (1989) *Sources of the Self*, Cambridge: Cambridge University Press.

Taylor, C. (1992) *The Ethics of Authenticity*, Cambridge: Harvard University Press.

Taylor, C. (1994) *Multiculturalism*, Princeton: Princeton University Press.

Taylor, G. (2007) *Ideology & Welfare*, Basingstoke: Palgrave Macmillan.

Taylor-Gooby, P. (ed.) (2007) *Risk, Trust and Welfare*, London: Macmillan.

Taylor-Gooby, P. (2009) *Reframing Social Citizenship*, Oxford: Oxford University Press.

Temkin, L. S. (1993) *Inequality*, Oxford: Oxford University Press.

Temkin, L. (2009) 'Illuminating Egalitarianism', in Christiano, T. & Christman, J. (eds) *Contemporary Debates in Political Philosophy*, Oxford: Wiley-Blackwell.

Thaler, R. and Sunstein, C. (2008) *Nudge*, New Haven: Yale University Press.

Thompson, E. P. (1978) *The Poverty of Theory*, London: Merlin Press.

Thompson, N. (2008) 'Hollowing Out the State: Public Choice Theory and the Critique of Keynesian Social Democracy', *Contemporary British History*, 22(3): 355–382.

Thoreau, H. D. (1995) *Walden: or, Life in the Woods*, New York: Dover.

Tilly, C. (2004) *Social Movements: 1768–2004*, Boulder: Paradigm Publishers.

Titmuss, R. (1968) *Commitment to Welfare*, London: Allen & Unwin.

Titmuss, R. (1970) *The Gift Relationship*, London: Allen & Unwin.

Todd, S. (2008) 'Affluence, Class and Crown Street', *Contemporary British History*, 22(4): 501–18.

Tooley, J. (1999) *Reclaiming Education*, London: Continuum.

Touraine, A. (1981) *The Voice and the Eye*, Cambridge: Cambridge University Press.

Touraine, A. (2000) *Can We Live Together?*, Cambridge: Polity.

Turner, B. S. (1993) *Citizenship and Social Theory*, London: Sage.

Turner, B. S. (1996) *The Body and Society*, 2nd edition, London: Sage.

Unger, R. (2005) *What Should the Left Propose?*, London: Verso.

United Nations Development Programme (2007) *Human Development Report, 2007–08*, New York: UNDP.

Vallentyne, P. (2009) 'Left-Libertarianism and Liberty', in Christiano, T. & Christman, J. (eds) *Contemporary Debates in Political Philosophy*, London: Wiley-Blackwell.

Van Oorschot, W., Opielka, M. & Pfau-Effinger, B. (eds) (2008) *Culture and Welfare State*, Aldershot: Edward Elgar.

Van Parijs, P. (1995) *Real Freedom for All*, Oxford: Oxford University Press.

Wall, S. (2003) 'Freedom as a Political Ideal', in Paul, E., Miller, F. & Paul, J. (eds) *Autonomy*, Cambridge: Cambridge University Press.

Wallerstein, I. (1974) *The Modern World System*, New York: Academic Press.

Walzer, M. (1983) *Spheres of Justice*, Oxford: Blackwell.

Walzer, M. (2003) 'Universalism, Equality and Immigration', in H. Pauer-Studer (ed.) *Constructions of Practical Reason*, Stanford: Stanford University Press.

Walzer, M. (2004) *Politics and Passion*, New Haven: Yale University Press.

Walzer, M. (2007) *Thinking Politically*, New Haven & London: Yale University Press.

Watson, S. (2000) 'Foucault and the Study of Social Policy', in Lewis, G., Gewirtz, A. & Clarke, J. (eds) *Rethinking Social Policy*, London: Sage.

Weber, M. (1991) *From Max Weber*, edited by H. H. Gerth & C. W. Mills, London: Routledge.

Weinstock, D. (ed.) (2007) *Global Justice, Global Institutions*, Calgary: University of Calgary Press.

White, S. (2003) *The Civic Minimum*. Oxford: Oxford University Press.

White, S. (2006) *Equality*, Cambridge: Polity.

Wilkinson, R. & Pickett, K. (2009) *The Spirit Level*, London: Allen Lane.

Williams, F. (1989) *Social Policy*, Cambridge: Cambridge University Press.

Wilson, W. J. (2003) 'Race, Class and Urban Poverty: a rejoinder', *Ethnic and Racial Studies*, 26(6): 1096–1114.

Wolf, M. (2005) *Why Globalisation Works*, New Haven, Yale University Press.

Wolfe, A. & Klausen, J. (1997) 'Identity Politics and the Welfare State', *Social Philosophy & Policy*, 14(2): 231–255.

Wolff, J. & de-Shalit, A. (2007) *Disadvantage*, Oxford: Oxford University Press.
Wollstonecraft, M. (1975) *Vindication on the Rights of Women*, Middlesex: Penguin.
World Bank (1994) *Averting the Old Age Crisis*, Washington DC: World Bank.
Wright, E. O. (ed.) (2006) *Redesigning Distribution*, London: Verso.
Wright, E. O. (2010) *Envisioning Real Utopias*, London: Verso.
Yeates, N. (ed.) (2008) *Understanding Global Social Policy*, Bristol: Policy Press.
Young, I. M. (1990) *Justice and the Politics of Difference*, Princeton, NJ: Princeton University Press.
Young, I. M. (2000) *Inclusion and Democracy*, Oxford University Press.
Young, I. M. (2009) 'Structural Injustice and the Politics of Difference', in Christiano, T. & Christman, J. (eds) *Contemporary Debates in Political Philosophy*, London: Wiley-Blackwell.
Ypi, L. (2010) 'Politically Constructed Solidarity: the idea of a cosmopolitan avant-garde', *Contemporary Political Theory*, 9(1): 120–30.
Yuval-Davis, N. (2006) Intersectionality and Feminist Politics', *European Journal of Women's Studies*, 13(3): 193–209.
Zald, M. & McCarthy, J. (eds) (1987) *Social Movements in an Organisational Society*, New Brunswick, NJ: Transaction Books.
Zald, M. & McCarthy, J. (eds) (1988) *The Dynamics of Social Movements*, London: University Press of America.
Zey, M. (1998) *Rational Choice Theory and Organizational Theory*, London: Sage.
Žižek, S. & Douzinas, C. (eds) (2010) *The Idea of Communism*, London: Verso.

Index